D0947187

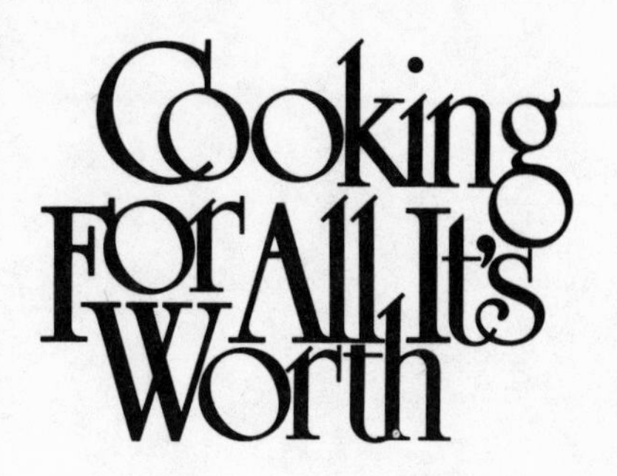
Cooking
For All It's
Worth

RFK: His Life and Death
The Color Encyclopedia of World Art
A History of Gastronomy
New York à la Carte
Winning the Restaurant Game

WITH OTHERS:

The Collector in America
The Horizon Book of Great Cathedrals
The Horizon Book of the Elizabethan World

Cooking For All It's Worth

Making the Most of Every Morsel of Food You Buy

Jay Jacobs

McGraw-Hill Book Company

New York • St. Louis • San Francisco
Hamburg • Mexico • Toronto

1 2 3 4 5 6 7 8 9 F G R F G R 8 7 6 5 4 3

ISBN 0-07-032155-8

LIBRARY OF CONGRESS CATALOGING IN PUBLICATION DATA

Jacobs, Jay.
Cooking for all it's worth.

Bibliography: p.
1. Cookery. I. Title.
TX652.J28 1983 641.5'52 82-13010
ISBN 0-07-032155-8

Book design by Roberta Rezk

In memory of
Everett Rattray
Gloria Durham
Ann Moray de Ceballos

Permissions and Acknowledgments

Recipes on pages 123, 124 (top) and 171 were adapted by permission from *The Cuisine of Hungary*, by George Lang, © 1971 by George Lang.

Recipes on pages 119, 122, and 166 were adapted by permission from *Italian Family Cooking*, by Edward Giobbi. Quotation on page 127 was reproduced by permission from the same source, © 1971 by Edward Giobbi.

The poem *Flower Soup* by Jin Hwa, © 1979 by the Wyoming Council on the Arts, is quoted by permission.

Recipes on pages 133–136 were adapted by permission from *Chinese Cuisine: Wei-chuan's Cookbook*, by Huang Su Huei, © 1971 by Huang Su Huei.

Recipes on page 139 were adapted by permission from *Gourmet* magazine.

Individual acknowledgments for any other recipes adapted by permission are given in the text.

· Contents ·

• WRITER TO READER •

CAVEAT LECTOR: I am a writer who cooks, not a cook who writes. Although you will find numerous recipes in these pages, this was not conceived as a cookbook in the generally accepted sense of the term and won't do you much good if you try using it as such. Rather, it was intended to be an examination, more or less in essay form, of home cooking in America today, and a corrective to what I see as widespread culinary irresponsibility and abuse, with selected recipes appended for whatever illustrative light they may shed on matters.

As the architect Louis Sullivan pointed out, form follows function. Because the intended function of this book differs from that of most conventional cookbooks, its form deviates somewhat from generally accepted norms, as do its content and structure. Because I am what I am, its style differs from most. And because one of the book's chief functions is to foster an approach to cookery in which improvisation plays a key role, many of the recipes are themselves improvisatory in nature and lack both the consistency of format and quantitative precision found in most cookbooks.

I am not a culinary pharmacist or accountant, and harbor no desire to be a culinary drillmaster. For the most part, my measuring cup is my cupped hand and my weighing device a practiced eye. Where precision is essential to the successful outcome of a particular dish, I've tried to be precise; where it isn't, I haven't, experience having convinced me that good instincts and culinary commonsense produce better food than does slavish adherence to dogmatic, often mindlessly arbitrary formulas. Two sprigs of parsley more or two sprigs less won't have a detectable effect on the outcome of a batch of stock, nor will the addition or subtraction of a clove or two of garlic irreparably damage a potful of stew.

To my way of thinking, the ingredients of a good dish do not begin and end with those that can be baldly enumerated and measured by weight or volume. Inevitably, whatever preparations we eat take some of their flavor, color, shape, texture and resonance from the history, lore, customs, literature and personal experience with which they have interacted through the years. For this reason, much to be found in these pages has little to do with the simple mechanics of cookery and may seem needlessly digressive if you're looking for nothing but practical step-by-step guidance. Sorry about that, but food to me is much more than the sum of its tangible components.

I cook seriously but not, I hope, solemnly. Most American cooks I know, professional and amateur, cook solemnly but not seriously. A good many others cook frivolously, dishonestly and wastefully, which last I consider to be morally indefensible. I derive immense satisfaction from working with food, and if an occasional dish is botched, so what? The worst punishment I suffer is having to eat it. Most cooks I know consider the actual process of cooking an onerous means to an ego-flattering end. I pity them.

Much of the cooking I see angers me. If the anger expressed in some of these pages strikes a raw nerve, well, in Harry Truman's words, "If you can't stand the heat, get out of the kitchen."

—J. J.

• TWO VIGNETTES • BY WAY OF A PROLOGUE

THE SCENARIO is painfully familiar. An elderly shopper stands bemused in a supermarket aisle, literally weighing alternatives in her hands, balancing a few thin slices of die-cut cheese against even fewer slices of some machine-made meat byproduct. She mulls her dilemma for long minutes, sorrowfully returns the more expensive item to the display case, adds a few pennies to what she has thereby "saved" and splurges on a single apple. She makes her way to the checkout counter, where coin by coin she relinquishes the price of her meager, joyless supper. For the same money she could have purchased three square meals.

NEARBY, perhaps in a "luxury" apartment above the same market, a hostess renowned in her social circle as a "gourmet chef" makes out a shopping list for that evening's dinner party. Her little bash for three couples will cost her upwards of fifty dollars, not including booze or wines, but the praises heaped on her by her guests not only will justify the expenditure but will more than offset the grousing of her husband when he opens the refrigerator later in the evening, to find not even the makings of a sandwich.

• PUBLISHER'S NOTE •

Asterisk (*) following a recipe name denotes	a recipe to be found elsewhere in this book.
<u>Underscored text</u> denotes	elements or compounds salvaged from earlier cooking efforts.
Bold italic type denotes	recipe ingredients you may have to buy if you don't have them on hand.

The State of the Art

1

GOURMET COOKING. Gourmet dining. Gourmet-this. Gourmet-that. The terms are as inescapable these days as they are ungrammatical. America today, like the Roman Empire in the years of its decay, is preoccupied with fancy eating and oblivious of the underlying logic and economy on which any cuisine worthy of the name must be based. A seemingly unstemmable torrent of cookbooks gushes from the nation's printing presses. National magazines devote cover stories to "The Cooking Craze." *The New York Times* consecrates up to ten pages each Wednesday to unbridled *gourmandise*. Expensive belly boutiques and chic kitchenware outlets proliferate like gerbils. Food processors and woks become the lares and penates of an era in which the ultimate status symbol is ownership of a professional kitchen range. Hitherto unheard-of ingredients are readily available at small-town shopping centers. Account executives and surgeons, stockbrokers and sculptors spend their weekends turning out meals worthy of three-star restaurants. Never before in our history have we been so eager to undertake the preparation of esoteric ingredients and costly, exotic dishes.

Yet few of us understand what good cooking is all about.

As was the case in Sallust's day—Sallust, who described the Romans of his effete era as "slaves of their stomachs"—and Seneca's (who grumbled that "men eat to vomit and vomit to eat"), cooking today has lost touch with reality. In place of integrity, we have razzle-dazzle; in place of basic knowledge, superficial knowledgeability; in place of husbandry, waste.

To regale favored guests with "The Shield of Minerva," a preposterously ostentatious dish of his own devising, the Roman emperor Vitellius sent fleets of ships to the farther reaches of the then-known universe in quest of flamingoes' tongues, peacocks' and pheasants' brains, the gonads of lampreys and the livers of pike. Precisely what became of those anatomical elements that *didn't* go into Vitellius' modest little ragout wasn't recorded, but of one thing we can be sure: Having extracted more pelf from the epicurian emperor than he might have paid had he ordered his fish and poultry whole, Vitellius' suppliers found someone on whom to unload all those fractionally mutilated birds, eels and pike, and at a handsome profit. If they were as shrewd as their modern counterparts, they not only filleted the fish and found lucrative use for the oddments, but reduced all those flamingoes and peacocks and pheasants to their component members before putting them on the market. Frank ("Don't buy a chicken") Perdue and his retailers got richer faster by merchandising chicken parts than whole birds.

Few present-day Americans cook as extravagantly or entertain as lavishly as did Vitellius, but for most of us the difference is less one of kind than degree. Like Vitellius, we think in terms of single showy dishes composed of one-shot ingredients excised at exorbitant costs from potentially more productive entities. We may not buy peacocks' brains—yet—but we buy skinned and boned chicken breasts, paying nearly as much for them in our shortsightedness as the whole fowl would have cost, and aborting a culinary parlay that might have produced not only the *supreme de volaille à la* something-or-other with which we meant to knock our dinner guests over, but also a fine soup, a couple of splendid appetizers and at least one additional main dish more palatable than the first. Similarly, we pay through the teeth for filleted fish, thereby gaining a few moments of "convenience" but losing in the process the bones, heads, tails and trimmings that are the essence of fine fish cookery. We reject, discard or are deliberately deprived of such useful, nutritious, potentially delectable items as vegetable skins, tops, pods, roots and parings; animal bones, fats, skins and all but a very few innards; poultry feet, necks, carcasses and skins; the heads, shells, roe and detritus of crustaceans; and all manner of recyclable materials, all of which are fundamental to really fine cookery and for which we pay dearly at the market.

The whole edifice of truly fine cooking—gourmet cooking, if you will—rests on the reduction of waste to the irreducible minimum. Virtually no part of any natural foodstuff, animal or vegetable, cannot be put to good, often elegant culinary use. Many of the most refined French soups, sauces, hors d'oeuvres and garnishes—the crowning glories of the Western world's most sophisticated cuisine—traditionally and necessarily have been the products of "garbage" such as modern Americans daily discard in quantities sufficient to feed whole nations handsomely and well. Collectively each week we scrape from our plates and jettison from our kitchens thousands of tons of potentially recyclable scraps, leftovers and oddments, and then proceed straight from the rubbish can or town dump to the market, there to pay out hard-earned money for the same items we have just discarded. On economic grounds alone, this throwaway mentality, morally unconscionable even in the best of times, is just plain idiotic today, when food costs are prohibitive, freezers of one sort or another are standard household equipment and few serious home cooks lack food processors or similar labor-saving devices.

A few years ago *Time* devoted a cover and more than seven pages to America's then-burgeoning, now-pandemic fascination with fancy cooking. "The amount spent on specialty foods by the average family has increased over the past five years by 20%," the magazine informed its readers.

> New cooks also are spending vast amounts on the steel, plastic, wire and wooden twiddlybits with which to turn their foodstuffs into ambrosial dinners. Zabar's, a Manhattan shop that stocks everything from French dry morels . . . to a $1,000 espresso-cappucino machine, has increased its sales sixteenfold over the past dozen years. Says co-owner Murray Klein: "We have never seen such an explosion of food buying." Super-

markets from coast to coast now stock such one-time exotica as game pâtés, Beluga caviar, imported mustards, goat and sheep cheese, leeks, shallots, bean curd, pea pods, bok choy, capers, curries, coriander and cornichons.

Warming to their subject, the *Time* writers went on to note that Macy's basement, "where women once battled with umbrellas for lingerie markdowns has become one of New York City's great gastronomic pleasure domes. At hand in Macy's Cellar are 200 varieties of cheese, 100 jams and jellies; 50 breads, a dozen coffees and forty teas—as well as an Aladdin's palace of equipment wherewith to transform the raw stuff into rare meals."

The raw stuff? *What* raw stuff? In its confusion of ostentatious gluttony with cookery, *Time* neglected to inform its readers (by then presumably agog at all those statistics and itemizations) just what sort of equipment, other than a knife, is required to spread factory-cooked jams and jellies, to cut commercially produced cheese or to slice commercially baked bread. To be sure, *Time* was able to cite a few examples of undeniably raw stuff, noting, for instance, that one Houston retailer "recently filled a client's request for 48 lbs. of African elephant meat (which was cut into steaks and broiled)." (This at a time when Africa's elephant herds were being tragically depleted by rapacious ivory hunters!)

"Yet," *Time* concluded (after acknowledging that its description of runaway epicureanism "sounds perhaps like the last days of the Roman Empire"), "Americans are certainly eating more wisely than in the days when a hunk of steer and a stack of fries were the banquet supreme." Ah, to what heights of gastronomic sagacity have we soared! Today's banquet supreme? A hunk of elephant and a stack of *pommes soufflées*.

If Zabar's has increased its sales astronomically over the past several years, your neighborhood greengrocer has not. Nor has the corner butcher, or the grocer or fishmonger in the next block. Given no significant population shifts from one sector to another of any city, it seems safe to say—even without supporting statistics—that *their* sales have remained more or less constant, if indeed they haven't sagged while all those newly fledged epicures were stampeding in the general direction of the belly boutiques. And therein lies the rub: In our fascination with culinary exotica we are paying no more attention than we ever did to culinary staples. Indeed, we may largely have lost touch with culinary fundamentals. We can open a tin of caviar as well as any world-class chef, but we don't know what to make of a chicken carcass or a mess of veal bones.

Our ignorance can be laid in part directly on the doorsteps of food writers who implicitly encourage waste and kitchen sloth in the name of temporal economy. To save time while cooking impressively, the tacit message goes, waste money, abjure the satisfactions to be derived from honest work well done and feed your loved ones ostentatiously at any cost. Recipes are conceived and meals whacked out willy-nilly, in isolation from one another, as though cooking were interchangeable with casual sex and as though a quick succession of one-night stands successfully can be substituted for an ongoing, building relationship. *The New York Times'* "60-Minute Gourmet" makes a sort of drag race of the preparation of a meal, almost invariably using cuts of meat, fish or fowl excised at considerable cost from larger contexts and, in the process, economizing on food with the sort of efficiency with which a supercharged racing car economizes on fuel. But if the *Times* recipes are extravagant, they are at least legitimate. Many others aren't.

In 1965, for example, when the current cooking craze was in its nascent stages, one Yvonne Young Tarr broke the culinary equivalent of the sound barrier with *The Ten Minute Gourmet Cookbook,* in which she not only managed to use the word *gourmet* as a verb ("a new way to gourmet") but gourmetly managed to work three different canned soups and a package of frozen seafood (thawing time presumably not included in the allotted ten minutes) into a single recipe for tomato crab bisque. Her book was dedicated to her two sons, "who learned about gourmet cooking the hard way."

Fifteen years later, with the cooking craze in full efflorescence, Judith Aronson, writing in *Vogue,* presented as part of an "Elegant Dinner for Company" a four-serving recipe for clam soup. The Aronson formula for company elegance entailed the opening of four cans, with a fifth listed as an optional supplement. For elegance on a grander scale—"Cocktail Supper for Twenty"—a single side dish, rice pilaf, called for no fewer than nine cans of commercially cooked and packed consommé and two of precooked mushroom caps.

The attitude embodied in this sort of cooking—if it can be called cooking—was baldly stated by Peg Bracken in the title of her popular magnum opus, *The I Hate to Cook Book,* which, if you choose to credit the flap copy, is "such a clever book that no one need ever know how much you do hate to cook." In a pig's eye, no one need ever know. Consider the Bracken recipe for Beef à la King, of which the author tells us, "Don't recoil from the odd-sounding combination of ingredients here, because it's actually very good. Just shut your eyes and go on opening those cans." The recipe calls for canned chicken noodle soup, canned cooked mushrooms and commercially packaged chipped beef (which last, when served on toast, was known to, and beloved by, a generation of GIs as "shit on a shingle"). Just shut your eyes indeed! If you have any respect for your insides, don't open your mouth either.

For a Bracken creation called Sweep Steak, the contents of a package of onion soup mix are dumped over a hunk of meat. For something else called Ragtime Tuna, canned macaroni-and-cheese and canned tuna are arranged in alternating layers, sprinkled with commercial grated cheese and baked. The first course of a "company" menu is vichyssoise—"cold, canned, topped with chopped green onions."

Intended or not, the message implicit in such fare is that the "cook" hates more than just cooking. To invite putative friends to dinner and set before them a soup poured straight from the can is to inform them that they are worth neither time nor trouble, to treat them to a show of contempt roughly comparable to spitting in their plates.

Cooking is above all an act of love. If you hate to cook, don't cook. A dish composed of bile, gall and spleen will taste every bit as hateful as it is. On the other hand, the most egregiously botched mess, put together by a teenage newlywed whose previous gastronomic experience might pass for an Andy Warhol retrospective, will have about it at least a faint bouquet of solicitude and affection.

A voice of reason cries out, almost inaudibly, from the *Time* article cited earlier. It is that of Jacques Pépin, "peripatetic teacher, author and *cuisinier* who was once the personal chef of Charles de Gaulle." After recommending that the home cook purchase "three good knives" and "a few basic strong pots," Pépin cautions: "Also try to avoid snobbism. Cooking is not for showing off to the neighbors."

Chef Pépin's sage counsel notwithstanding, the cooking craze of the past several years is in large part a matter of showing off to the neighbors and the fact might as well be faced. We no longer invite our friends over for pot roast or fried chicken but regale them instead with rarefied dishes that rival, and often excel, examples to be found in the best restaurants. We one-up one another constantly, ever on the lookout for an opportunity to beat the Joneses next door to some esoteric ingredient, a recipe that will knock their socks off or a meal that will be the talk of our social set . . . until it is topped by a rival hostess. We cook as we dress and as we play, seduced by whatever is in vogue at a particular moment, discarding ingredients and dishes like last year's rags whenever some culinary couturier decrees a new seasonal line.

Beef Wellington, the dumb but ubiquitously chic dish of a decade or so ago, gives way to *quiche lorraine*—a bourgeois standby that temporarily gets itself mistaken for *haute cuisine*. Fettucine Alfredo makes a momentary splash, to be supplanted in turn by spaghetti *primavera*, angel's hair in truffled cream sauce or whatever. Snow peas are all the rage until the culinary avant-garde happens on sugar snap peas. Bibb lettuce becomes as déclassé as iceberg once ruby lettuce makes the scene, only to be superseded in turn by arugula, *radicchio* and *mache*. Green peppercorns are the spice of the good life until brown szechuan peppercorns arrive, then the latter are bounced in favor of *baies roses*. "Spaghetti squash" is the culinary buzzword one year, "asparagus beans" the next. If you still crave apple pie, you're half-safe with *tarte Tatin,* but be advised: Jones next door knows that *clafouti aux kiwis* is really where it's at.

Cooking in America today intensely reflects the need of most Americans to be "with it" at whatever cost. It has supplanted the automobile as our prime vehicle of ostentation. As *Time* quotes the cartoonist William Hamilton, "It's as though you say, 'Take and eat, for this is my ego.' "

Well, it may be asked, if the home cook outdoes the restaurant chef, what's the problem? The problem is precisely that the amateur cooks with his ego, not his head or heart. Unfettered by the economic or logistical realities of professional kitchen management and given as much time as he feels like wasting to produce a dish of his own choosing, any reasonably proficient home cook has every advantage over the professional chef. He can spend the better part of a Saturday—and the equivalent of his gardener's weekly earnings—shopping at some suburban belly boutique that stocks 467 varieties of cheese, 83 variously flavored vinegars and hundreds of pounds of the spinal marrow of sturgeon . . . but no flour or yeast or common table salt. He can purchase the most refined cuts of the rarest viands, trimmed for him with lapidary precision, at a cost just fractionally below that of cutting the Kohinoor diamond. He can cook them to roseate perfection, undistracted by the exigencies of volume feeding or the disparate demands of a roomful of people ordering individually from an extensive menu. He can smother each portion of meat under an unconscionable abundance of *foie gras* curls, slivered truffles, infant string beans, chanterelles and/or any other pricey little delicacies his vanity impels him to pile on. His concerns begin and end with the meal of the moment, with no thought given to what has preceded or will follow it.

The meat delivered to the restaurant, on the other hand, is butchered (i.e., divided into its component parts and trimmed) in the kitchen, where costs must be cut by making good use of every possible scrap in a logical serial method of food preparation and meal production, a method with which most of our grandmothers were thoroughly familiar but which is as little known to most contemporary cooks as the far side of the moon. Moreover, dilettante cooks easily can impress their friends and neighbors by mastering a very limited number of showy recipes (or even just by throwing together commercially prepared ingredients in the manner of the hostess who brings home a pound of fresh linguine and a pint of store-bought *pesto* and has only to boil up some water to earn a reputation as a dynamite Italian "chef"). They are instant Escoffiers who haven't learned the fundamentals of the craft. In essence they are not cooks at all but shoppers, and wildly extravagant shoppers at that. In matching a trained professional at his own game they have accomplished nothing more than has the chess *patzer* who is offered a draw by the grandmaster who simultaneously takes on six dozen opponents.

The ostensible justification for the purchase and use of prepared culinary components and precooked delicacies is that they are too complicated, time-consuming or expensive to make at home from scratch, but a visit to any fancy food shop indicates otherwise. Dean and Deluca, one of Manhattan's most popular fancy food shops, maintains an outpost in the Long Island village of East Hampton. A random browse through the spinoff venture turned up these items: fresh chantrelles, $26 per pound; smoked goose breast, $12; *gravlax*, $17.50; fresh tortellini, $3.65 for a priggish 15 ounces; 7½ ounces of green pepper mustard, $4.50; pickled beets, $3.05 per 16-oz. jar; cherry preserves, $4.65 for a 9-oz. jar; and Dilly Beans at $4.65 per 16-oz. jar.

Of the foregoing only the staggeringly pricey chanterelles can be termed an honest-to-God scratch ingredient, something any home cook could not produce herself. Everything else can be produced in the home kitchen with little effort or expenditure, and at a fraction of the cost of the store-bought merchandise.

And what, it may be asked, are Dilly Beans? What manner of manna more costly than beefsteak? Well, they are a handful of string beans—a couple of dimes' worth, to give their producers the benefit of the doubt—packed, with perhaps a penny's worth of herbs and condiments, in a blend of vinegar and water. In an hour or so the shopper who lays out $4.65 for a pint of Dilly Beans (perhaps enough to make a meager cocktail accompaniment for three or four couples) could have put by a year's supply of pickled beans for little more than the price of a couple of jars. Chances are they would have tasted better, too.

• DILLED PICKLED BEANS •

Using the freshest, straightest, most uniform produce available, trim the ends from 8 lbs. ***green beans.*** In a large pot bring 3 gals. water t a high boil, add beans and cook 1 minute. Using a colander, quickly drain beans and plunge them immediately into 3 gals. ice water. When beans are thoroughly chilled, pack them upright into hot sterilized 16-oz. canning jars. To each jar add 1 whole peeled ***garlic clove,*** 2–3 sprigs ***fresh dill,*** 1 tbs. coarse salt and, if desired, ***hot pepper flakes*** to taste. In a pot combine 2 qts. ***white wine vinegar*** and 1 qt. water and bring to a high boil. Pour vinegar mixture over beans, filling jars to overflowing, and seal jars immediately. Yields about 12 pts.

Admittedly, making tortellini at home is a time-consuming job that may make the Dean and Deluca price and product seem attractive to anyone accustomed to earning more than the minimum wage. Still, time spent in the kitchen can no more be reckoned solely in terms of its cash value than can time spent in the bedroom. To make tortellini (supposedly modeled on the navel of Venus) is, if not to make love, to engage in languorous foreplay at the very least. The cash outlay for a pound of the homemade product, filled according to taste or whim with the planned-for detritus of previous fine dinners, is but a fraction of the cost of the commercial product (with *its* unchanging dictatorial character), but that hardly matters in this particular case. To make tortellini, as to make sausage by hand, is to abandon one's self to sweet sexy dreams that have nothing to do with bottom-line realities.

Gravlax is another story altogether. On the same day that

this cured salmon sold for $17.50 at Dean and Deluca, fresh salmon was available from three nearby fishmongers at under six dollars. True, to attain its optimum ambrosial characteristics, *gravlax* requires time. It must lie for many hours under weight, allowing its juices to flow and slowly building the spicy-sweet sensations and toning the flesh that ultimately will transport those who partake of it. But all that goes on in the dark privacy of the refrigerator, interrupted only for a moment every twelve hours or so. The actual working time expended in the preparation of *gravlax* is a matter of minutes and the saving for the home cook is a considerable eleven dollars and more per pound. And what an elegant, memorable Sunday brunch the stuff makes with its thick suave mouth-filling flavor! And how felicitous are the orts, missed on the first go-round by the long supple slicing knife, when carefully, frugally pared from the silvery hide and incorporated into an omelet, a salad or a pasta dressing!

• GRAVLAX •

Split a 2½-lb. piece of unskinned ***salmon,*** preferably from the muscular tail end, from back to belly. Remove the central bony structure, reserving it for other uses. Run the fingers over the flesh, feeling for fine bones, which should be drawn out with pliers. Combine ½ cup ***sugar,*** ⅓ cup salt and ¼ tsp. crushed ***peppercorns.*** Rub the mixture into the fleshy sides of the fish and sprinkle each side evenly with 1 tbsp. ***dill seed.*** Arrange 3 or 4 springs of ***fresh dill*** on the bottom of a walled dish, place one fish-half skin-side-down in the dish and loosely strew the fleshy surface with sprigs of fresh dill. Fit the second fish-half atop the first, flesh-to-flesh as in life, and top it as the first was bottomed, with fresh dill.

Pack any remaining salt-sugar-pepper mixture around the sides of the fish, along with a few more sprigs of dill. Cover the salmon loosely with wax paper or plastic wrap and cover *that* with a flat dish a little smaller than the walled dish. Weight the second dish with a brick or anything about as heavy and refrigerate 48 hours or more, turning the fish and replacing the weight every 12 hours. Before serving, drain off the liquid that will have leached out of the fish and rub the surfaces clean of seasonings with cheesecloth or paper towels. Slice the *gravlax* laterally, at a shallow angle, in translucently thin slices, flattening the knife parallel with the skin at the end of each stroke. Serve on thin slices of dark pumpernickel with Mustard Dill Sauce on the side. The number of portions will vary according to use.

• MUSTARD DILL SAUCE •

In a processor or blender combine ⅓ cup each ***Dijon*** and ***brown mustard,*** 2 tbs. ***fresh dill*** (stems removed), ½ tsp. ***sugar*** (if wanted), and salt and pepper to taste. With machine running, gradually add olive oil in a thin stream until the mixture takes on the consistency of thick sour cream. With machine still running, add 1 tbs. ***tarragon vinegar*** to thin sauce slightly.

There is little need to dwell at length on the rest of the list. The ingredients for seven-and-a-half ounces of green pepper mustard ("mustard, vinegar, salt, green pepper," according to the label) will set you back less than a dollar at the nearest supermarket. The preserves and pickled beets, needless to say, were another generation's thrifty means of having fruits and vegetables out of season and can be put up still, as they were in the not-too-distant past, for pennies, not dollars. Finally, anyone who develops an addiction to smoked goose breast—a twelve-dollar-per-one-pound-fix habit if the pusher is Dean and Deluca—would be well advised to purchase or construct an inexpensive smoker. For twelve dollars you can buy a lot more goose than a mere pound of its breast, and the rest of the bird can be put to so many good uses that the cost of the smoking device will be more than offset by the time you're into your third goose or vice versa.

But what about the vast majority of America's home cooks, the good thrifty folk who are not seduced by the snob-appeal of specialty shop delicacies? Alas, their situation usually is worse. In all but a relatively few cases they are gulled by the same scams, on a lower level of connoisseurship, as are the patrons of the belly boutiques. Packaged "convenience" foods and prefabricated meals beckon from the supermarket aisles, outpulling honest raw ingredients. If the individual extravagances are not as whopping as at the gourmet shoppes, their aggregate outstrips by cosmic numbers the sums spent on such limited-appeal items as Dilly Beans, esoteric mustards and smoked goose breast.

At a supermarket across the street from the Dean and Deluca branch already discussed, the quantities of presumably edible junk that are trundled past the checkout counters are blood-curdling and the ratio of scratch ingredients to processed kitsch is appallingly low. Simple charity will spare us much description of the grandmotherly types whose shopping carts are veritable Himalayas of pop edibles: putative breakfast cereals that turn out to be sugar-glazed styrofoam toys; canned limp pastas in bilious, sugar-saturated sauces; between-meals fodder concocted of synthetically flavored sawdust; baby foods calculated to foster lifetime addictions to sugar; Play-Doh pastries for gastronomic cretins; cryogenically preserved French fries; test-tube "lemonade" . . . and all the irresponsible, wasteful, unconscionable rest of it.

In a region where sweet fresh clams can be had for the taking, shoppers buy Campbell's relatively clamless New England clam chowder at $.57 the can, which yields two not very generous servings only after its volume has been doubled with milk or tap water. They spend $.69 for 4½ ounces of tin-flavored clam spread, $.97 for 6½ ounces of equally metallic minced clams of an extraordinarily mushy consistency, $1.39 for a half-dozen frozen stuffed clams (eleven ounces in all, half-shells, filler and chemical additives included).

They pay $.83 for a pound loaf of white bread that is indistinguishable to most palates from toilet tissue (it's no great coincidence that the manufacturers of both commodities invite prospective customers to squeeze their products), and precisely the same price for *six ounces* of virtually the same stuff in the form of seasoned croutons. They pay $1.99 per pound for Italian-style pork sausage, which is displayed, as it happens, alongside $.99-a-pound fresh pork shoulder, from which a far tastier product can be made at home with little effort. They invest

$1.55 in a six-ounce can of mushrooms containing perhaps a penny's worth of butter, when the same mushrooms are $.40 cheaper unbuttered, and fresh mushrooms enough to fill three or four of those cans cost only $.40 more than a single tin of the processed product. For the alleged convenience of slapping up six cups of Stove Top stuffing mix (i.e., minimally gussied-up bread that, according to the proud declaration on the package front, requires "only" fifteen minutes of kitchen work to put into some semblance of palatability) they shell out $1.65, when they could prepare their own much better stuffing in less time at a fraction of the cost.

If the belly boutique patron buys his *pâté de canard* ready-made, he has little reason to sneer at the supermarket shopper who stocks up on stuffing mix. For both, the next logical step would be to purchase the Sunday roast, done to a turn, from the corner deli. In large part the meals in which both take varying degrees of pride are not really cooked but catered. Moreover, even the caterers can't be depended on to work from scratch. One New York City specialty shop, the Food Emporium, for example, advertises (with more candor than logic) "17 different, thick, chunky salads with homemade goodness—because they're made with Hellmann's Mayonnaise."

The Conscientious Cook 2

WITH NEGLIGIBLE differences of phraseology, most dictionaries define a cook as one who prepares food for eating. *One* who prepares food—not one in collaboration with all manner of assembly-line workers, canners, chemists, embalmers, packagers, merchandisers, and flash-freeze technicians. As the hoary adage had it long before *The Ten Minute Gourmet Cookbook* proved the point by making a triply egregious potage out of three meretricious commercial soups, too many cooks spoil the broth.

In essence the art of cooking is the art of combining elementary ingredients to produce a palatable and nutritious compound. An elementary ingredient cannot itself be a compound but must be an irreducible culinary substance. Thus salt, pepper, celery, trout and lard are elementary ingredients, whereas mayonnaise, pâté, *gravlax* and ravioli—not to mention Dilly Beans and Stove Top stuffing mix—all are compounds. With very few exceptions (an unseasoned boiled egg, a raw oyster sans condiments or sauces, a sliced pear), the finished dishes we set upon the table are compounds, whether simple or complex.

To "cook" with commercially prepared compounds, however fine a few of them may be, is analogous to producing a landscape from one of those paint-by-the-numbers kits. Cooking, like painting, is (or should be) an art of self-expression. Whose self is expressed by slapping together the pre-cooked compounds of anonymous factory workers; workers who, using measurements, proportions, formulas and, to all intents and purposes, ingredients known only to themselves, dictate which flavors the consumer shall experience, which chemicals he shall ingest?

To cook in any meaningful sense of the term is to prepare foods from scratch, but to cook from scratch doesn't necessarily entail utter fanaticism. Even the finest cooks, amateur and professional, will make sparing use of decent commercially prepared compounds if their pedantic avoidance makes neither culinary nor economic sense. It would take the mentality of an Ayatollah Khomeini, for example, to liquefy cayenne peppers and combine them with salt and vinegar merely in order to add a couple of drops of pizzazz to a bloody mary. In this case such commercially bottled products as McIlhenny's Tabasco sauce are pure, inexpensive, and as good as, or better than, any approximation the home cook is likely to produce. Similarly, one's integrity is not compromised beyond redemption if a dab of factory-made Dijon mustard is combined with egg yolks, oil, lemon juice and salt to produce homemade mayonnaise. Again, the commercial product is honestly made stuff and costs so little that the home cook hardly would be justified in taking the time and trouble to attempt its duplication in small quantities.

On the other hand, there is no excuse for the inclusion in any context of a Herb-Ox (or any other commercial) bouillon cube, despite the manufacturer's assurance that it is "a quick and easy, flavorful base for sauces, soups, stews, gravies, casseroles" and that it "adds real zest when cooking vegetables, too." What the product adds to anything in which it is used is, among other things, salt, hydrolyzed vegetable protein, sugar, autolyzed yeast, beef fat, malto-dextrin, caramel, disodium inosinate and disodium guanylate (a guano derivative?), along with a distinctly pharmaceutical bouquet and the catalyst for a few hours of mild heartburn. In no way is this potpourri of salts, sugars and laboratory chemicals an acceptable substitute for good honest homemade stock.

Many other commercial compounds are all too often mistakenly regarded as scratch ingredients. Store-bought curry powder, for one, is not a legitimate culinary element but a factory-produced blend of readily available ingredients, as are commercial chili powders, crab boils, pickling spices, onion salts, "flavor enhancers," chutneys and other relishes, egg noodles, sausages and most canned or frozen meats, fish, fruits and vegetables.

Precisely where the home cook (or restaurant chef for that matter) is to draw the line on the use of commercially processed ingredients is a matter of individual conscience and common-sense practicality. Ideally, for example, a marinara sauce should be made with fresh vine-ripened tomatoes, but a reliable brand of factory-canned tomatoes is infinitely preferable to the zombie produce that passes for tomatoes in most parts of this country except during short local growing seasons. Similarly, if a given dish calls for anchovies or olives, jalapeño peppers or water chestnuts, soy sauce, *escargots* or truffles, there is little or nothing most Americans can do but choose the best available commercially packed article.

The Tools of the Trade

As the earliest English recipe writers tried to make clear once and for all, with their "Smite ye checkyns" and "Hew ye hares to gobbets," cookery should be attacked amain. The kitchen is no place for diffidence or primness, whether the task at hand be the butchering of a side of beef or the decorative carving of a radish. A good resourceful cook will, if circumstances so dictate, prepare a meal in a coffee can or make a work counter of a plank and an oil drum, but day-in-day-out cooking calls for sturdy tools, durable utensils and solid, easy-to-clean surfaces. Your battery of kitchen equipment need not be extensive, but what you choose to work with should be up to the tasks set it. A good thick pot has all the capabilities of a flimsy thin one but the reverse does not hold true, and if you can't safely administer a healthy whack to a slab of meat with the side of your chef's knife, the knife wasn't worth buying.

A few absolutely essential items aside, no home cook should attempt to equip a kitchen at one go, before he (or she—and enough of *that*) has a reasonably good idea of how his style and repertory are likely to evolve. Good kitchen equipment doesn't come cheap and, even if it did, should not be acquired prematurely or for the wrong reasons. Until you are certain you can't function without it, regard with a wary eye any utensil or gadget designed for a single purpose. A gleaming array of duck presses, turbot poachers, couscoussières, truffle cutters, blini pans and the like may impress your guests mightily, but such highly specialized gear contributes little except to kitchen clutter if it is seldom or never used.

Beware too of gadgets whose usefulness decreases in inverse ratio to increasing skills. The fancy "foolproof" clam opener, for example, that may seem indispensable before one learns to split clams with a thin knife, will never be used once this very simple technique—which happens to be faster, cleaner and safer—is mastered. Nor will the garlic press, once it is discovered that a knife can do just what *that* superfluous tool is supposed to do, and do it a lot better.

As noted earlier, good kitchen equipment costs money. Much of it, however, need not cost anything like what is charged in the smart kitchenware shops that have proliferated apace from coast to coast since the onset of the cooking craze. True, a set of fine knives will set you back a pretty penny, but a first-rate kitchen knife will probably outlast its owner and in fact costs no more than did the designer jeans you haven't been able to get into since the neighborhood belly boutique started stocking *crème fraiche*.

Good kitchen knives seldom turn up at yard and garage sales, church bazaars, thrift shops or flea markets, but a surprising amount of other fine kitchenware does. With a little patience and a modicum of elbow grease, one can put together the bulk of a perfectly serviceable *batterie de cuisine* in the course of a few visits to such sources, and the cash outlay will be relatively small. (A single yard sale visited around the time of this writing yielded a heavy aluminum two-and-a-half-quart pan, a sturdy six-quart stainless steel pot, an enameled Dutch oven in mint condition and a magnificent copper bowl, for a total outlay of about what the least expensive of those items would have cost at any store.) Moreover, used implements often have the advantage over their new counterparts of not having to be broken in. A veteran rolling pin, for example, with the patina of use, *knows* its job and does it without hesitation, as does a properly cured, properly cared-for black iron skillet. Battle-scarred as these hand-me-downs may sometimes be, they take their users' hands with easy familiar warmth. Anthropomorphizing just a bit further, it might almost be believed that, rejected by their original owners after years of faithful service, they are capable of gratitude toward their adoptive parents.

Other good, relatively inexpensive sources of kitchen equipment are restaurant and institutional supply houses, restaurant and hotel liquidation sales and estate auctions. And if you travel in such countries as Italy, Spain and Mexico, don't overlook the internally glazed brown earthenware cooking vessels to be found in shops and markets patronized chiefly by the poor. They are dirt-cheap, uncommonly handsome and versatile and require far less maintenance than metal utensils. True, lugging them through customs and home is a bit of a nuisance (and dropping one onto a hard surface a major tragedy), but once you have the hang of working with them, a bond of affection develops between cook and pot that only so common a substance as the clay of which both are made seems to generate. To cure a terra cotta vessel (such as Velazquez painted) for use, either in the oven or in direct contact with flame or electrical coils, fill it with cold water, place it on a burner and slowly bring the water to a boil. The inner glaze will craze (i.e., develop a network of fine cracks), but this is an asset, not a detriment, to the vessel's utility.

A WORD ABOUT PROCESSORS

That both home and professional cooks managed for millennia without the benefit of food processors should not be held against these devices. There is nothing these culinary R2-D2s can do that cannot be done by hand, and in most cases better, but the very significant amounts of time they save more than offset both their occasional aesthetic deficiencies and their considerable cost.

It should be borne in mind, however, that the speed with

which processors accomplish their tasks can be illusory in some cases, as when the time expended in cleaning the work bowl of the adhesive remnants of a small batch of mayonnaise exceeds the time handwork would have required. As a consequence, many processor purchasers use the machines with steadily decreasing frequency once the novelty of their toy wears off. Nonetheless, a good processor, with its multiplicity of uses, can be an invaluable labor saver when assigned to such tasks as slapping up a batch of pastry dough or a *large* batch of mayonnaise.

The most versatile kitchen tool of them all—the ultimate kitchen tool—is what the French call *la fourchette d'Adam:* Adam's fork, the human hand, the only implement yet devised for many culinary chores. The most obvious use of the hand in direct contact with foods is of course as a vise that holds them firmly in place while they are worked on with other tools. Its less obvious uses, though, are manifold and in many cases unique to the hand itself. In the boning of meats and fowl, for example, the hand "sees" where the eye cannot. A forefinger stabbed into a saucepan and licked will tell you more about your béarnaise or whatever than will the breath-cooled content of a wooden spoon dipped into the same sauce. To distribute oil and onion evenly in a white bean salad without bruising the beans, nothing will do the job as quickly and effectively as your own two hands, slightly cupped and plunged right into the bowl. However well your processor makes short-paste dough, a few quick finishing smears with the heel of the hand will blend fats and flour more evenly. Bread and pasta doughs will not transmit essential information to the brain without the intervention of the hand. Meatballs and patties; croquettes and *gnocchi; paupiettes* and *sushi;* pretzels and pita—all these preparations and countless others require direct shaping, feeling contact between human flesh and foodstuffs. To cook well you must get your hands into the work like a Rodin communicating with clay. As Julia Child and her confederates put it in the most telling line they ever wrote, *"Il faut mettre la main à la pâte!"*

Mention of Julia Child leads naturally to the subject of cookbooks. Which and how many should you own? As is the case with kitchen gear, circumspection is called for here. To amass a multi-volume library before you have discovered and defined your spheres of culinary interest leads only to clutter, redundancy and waste. *1001 Ways to Prepare Camel Meat* may just turn out to be a poor investment if the local supermarket somehow neglects to stock bactrian steaks or dromedary chops, and *Eskimo Cuisine* will avail you little if you happen to be on a low-fat meatless diet. The ownership of *Cajun Crawdad Cookery* makes little more sense if you're allergic to crustaceans or can't readily come by crawfish, and *Feasts from Rural Picardy,* definitive though it may be, will be somewhat supererogatory if you already own an exhaustive compendium of provincial French recipes.

The more specialized the cookbook, the less likely it is to earn out your initial investment or to justify the shelf space it occupies. Pass up *Trout to the Table* if you already own *Everything You Can Do with Fish,* and resist the latter if you've already become the proud possessor of *Positively Everything You Can Do with Food.* A good comprehensive volume on the cookery of Spain will comprise all you may want to know of the cookery of Asturias but the reverse doesn't necessarily follow.

According to James Beard, "There is such a wealth of ideas in good cookbooks that no one can collect all of them in a lifetime." Well, there are ideas in cookbooks only for those cooks with a propensity toward ideation and a reasonably firm grasp of underlying culinary logic. Shun the cookbook that appears to bubble with bright new ideas—ideas such as this brainstorm from Valera Grapp Blair's *The Cook's Idea Book:* "Form 2 cupfuls of cheese spread into a ball and roll in finely chopped parsley and ground almonds. Store in the refrigerator. Before serving, bring to room temperature and insert small thin pretzel sticks into the ball to make it resemble a porcupine." At this stage of an ancient game there *are* no bright new ideas but only minor variations on well-worn themes. (Regardless of all its attendant hype, the essentials of the so-called *nouvelle cuisine* of France have been known to various cultures, especially in the Orient, for millennia.) What hasn't been done before hasn't been done for good reason. Pouring fudge sauce over a flatfish will not make a latter-day Carême of you. To quote the gist of an observation by the French food writer Robert Courtine, the fool who shoves a banana up a duck has not invented a new dish.

Avoid cookbooks with smarty-pants titles. With very few exceptions they are meretricious potboilers. Beware of cookbook authors who bring out a volume a year. In most cases they are simply milking the public by selling a single book in puffy installments. Like any other kitchen tool, a good cookbook should be viewed as a long-term investment. Hence paperback editions are best avoided as a false economy. They lack durability and won't lie flat, leaving the hands free to work. Beware above all of cookbooks that put forth extravagant claims to ease, speed and simplification. No job of work should take more time or effort than it requires but neither should it take less. As Robert Farrar Capon puts it in *The Supper of the Lamb* (a dispensable collection of recipes caboosed onto an altogether indispensable series of culinary meditations), "I despise recipes that promise results without work, or success without technique. . . . Technique must be acquired, and, with technique, a love of the very process of cooking. No artist can work simply for results; he must also *like* the work of getting them."

In building a library of cookbooks (a dubious pursuit at best), it is wisest to work your way from the general to the particular. If you first familiarize yourself with an encyclopedic volume such as *Larousse Gastronomique,* you later may find no need to clutter your kitchen or your life with scores of more specialized treatises. Know your book before you buy it. Be sure you're comfortable with its style and format. Not everyone is receptive to every style of presentation. If you just can't work comfortably and confidently unless each set of instructions is preceded by a table of measured ingredients, *Larousse* is not for you and neither are the terse recipes of Escoffier, which presuppose considerable expertise on the reader's part. If, on the other hand, you want only a general idea of a given dish and the freedom to adapt it to your own informed taste, you may find Child's meticulous detail and lock-step guidance too constricting and turn gratefully to Waverley Root, whose books are not cookbooks at all in any generally understood sense of the term but can be used as such by reasonably accomplished home cooks.

To repeat, Know your book before you commit yourself to its ownership. Borrow it from the library or borrow it from a friend. If need be, alienate your bookseller by perusing his wares at length before rejecting them. Be certain *any* cookbook is one you can't do without, now and in the future, before you buy it. There is nothing as useless as an unused book.

FALSE ECONOMY: DISCOUNT COUPONS AND RELATED SCAMS

A new sort of media celebrity has emerged in recent years. She is the *hausfrau*–turned–author–turned–talk show guest, whose particular shtick is shopping for food with discount coupons and applying for mail-order refunds. By means of paperwork and calculation that would occupy all the spare time and boggle the mind of an IRS auditor, she amasses mountains of groceries for a cash outlay only fractionally commensurate with their putative worth. Like a magician pulling rabbits from a hat, she extracts fifty, seventy, or a hundred packages from a train of shopping carts, buries the checkout clerk under an avalanche of newspaper, magazine, and flyer clippings, and triumphantly announces that her month's supply of comestibles has cost her a mere six dollars and fourteen cents. On examination, that turns out to be just about what it's worth. She has attempted to con the con artists, with predictable results. Not two items in the scores she has amassed are legitimate staple foodstuffs. She and her family will subsist on marginally edible trinkets that afford no gastronomic satisfactions, pose no culinary challenges, and provide a lot less nutrition than might have been the case had she not played into the hands of corporate mountebanks whose wealth is built on the impoverishment of her table.

You won't find discount coupons or refunds for many honest staples because it is not in the producers' interests to issue them. Should you find eggs, butter, meats, or produce offered on these terms, by all means avail yourself of the savings. But don't hold your breath waiting for it to happen.

The old hunter's axiom, "Eat what you kill" (tauntingly directed at Richard Nixon during the war in Vietnam), should be conspicuously posted in every American kitchen. Whether we actually terminate with our own hands the lives of the creatures and plants on which we subsist or have surrogates do the deeds for us, we all depend for our own lives on the mass extinction of other organisms. Kill them we must, but there is no moral defense for wasting that which we have slaughtered. Nonetheless, most of us eat but a fraction of what we kill.

It wasn't ever thus, and it still isn't in most parts of the world. In an earlier America, when much of what we killed we killed personally, food waste was all but unknown. Moreover, those organic parts that could not be eaten were put to other productive uses. The per capita production of garbage was minuscule, whereas it is staggering today.

Much of the food waste that occurs in this country today can be laid directly to the food industry and various overnice governmental agencies. With the tacit acceptance of the consuming public, foodstuffs considered delicacies elsewhere are effectively excluded from our use. Various animal and vegetable elements of which the rest of the world makes nutritious, delectable use seldom or never appear in the American market. The chickens' feet essential to Grandmother's soup (or was it Great-grandmother's?) are scarcer today than the proverbial hens' teeth. Ducks are delivered de-livered to market. The hearts, lungs and testicles of various domestic quadrupeds—all considered delicacies in many parts of the civilized world—are harder to find in today's shopping centers than elephant steaks. Shrimp come to the fishmonger's minus the heads used to make celestial soups and sauces in the Mediterranean and Oriental worlds. Carrots, turnips and radishes undergo similar decapitation at the source of supply, although their green tops are (or would be) marvelous additions to the stockpot or salad bowl. Squash blossoms, numbered among the major delights of Italian cuisine, never make it to the A&P, which sells Brussels sprouts at fancy prices but not the broad upper leaves of the plant that produces them—greens that happen to be as tasty as, and more versatile than, the sprouts themselves. The shallows of the northeastern seacoast teem with periwinkles, the beaches of Florida with coquinas, but try to find either in the local markets. Cocks' combs are as highly esteemed in France as ducks' feet and fish maws are in China. Try to find any of those in your belly boutique, let alone your supermarket. For that matter, try to find a tough old stewing fowl, full of character and flavor, in a land where the spirit of the aptly named Frank Perdue presides over millions of banal dinners each Sunday.

The edible wild plants on which our forebears feasted at the cost only of time well spent in the open are virtually unknown in America today, the missionary zeal of the late Euell Gibbons notwithstanding. Only a minuscule number of the millions of us who grow garden flowers eat such potentially delectable items as violets, roses,chrysanthemums, lilies and nasturtiums. Chive blossoms, which would make a pretty, pungent garnish for soups, salads and omelets, go to seed unplucked and uneaten. To be sure, not every cook willingly will sacrifice the visual satisfactions of the garden to the gustatory satisfactions of the pot, but let us pause momentarily to consider the lilies of the field—daylilies to be precise. Their blooming is of the briefest; they die as darkfall blinds us to their beauty. Why not gather them at dusk for the evening meal, thereby both prolonging and adding another dimension to the delight they afford us? Strip them of their petals and bestrew your green salad with these tongues of orange flame, adding if you like a couple of similarly stripped zucchini blossoms and just a *few* peppery green leaves and variegated petals from your precious border of nasturtiums. You have arranged an edible bouquet to gladden the eyes and hearts of its recipients. Or rinse the whole blossom to dispossess any resident ants, gently shake off the few beads of water that accumulate on the petals, tow the bloom by its stem-end through water-thinned beaten egg, dust it lightly with flour and deep-fry it for seconds in safflower oil. A lovely accompaniment to light meats or fish; the crowning glory of a *fritto misto di verdura*.

The waste of all these untapped culinary resources and hundreds more sorely impoverishes American gastronomy. Cooking craze or no cooking craze, we remain among the least imaginative feeders on earth. In quantitative terms we may be the very best-fed of nations, but from an aesthetic point of view we are among the worst-fed. In a sense we undereat even as we overeat. But wasteful as our neglect of many delicious and adventurous forms of nutrition may be, it is as nothing beside the waste we make of those less-esoteric items that we actually buy and pay for.

To cook in any meaningful sense of the term we must cook responsibly, lovingly and thriftily, making maximal use and prolonging to the utmost extent the working life of anything and everything with which we choose to stock our larders. In short we must make every possible effort to eat *all* of what we kill.

For the overwhelming majority of Americans an outsized hunk of grilled sirloin epitomizes good eating. The "gourmet" may substitute a sautéed filet mignon or two and gussy it up with flamed brandy, crushed peppercorns, shallots, herb butter or whatnot, but he, his barbecue-oriented brother, and the lion rending the carcass of an antelope are all three the same breed of cat at bottom. Lion and men will gorge until sated on more meat than they need at the moment, then regard anything left unconsumed as fit only for scavengers.

It is not the object of this book to banish steak from the American table. It *is* its object, though, to convince you that you can have your steak *and* eat two or three other, possibly better meals for the cash outlay the steak alone commands. The method is simple enough; it merely entails a slight realignment of prevailing culinary attitudes.

In *The Supper of the Lamb,* Robert Farrar Capon perceptively divides cooking and eating into two categories: festal and ferial (the latter from "feria," a day of the ecclesiastical week on which no feast is observed). Whether the dish brought to the table be the lowly hamburger or something as refined as *poularde en demi-deuil,* most cooking in this country is festally conceived; it addresses itself to the satisfactions of the moment with no thought of the morrow. Ferial cooking (which might more accurately be called *serial* cooking), on the other hand, "involves the wholesale and deliberate manufacture of leftovers, the creation of . . . dishes from carefully precarved and precooked meats."

The wholesale and deliberate manufacture of leftovers is precisely what good cooking—and the main thrust of this book—is all about. Any fool with money in his pocket can make a splendid meal of caviar, *foie gras,* truffles and the like, but only a true cook can make tomorrow's dinner of tonight's and produce a better meal in the process.

The term "leftovers" is freighted with negative connotations: nightmarish visions of sandwiches, salads and hashes begat generation upon generation by the Thanksgiving turkey, Easter ham or Sunday roast; offerings that grow progressively more monotonous and less palatable with each succeeding day until, finally fed up with this dreary parade of anticlimaxes, we escape to a fine restaurant, there to dine elegantly on *bisque d'homard, émincés de boeuf bordelaise* and *île flottante*—in plain English, recycled leftovers.

The problem with leftovers (and, by extension, cooking) in this country is that they are not the products of wholesale and deliberate manufacture. It is in large part—nay, wholly—a matter of attitude: The American home cook buys a ham, beef roast, turkey or whatever and prepares it with a single meal in mind, hoping that somehow it will be consumed at one go, thereby obviating the need to consider disposition of the remains. Whatever is not finished off on the occasion either is trashed or disdainfully suffered, like a guest who has overstayed his welcome. ("There's *still* half a ham in the fridge. Make yourself a sandwich. Make yourself *two* sandwiches. We've *got* to use it up.")

Consider, on the other hand, the happy expectations of the true cook: "If I buy and bake this ham, no more than half will be eaten at dinner tonight. Consequently I can slice and store some of the unmutilated portion for eggs benedict, *jambon à la crème,* ham and winter melon soup, *caldo gallego* or a good old country breakfast with redeye gravy. I can cube a few ounces and freeze them for later use in *jambon persillé* or a pâté, a galantine or *sopa al cuatro de hora.* I can purée some in the processor for a ham mousse *en gelée* or for a soufflé with spinach or asparagus. I can cut an ounce or two in julienne strips and combine them with some of yesterday's chicken and some cheese for a light-lunch chef's salad. I can chop a little, with its fat, to add interest to pork sausage or stuffed turkey legs, or mince some to combine with *gnocchi* dough. All those ragged little scraps will go into future gumbos and jambalayas, quiches and omelets, stuffed artichokes and—blended with bits of chicken salvaged from the stockpot—*tortellini* filling. The fat will be used to bind and add lightness to all manner of forcemeat preparations. The rind, pan gelatine and deglazed bits and juices will add viscosity, color and a haunting whiff of smokiness to next week's stock and the sauces that issue therefrom. The bone—precious bone!—will add resonance and character to my black bean or split-pea soup. I and mine will sup superbly off and on for months on this ham, conferring virtual immortality on the pig whence it came, and never know gastronomic ennui."

• INTERLUDE •

The Ham What Am – and Am and Am . . .

IT IS NOT the purpose of this book to add still another compilation of discrete recipes to an existing glut of essays in the genre. Its purpose rather is to reintroduce American cooks to a culinary concept that, although old as cookery itself, has been largely discarded, to the impoverishment of our tables and our lives. The overriding concern here is not with *what* to cook but *how* to cook; not to present recipes as solitary entities but rather to use them as illustrative examples of a process that might be termed Connective Cooking. Hence no attempt has been made either at comprehensiveness or conventional cookbook organization. One-shot recipes abound and have been replicated with only minor variations in thousands of cookbooks that will tell you all you need know about dishes considered in isolation from one another and from a larger culinary context. Our concerns here are not with the parent dish but with its multifarious progeny.

Whether any recipe devised since the Neolithic era legitimately may be termed original is questionable in the extreme. The laws of probability suggest that it cannot. The term "original recipe" as used hereafter denotes nothing more than a dish conceived in ignorance of any prior claims to authorship that may exist. The hope is that the recipes chosen will impel you to create good workable "original" dishes of your own.

To cook well with frugality and integrity we Americans must reorder our priorities. The dish-of-the-moment must be considered not as an end but a beginning. Every major culinary element must be parlayed from compound to compound until its every potentiality has been realized and its usefulness exhausted. In sum we must not only eat what we kill but extend its working afterlife to the fullest extensible degree. Admittedly all this takes time, effort and imagination. Whether it is worth it to you, you alone must decide. Of four things you can be sure, though: Effortless cooking is not. Extravagant cooking is not. Unimaginative cooking is not. Loveless cooking is not.

You have cooked your ham for the Sunday dinner or party buffet and there its ravaged remains lie on the table or sideboard, surrounded by the debris of its various accompaniments while the roasting pan clamors for attention in the kitchen. Look at this mess! Yes, look at this mess; look at it carefully and long for there is much here to gladden the heart. Those heeltaps of wine and unconsumed crusts will not be wasted. The wine will be rebottled and refrigerated for later use in marinades, stews and sauces; as a poaching medium for fish or fruits; as a braising medium for meats; at the very least as an addition to the vinegar bottle. Those unsightly hunks of bread will be gathered and dried, then crumbed in the processor for a multitude of future uses. If it hasn't already sauced your ham, the deglazed pan detritus will spark a gravy or enrich the stockpot. The ham itself will go into any or all of the dishes to follow, depending on how much has been left unconsumed.

• HAM AND WINTER MELON SOUP •
(Cantonese cookery)

Soak 3 dried black ***Chinese mushrooms*** 30 minutes in warm water, then rinse and quarter them, discarding the tough stems. In a heavy 2-qt. pot bring 3 cups ***chicken consomme**** to a boil and add mushrooms, 2 oz. of your ***diced cooked ham*** and ½ lb. ***winter melon*** (seeds and rind removed) cut into 1-inch squares ¼-inch thick. Simmer 15 minutes and serve piping hot to 6.

• CZECHOSLOVAK TRIPE SOUP •

If tripe does nothing else it stands as an irrefutable indictment of American gastronomy and American food waste. The stomach of every ruminant we kill is lined with tripe—an annual yield that runs to tens of millions of pounds—but our consumption of the potentially delectable stuff is so infinitesimal that, even without supporting statistics, it is safe to say that its per capita intake can be measured in fractions of grams. Few culinary elements are more highly prized in many parts of the world and few experiences are as soul-stirring as an encounter with a well-made dish of *tripes à la mode de Caen*. To all but an insignificant number of Americans, though, tripe is "Anything with no value; rubbish" (The American Heritage Dictionary of the English Language).

* * *

In a heavy kettle cover 1 lb. well-washed ***beef tripe*** with water, bring to a simmer and cook about 90 minutes until tender. Drain, rinse with cold water and reserve tripe. In the same kettle sauté 1 small chopped ***onion*** in 3 oz. ***rendered ham fat*** until onion begins to color. Add ¼ cup ***flour*** and 1 tbs. ***sweet paprika*** and cook over low heat 5 minutes, stirring constantly to prevent scorching of the paprika. Add 1½ qts. heated ***beef stock**** and 1 pt. ***ham broth*** to mixture and cook slowly, stirring often, for ½ hour or until soup is creamy, adding additional stock if soup over-thickens. Add tripe and cook 5 minutes longer with salt and pepper to taste, 2 tsp. dried ***marjoram*** and 2 crushed ***garlic cloves.*** Serves 8–10.

• THE COACH HOUSE BLACK BEAN SOUP •

This heart-warmer has attained legendary status among patrons of The Coach House restaurant in New York's Greenwich Village, and deservedly so.

* * *

In a large heavy pot bring to boil 15 cups water, 3 lbs. ***beef bones,*** ¾ lb. ***beef shin,*** 3 lbs. ***ham shank*** (including bone and rind), ¾ tsp. black ***peppercorns,*** 3 whole ***cloves*** and ¼ tsp. ***celery seed.*** Reduce heat and simmer half-covered 8–10 hours. Strain, discard bones (reserving beef marrow for other uses), reserve meats for other uses and refrigerate stock. Soak 2½ cups dried ***black beans*** overnight in refrigerator in 10 cups water. Next day, remove congealed fat from top of stock, reserving 2 tbs. (The suggestion here—despite any cries of anguish from incorrigible chiliheads, who will yelp like coyotes no matter what is said on their favorite subject—is to store the remaining fat for use as a sauté medium when preparing chili con carne.)

In a large pot cook 1 cup chopped ***onion*** and ½ cup chopped ***celery*** in ***reserved fat*** until soft. Add drained ***beans,*** 2 cups water, 7 cups ***reserved stock*** (adding water if stock is of insufficient quantity) and 1 tsp. chopped ***garlic.*** Simmer uncovered 2½ hours, stirring occasionally and adding water as needed to cover the mixture. Purée mixture coarsely through a strainer or with the machine of your choice. Reheat, adding ¼ cup ***sherry*** and salt and pepper to taste. Add 2 chopped ***hard-boiled eggs*** to soup, mixing lightly, and top each serving with a thin round of ***lemon*** dipped in chopped ***parsley.*** Serves 10–12.

• BLACK BEAN SOUP ANOTHER WAY •

Admittedly this lacks the Beethovian resonance of the Coach House reading but it is still no mean soup and requires much less cooking time.

* * *

In a large heavy kettle generously cover your ***meaty ham bone*** and 1½ lbs. dried ***black beans*** with a half-and-half blend of cold water and cold ***stock.**** Add 1 large ***onion,*** chopped fine, a couple of ***bay leaves,*** the seeded and de-ribbed diced flesh of a ***green bell pepper*** or two (you be the judge), a minced ***garlic clove*** (or two or three) and ½ ***celery stalk,*** chopped. (On second thought, make it a *whole* chopped celery stalk and toss in a ***chopped carrot*** or any fraction thereof for added sweetness.) Bring to boil, reduce to a gentle simmer and cook about 3 hours until beans are tender. While beans are cooking and the Dolphins are trouncing the Giants, brown 1 cup or so ***diced cooked ham*** in its own ***rendered fat*** and add 1 chopped ***onion*** and 1 or more minced ***garlic*** cloves, sautéeing the two members of the lily family until wilted. Remove ham bone from the kettle, strip off all meat adhering thereto and return it (the meat) to the pot. Jettison the bay leaves, add ham-onion-garlic mixture and a belt of dry sherry to taste, cooking the whole business long enough to take the alcoholic edge off the wine. Skim off any risen fat or other undesirables and purée ¾ of the soup in the machine of your choice. (Do this in stages, taking care not to splatter the ceiling or your person.) Roughly machine-chop the remainder of the mixture, return it to the soup and garnish as indicated in the preceding recipe. The finished soup may be served over *leftover cooked rice* and, if you like, further garnished with chopped raw onion moistened with oil and vinegar. Serves 6–10, depending on whether or not rice is included.

• SOPA AL CUATRO DE HORA •

Although it takes a few minutes longer to prepare than the fifteen minutes its name suggests, this traditional Spanish soup won't occupy your undivided attention any longer than that, leaving you free to assemble a salad while the pot boils.

* * *

In a heavy 2-qt. pot light brown *2 or 3 oz.* of your cubed ***cooked ham*** in 2 tbs. ***olive oil.*** Remove meat with slotted spoon and set aside, reserving oil in pot. Seed and roughly purée 2 small ripe ***tomatoes,*** skins included (or substitute ¼ *pt.* home-canned *purée*), and set aside. Fine-chop 1 ***hard-boiled egg,*** add it to ⅓ cup shelled ***peas*** and set aside. In 2 cups water brought to a fast boil scald 2 or 3 tbs. ***raw rice*** for 3 minutes, rinse in a strainer under cold running water and add to the foregoing mixture. Shell and set aside ½ lb. small ***raw shrimp.*** In a heavy covered pot steam 12 or more well-scrubbed hard clams just until the shells part. Half-shell clams and set aside, reserving pot liquor.

Strain reserved claim liquor through a damp cloth, or dispense with this nicety by pouring the broth off with care, allowing any heavier-than-water grit to remain harmlessly in the pot. Fine-chop 1 medium ***onion*** and sauté it in reserved olive oil until it colors lightly, meanwhile bringing 4 cups water to a hard boil. Add tomato purée to onion and cook 5 minutes over moderate heat, then remove pan from heat and blend in ½ tsp. ***mild paprika.***

The final fifteen minutes

Add the boiling water to the onion-tomato mixture, along with the reserved pea-rice mixture and white pepper to taste. Boil soup 15 minutes, adding seafoods 2 minutes from finish and ham at the last moment. Garnish with chopped egg and serve to 6.

NOTE—Most recipes suggest the full 15 minutes of cooking time for the shrimp, which is why most American versions of *Sopa al Cuatro de Hora* appear to have been made with shrimp-shaped erasers. If your crustaceans are fresh, the less they are cooked the better. Leftover ***cooked rice*** may be substituted for raw rice, in which case add it to the soup just before the shellfish go into the pot.

• A NON-RECIPE FOR GUMBO •

A sedulously measured and itemized recipe for Gumbo is a contradiction in terms, for Gumbo as it is known in the American South originated as a slave dish that made use of whatever ingredients were available. It was, as one early-nineteenth-century sojourner in New Orleans put it, "made of every eatable substance." The name derives from the Bantu word for "okra," hence any "Gumbo" made without okra is no Gumbo at all, advocates of powdered sassafras leaves as an alternative thickening agent notwithstanding. Some people harbor an almost phobic distaste for okra. Well, some people find sex distasteful too, and others see no merit in gin. A proper Gumbo is a full meal.

The highly personal view here is that the traditional *roux* (flour-and-fat) with which most gumbos are begun merely clouds the issue, that ***fish stock**** ***chicken*** or ***turkey broth***,* or leftover ***lobster bisque***,* singly or in any combination, makes a fine Gumbo base and that plain water will do in a pinch. Whatever the base liquid of choice may be, pour a couple of quarts into a good-sized pot, add a pound or more of sliced ***raw okra*** and as much ***oyster liquor*** as you may have salvaged from an earlier dinner of fried oysters, a pan roast, Hangtown fry or whatever. Cook the mixture at a slow simmer, stirring often, until the okra is tender. Add a cupful or so of hand-crushed ***tomato*** (seeded and peeled or not, as you like), a couple of sliced sautéed ***onions***, a few bits of your favorite ***hot chili pepper***, a clove or two of crushed ***garlic***, two or three ***bay leaves*** and as much Tabasco as you deem fit.

Simmer all the foregoing for half an hour, then add any or all of the following items husbanded from earlier meals, in quantities sufficient to add up to at least half a pound: your diced ***cooked ham***, diced ***cooked chicken***, diced ***cooked turkey, crabmeat***, etc. (a few cooked ***mussels***, sans shells, won't endanger the enterprise, nor will any scraps of non-oily ***fish*** that may be lying around, cooked or raw. The odd ***soft-shell crab***, hacked into conveniently mouthable morsels, will endow it with sublimity.)

Continue the simmering process another twenty minutes or so and just before serving add a quarter-pound or more of butter-sautéed ***shelled shrimp*** (fantails removed or not, as the spirit dictates) and a dozen or more shucked ***oysters*** (whose precious bodily fluids have presumably already entered the pot). Stir well, adjust seasonings and serve over boiled rice in generous portions.

> **NOTE**—just how many portions will depend on the density of your Gumbo and the capacities of all concerned. The Gumbo may be thinned by adding liquid but shouldn't be diluted to the point where its natural okra-induced viscosity is impaired. A spoonful of the liquid should not drip like a leaky faucet when tipped but slowly let down an unbroken mucilaginous thread.

• CALDO GALLEGO •
(Galacian cookery)

In a heavy, preferably earthenware, 3 qt. pot cover ¾ cup dried ***white beans*** with cold water. Add ¼ lb. ***lean slab bacon*** and a ¼ lb. slice of your ***cooked ham***. Simmer slowly, covered, 2 hours until beans are tender. Add ½ ***onion***, sliced, and, hacked into bite-sized pieces, ½ head white cabbage and 3 turnips with their green tops. Add salt and white pepper to taste, mix all ingredients gently and simmer 90 minutes longer. Serve hot, with the meats cut up, to 4 as a midday main course or 6 as a first course at dinner.

• HAM WITH REDEYE GRAVY •

In a black-iron skillet lightly greased with ***ham fat*** fry as many slices as desired of your ***cooked ham***, allowing one ¼-inch-thick slice per serving. When ham is lightly browned on both sides transfer it to heated serving plates. Drain fat from skillet, deglaze remaining pan juices with 1½ tablespoons strong ***coffee*** and pour gravy over ham. Serve with ***grits*** and hot ***biscuits.***

• JAMBALAYA (Creole cookery) •

As the name of the dish (derived originally from the Spanish *jamon* and, later, the French *jambon*) implies, ham is the indispensable flashy component of Jambalaya but, as is the case with both gumbo and the *paella* from which the dish itself derives, Jambalaya is hospitable to poultry, sausage and seafoods as well.

* * *

In a large skillet melt 1 tbs. ***shortening*** or ***ham fat.*** Add 1 pound cubed ***cooked ham*** (or any combination of ham and cubed leftover ***poultry, crabmeat, sausage,*** etc.). Cook 5 minutes over moderate heat, stirring frequently, then add 1 tbs. ***flour,*** stir until smoothly blended and cook 90 seconds longer. Add ¾ pound cooked ***shrimp*** (more or less), 4 large ***tomatoes,*** peeled and diced, 2½ cups warm water, 1 large ***onion,*** sliced, 1 clove ***garlic,*** minced. Bring to boil and stir in ½ cup diced ***green pepper,*** 2 cups ***long grain rice,*** a pinch of ***dried thyme,*** 2 tbs. ***Worcestershire sauce*** (if desired) and salt and pepper to taste. Cover and cook 30 minutes over low heat until all liquid is absorbed. Serve, sprinkled with chopped ***parsley,*** to 8.

• HAM SOUFFLÉ •

The natural affinity of ham and eggs can be put to few more refined uses than in a soufflé.

* * *

In a saucepan melt 2 oz. ***sweet butter*** and thoroughly blend in 2 tbs. ***flour.*** Add 2 cups ***milk*** and cook over low heat, stirring constantly until mixture thickens. Remove from heat, and add 2 cups cooked ***ham,*** chopped fine, 3 ***egg yolks,*** lightly beaten, and 2 tbs. fresh grated ***Parmesan cheese*** (no substitutes please). Fold in 3 ***egg whites*** beaten stiff, and pour mixture into a greased 1-qt. soufflé dish. Smooth surface of mixture with a rubber spatula, bake 25 minutes in a preheated 350° oven and serve immediately to 4.

NOTE—For ***Ham-and-Spinach*** or ***Ham-and-Asparagus*** soufflés, substitute for ⅓ the volume of ham a proportionate amount of the desired vegetable, puréed and cooked in a little butter in a moderate oven until most of its moisture has evaporated.

• HAM À LA CRÈME •

Authentically, this dish from central France requires ham baked on a bed of vegetables, mushrooms and herbs but this adaptation works quite well. The number of servings will be determined by the amount of leftover ham you have.

* * *

In a saucepan combine ***pan drippings*** with ¾ cup ***rich stock****, 1 jigger ***Madeira***, 6 chopped ***mushrooms***, a *bouquet garni*. Bring to a lively boil and reduce liquid by one-third. Add ½ cup ***heavy cream*** and salt and pepper to taste. Simmer 6–7 minutes until sauce thickens and strain. Pour half the sauce over thin slices heated leftover ***ham*** and serve, passing the remaining sauce in an appropriate receptacle.

• CZECHOSLOVAK HAM SALAD •

This simple preparation is a first-course mainstay of Czech cookery.

* * *

Cut into julienne strips ½ lb. sliced leftover ***ham***, ½ lb. ***salami***, 4 medium ***dill pickles*** and 3 small ***green apples***, peeled and cored. In a bowl blend the foregoing with 5–6 tbs. ***Mayonnaise****, 2 tsp. ***Dijon mustard***, juice of ½ ***lemon*** and, if desired, a few drops of ***Worcestershire sauce***. Taste and add more mustard or lemon juice if desired. Refrigerate overnight and serve to 4 on beds of lettuce garnished with sliced tomato, lemon wedges and parsley.

• JAMBON PERSILLÉ •

In its more orthodox form this traditional Burgundian Easter offering is made by cooking a whole ham in white wine with veal knuckle, calves' feet and aromatics. The following adaptation achieves much the same effect, albeit on a more modest scale, by making judicious use of husbanded elements and compounds prepared separately in advance.

* * *

Trim all exterior fat from 1 lb. leftover baked or braised ***ham*** and cut the meat into large cubes. In a heavy pot combine ham with enough accumulated ***white-wine heeltaps*** to cover. Add a *bouquet garni,* bring wine to boil and reduce heat to maintain a steady simmer. Cover and cook 1 hour until ham is quite tender. Remove meat from liquid, drain, flake with a fork and pack loosely into a 1-qt. rectangular mold. Strain ⅓ of the cooking liquid through a damp cloth and combine it with 1 tbs. ***tarragon vinegar*** and 1 cup warm, well-reduced ***consommé****. The consommé should be gelatinous enough to form a very stiff aspic when chilled. Failing this, 1 envelope ***powdered gelatine*** should be dissolved in it. Allow liquid to cool until it begins to set and stir in 2–3 tbs. chopped ***parsley.*** Pour mixture over ham to cover and refrigerate until thoroughly jelled. Unmold and serve in ½-inch slices as a luncheon entrée or first course at dinner. Yields 14–16 single-slice portions.

• COLD HAM MOUSSE •

In a processor purée 1 lb. leftover ***ham*** combined with 1 cup very concentrated ***clarified stock****. Transfer mixture to a serving bowl, cool, stirring occasionally, and fold in 1 cup plain ***whipped cream.*** Chill thoroughly and serve as an hors d'oeuvre with toast points and a garnish of chopped ***aspic****. Serves 8–12.

The Bottomless Pot 3

THE STOCKPOT is the alembic of the kitchen, the repository of the philosophers' stone whereby the alchemists of yore dreamed of transmuting base metal to gold. It is the greatest boon to Connective Cookery ever devised. From it and the kitchen dross that simmers therein issue forth usable compounds in limitless number.

The chief products of the stockpot obviously are stocks, which the logical French call *fonds de cuisine*—the foundations of cookery. Treated one way or another, stocks serve as the bases for various soups, sauces, glazes and aspics, as well as flavoring agents for the thickeners known as *roux*. The stockpot antedates most of these uses, however, and derives directly from the cauldron of Medieval Europe, which perpetually hung over an open fire, to supply scraps and moisteners for such dishes as frumenties, mortrews and brewets, to be added to or subtracted from more or less continually and to be emptied and cleaned only at Lent.

The stockpot with its multifarious products could have evolved only where it did—in relatively cold climates where fuel was in good supply. A handful of exceptions notwithstanding (e.g., the *couscous* of North Africa and *bollito misto* of Italy), stockpot cookery is alien to the cuisines of the Mediterranean littoral, where timber historically has been scarce and a benign climate in any case obviated the need for long-burning fires. It is indigenous to the north of Europe and France in particular, where conditions were optimally propitious for its development: where indoor fires had to be maintained throughout long winters and cauldrons could be hung to simmer perpetually above them, their contents taking on ever-more-complex resonances as various items were added to the pot.

Recipes for basic stocks abound and are analogous to written scores for Dixieland jazz. By its very nature stock is improvisatory and, within certain self-evident limits, the stockpot is a catchall; a celestial garbage-disposal unit whence emanate compounds of great elegance and character, along with simple boiled dinners of one sort or another. According to conventional wisdom the uses of the stockpot stop there. The perspicacious cook will find, however, that the stockpot is a virtually inexhaustible source of good things to eat; of whole meals, indispensable ingredients and a marvelous array of hors d'oeuvres, salads, garnishes and main dishes, all constructed with recycled elements normally deemed to have been drained of their usefulness.

• A NON-RECIPE FOR STOCK •

Meat, game and poultry stocks fall into two basic categories, brown and white. Of these the second is used primarily as a basis for white sauces, uncolored soups and a flavoring for *roux*. In essence both are cooked in the same way, except that the elements of brown stock are first cooked in fat until they take on color, whereas those of white stock are simply cooked in water.

Before starting a stock the frugal connective cook will ransack the freezer for usable components. Presumably he will find there the ***carcasses*** left over from his last two or three ***chicken*** dinners: an assortment of ***bones***, perhaps including the invaluable cartilaginous ***rib ends*** prudently put by during the preparation of a rolled stuffed breast of veal; the ***rind*** stripped from a ***ham*** before the latter was baked at Easter and a couple of slices of ***lean meat*** from the same festive meal; all those ***poultry necks*** and ***gizzards*** that have been added over the past couple of months to a Ziploc bag reserved for that purpose; the ***fat*** that formed in a thick hard layer atop his *last* batch of stock when it was refrigerated; the unconsumed ***remnants*** of several ***steak*** dinners and perhaps the ***end of a roast***; possibly a hunk or two of ***shin of beef*** snapped up when the stuff was on sale at the local supermarket; and the accumulated raw ***trimmings of meats*** used for various purposes.

To the foregoing will be added whatever else turns up of a congruous nature: perhaps the ***skeleton of a duck*** served three ways at one meal, the odd ***turkey drumstick***, the savory gelatinous ***pan juices and scrapings*** from a couple of previous roasts, etc. To all this our cook will add an unpeeled ***onion*** stuck at each end with a ***clove;*** some chopped pan-browned onions, if he is so inclined; a few ***carrots*** and any ***carrot tops*** that happen to be lying around; a fat ***leek:*** any other ***root veggies*** (beets excluded) that come to hand; a few cloves of ***garlic;*** one or two hacked stalks of ***celery;*** and a *bouquet garni* made up of ***parsley stems, thyme, bay leaves, rosemary, tarragon*** or whatever. (Classically the *bouquet garni* is tied in a bit of cheesecloth but it can be stuffed into a metal teaball or, for that matter, strewn directly into the pot, along with a half-handful or so of coarse salt and a scattering of ***peppercorns.*** The hallowed Auguste Escoffier will tell you to omit the salt and most authorities will maintain that the peppercorns embitter your stock if added too early. What do *they* know? Almost any standard cookbook will imply that the eclectic, not to say eccentric, foregoing mix of elements is somehow impure; that it violates certain firmly established tenets; that a stock should be a *veal* stock, a *game* stock, or whatever. Where certain very specific uses are concerned their argument is valid. Obviously you can't make, say, a proper pheasant consommé if your stock is devoid of pheasant. For general purposes, though, your polymorphous stock will do just fine, and in any event the principles outlined here apply to stocks of any specific type. For veal stock, to take one example, use a preponderance of veal and veal bones, omitting any other animal matter—e.g., smoked ham—whose flavor might overwhelm that of the salient element.

Having turned your work surface into a charnel house, have at those poultry carcasses and ham rinds with a heavy knife or cleaver, smiting and hewing them with merry Medieval abandon. Insofar as it is possible, crack and split the bones of your quadrupeds too, using a mallet and chisel from the family tool chest if need be. (The hacksaw will come in handy on long narrow bones.) The ultimate richness of your stock resides in all that bony and cartilaginous matter, and this fracturing and flailing will facilitate its release.

At this juncture, if your finished product is to be a brown stock, melt a few ounces of that ***salvaged fat*** and coat the bottom of a large roasting pan with it, reserving the rest. Into the pan goes everything but your seasonings and *bouquet garni,* there to brown in the oven, brushed occasionally with the ***remaining fat*** and turned from time to time so that it may color evenly. Once browned, the contents of the pan—drippings, juices and scrapings included—go into the stockpot along with the *bouquet garni,* salt, pepper, and water enough to submerge the whole mess in considerable depth. Your nascent stock then is brought to a rolling boil, whereupon the heat is turned down and the pot is left to simmer gently.

At this point you will find a good deal of grayish scum bubbling malevolently on the surface. A few passes with a large spoon will clear off this unsightly dross but there is no need to rid the pot of every last vestige of it—a procedure advocated with utter fanaticism by most authorities. Indeed, there is little need to skim off *any* of the stuff, for as the liquid reduces virtually all the unwanted material will adhere to and dry up on the upper surfaces of the pot, leaving the finished stock unsullied by surface impurities.

Having allowed the stock to simmer, half-covered, for five or six hours, remove it from the fire and pour it through a large strainer sturdily mounted on a second pot capacious enough to accommodate the liquid, reserving the solids that accumulate in the sieve. Allow the stock to cool and then refrigerate it for several hours until the risen fat has set solidly on its surface. Eventually this fat must be removed—a procedure easily accomplished by running the point of a knife around its perimeter and gently lifting off the congealed mass with a spatula or some similar device. (Once removed, the fat may be frozen for use as a browning agent for a subsequent stock.) There is no hurry about this operation, though, especially with that strainerful of trash awaiting disposition of some sort. We'll return to the stock and its uses anon. Meanwhile, as it jells quietly in the fridge, let's turn our attention to

The Uses of Stockpot Solids

We have come to the moment of truth, the ultimate test of resolve for the would-be connective cook: That mess in the strainer must be dealt with. To put it bluntly, what confronts you at this point is the dirtiest, most tedious job Connective Cooking entails, and the natural impulse is to consign the whole odious business to the garbage can and have done with it. Resist the urge, for all that ill-assorted deliquescent ordure is the stuff of meals fit for the gods.

Pour yourself a stiff drink and have at it. Plunge in with both hands and separate the red and white meats. Strip those chicken necks of their meat, carefully feeling for and discarding pinhead-sized bits of vertebra. Slip the flesh from the carcasses of your birds (there will be a surprisingly large amount, however meticulously they may have been worked over at table). Again using the fingers as sensors, separate the soft gray bony matter from those poultry carcasses and reserve it (run through the processor it will be an eminently edible component of a delicious mousse). Divest those veal bones of their meat and set it aside. Salvage those bits and pieces of ham. The larger pieces of beef will make a fine dinner when reheated in a little of the stock, served with boiled vegetables and accompanied by fresh grated horseradish, a simple tomato sauce or this traditional Italian relish:

• SALSA CON CAPPERI ALL'OLIO •

In a blender or processor beat together ½ cup ***olive oil*** and 3 tbs. ***lemon juice.*** Add ½ cup drained ***capers*** and chop them very roughly.

Another good hearty use to which that beef can be put takes the slightly modified form of a venerable Latin American favorite:

• ROPA VIEJA •

Originally, the meat used for this dish was provided by tough old goats and dried on clotheslines. Hence the name, which translates as "old clothes."

* * *

Using the fingers and working with the grain, pull 2 lbs. ***cooked beef*** apart in uniformly thin strands and place them in a deep flameproof casserole. In a large skillet warm ⅓ cup ***olive oil*** and add 1 large sliced ***onion,*** 1 sliced ***green pepper,*** and 3 cloves mashed ***garlic.*** Sauté the mixture 10 minutes over low heat, then add 1¼ cups ***tomato sauce,*** ⅓ cup

white wine, and 3 ***bay leaves*** and continue to cook another 10 minutes. Add contents of skillet to beef casserole, pour in 1 cup of the ***stock,*** salt to taste and cook 30 minutes over moderate heat, stirring occasionally to prevent sticking. Just before serving add 1 oz. ***Spanish pimientos,*** cut in thin strips. Serve over cooked rice with a garnish of ***fried diced potatoes, small peas*** and, if desired, ***white asparagus tips.*** Serves 6 generously.

A CAUTIONARY TALE

On a wintry day between Thanksgiving and Christmas a benighted chap who here shall be called J chose to ignore the Jacques Pépin admonition quoted earlier: "Cooking is not for showing off to the neighbors." Laboriously and at considerable expense, he set out to impress a group of party guests by constructing a sizeable pâté composed primarily of duck and rabbit, liberally truffled, studded with black walnuts and generously laced with the finest cognac he could afford. While it baked, J confidently envisioned the reception his glorified meat loaf would be given when, clad in golden pastry embellished with all manner of relief sculpture, it was borne triumphantly to the buffet.

Pride goeth before a fall. J removed his creation from the oven, weighted it successively with a piece of pine planking tailored to fit precisely within the confines of the pâté mold, a slab of marble and the miniboulder he normally used as a sauerkraut press. Having left his *chef d'oeuvre* to cool on the deck of his country residence, he repaired to a nearby Chinese restaurant. He returned home several hours later, after gorging at leisure on *chow cham shee,* to discover that one or more raccoons had gorged at leisure on his pâté. The black-masked burglars had done their work with consummate professionalism. The weights had been neatly disposed around a mold licked so clean that it might have come directly from the dishwasher. Whether by inadvertence or nasty design, the furry epicures had left just a single nut in the bottom of an otherwise spotless utensil.

Sadder but wiser, J salvaged what he could of the day's efforts by producing a couple of quarts of *consommé double* and a dish that might be called the poor man's *pâté de foie gras* (or, more accurately, the recently impoverished fool's *pâté de foie gras):*

• MOUSSE DE RATON LAVEUR •
(Original recipe)

In a metal mold 2½″ × 4½″ × 13″ bake a pâté of rabbit and duck and (optimally) serve it to a family of raccoons or a gathering of humans. In a roasting pan brown the broken-up ***carcasses of the rabbit and duck,*** both of which presumably will have some meat adhering to the bones, along with the ***duck's neck and giblets*** and the usual ***stock vegetables.*** When these elements are well browned, toss them into the stockpot and proceed in the manner outlined in A Non-Recipe for Stock.

Having separated the cooked stock from the solids, strip away all remnants of flesh to be found on the duck and rabbit carcasses and duck neck. (Assuming you didn't ply a surgical scalpel for two or three hours on the first go-round, while assembling the late, lamented pâté, the yield should approach 2 cups.) Sauté in 1 tbs. ***butter or duck fat*** until well browned 4 or 5 ***chicken or duck livers*** and, if you like, flame them with a splash of that V.S.O.P. you bought for use in the pâté *perdu.* (In the fortuitous event that you neglected to include the rabbit innards in your pâté, sauté them too.)

In a processor combine all the meats, including the duck giblets, along with 1 red bell ***pepper,*** roasted, peeled, and seeded, ⅔ cup of ***rendered duck or goose fat,*** any available soft gray bony matter gleaned from stockpot chicken carcasses, if available, ½ tsp. white pepper, salt to taste, and 4–5 crushed juniper berries, if available. Process the mixture, using the steel blade, until absolutely smooth, then pack it into a crock and level the surface with a rubber spatula, leaving room at the top for a ¼-inch layer of ***melted duck or goose fat.*** After adding that last, refrigerate for at least 4 hours before use.

The mousse, which will keep 2 weeks or more in the refrigerator if covered with rounds of white paper, is notable for its savory richness and buttery consistency. Serve it well chilled with toast points or thick hunks of crusty bread.

To return to the matter at hand, it may be asked what all these rabbits, ducks, raccoons, pâtés and mousses have to do with the stockpot detritus we were concerned with earlier. Well, the point is that an underlying principle is at work here and that a slightly less rich but nonetheless delectable variation on the duck-and-rabbit preparation can be made from just those humble gleanings. Simply combine your ***salvaged chicken and veal*** (and, if you like, the ***ham*** too) with the ***soft bony parts of the chicken carcasses***. Add the remaining elements of the foregoing recipe in roughly the same proportions and proceed precisely as for the "raccoon" mousse.

Other Uses of Stockpot Solids

Because the additional uses to which your stockpot gleanings can be put, and the standard dishes to which they can be adapted, are all but limitless, no attempt will be made here to deal exhaustively with them. A few examples should suffice to demonstrate that the options open to the connective cook are limited only by the quantities of material at hand and the scope of his own imagination, and run a gamut from simple homely fare to dishes and garnishes of great elegance and refinement.

• BOUDINS BLANCS •

Aside from stockpot solids, the salient ingredients for these very stylish white sausages (an essential component of a traditional New Year's Eve supper in France) should come readily to hand from the larder of any dedicated connective cook, especially one who has been prudent enough to freeze a quantity of egg whites, having used the yolks for other purposes. When freezing egg whites it's a good idea to keep track of the number stored in a given container by appending a notation thereto. Alternatively, the whites may be frozen individually, one to a compartment, in an ice-cube tray and then bagged together. Salted pork sausage casings, which will keep almost indefinitely under refrigeration, are available at many Italian pork butchers. A simple, very inexpensive device for filling sausage casings takes the form of a metal funnel with a short wide spout (obtainable at Italian food and kitchenware shops). Before use, the sausage casing should first be soaked in warm water, then fitted at one end over the spigot of the kitchen sink and flushed through with warm running water. The casing is then fitted over the funnel spout, tied at the opposite end, and worked up with the fingers until its entire length has bunched around the spout. Finally, the stuffing is pushed by hand through the funnel and into the casing, which gradually works its way free of the metal spout, to be tied off with string at the desired intervals.

* * *

Boil 2¼ cups ***milk*** and pour it into a saucepan over the 2 rounded tbs. ***raw rice.*** Stir well and cook over moderate heat until rice is soft and mixture thickens. In the processor purée the rice-milk mixture together with the ***white meats*** salvaged from the stockpot, ½ lb. cut-up ***boneless pork*** loin, ½ lb. fresh pork ***fatback,*** 10 beaten egg whites, 1 tsp. ***ground white pepper,*** salt to taste and a pinch each of ***ground gingerroot, ground cloves,*** and ***ground nutmeg.*** Stuff the resultant paste into ***sausage casings,*** tying the latter off at 4-inch intervals, and poach sausages 20 minutes in gently simmering water, using some such device as a vegetable steamer or French-fry basket to facilitate lifting them safely from their hot bath. Drain sausages thoroughly and refrigerate, covered loosely with plastic wrap, for several hours. Before use, the sausages should be pricked in several places with a heavy needle, then brushed with melted butter and either grilled or gently pan-fried in butter. Serves 6–8.

NOTE—Either leftover ***cooked rice*** or ***white bread*** may be substituted for raw rice. In the latter case a *panada* should be made by moistening 10 oz. of ***crustless white bread*** in ***hot milk*** and then hand-squeezing the mixture to express as much of the liquid as possible. In small quantities, any or all of the following may be added to the sausage filling: ***whole beaten eggs, heavy cream, puréed onion*** (raw or sautéed to the transparent stage), ***chopped parsley, shallots, chives, tarragon.*** Nor is it likely that your dinner guests will object strenuously to the odd truffle paring, though your fiduciary may.

The ideal accompaniment to these sausages can be made with leftover ***boiled or baked potatoes***. (If baked potatoes are used, save those jackets for service as Baked Potato Skins.*) Just hack the peeled spuds roughly into segments, heat through in simmering stock and purée potatoes in the processor with butter, salt and pepper to taste, gradually adding stock until the consistency of the mixture is a little looser than that of ordinary mashed potatoes.

Boudins Blancs may be eaten unsauced or sauced variously. If you choose to sauce them, try a reduction of veal stock* swirled with a little butter and enriched with a beaten egg yolk stirred in off heat.

• STOCKPOT QUENELLES •

The airy dumplings known in their native France as *quenelles* generally are made with raw fish, chicken or meat. Since some of the flavor will have cooked out of your stockpot solids, this recipe calls for heavier spicing and more emphatic saucing than most. The same holds true for most treatments of stockpot solids.

* * *

Prepare and chill a *panada* of 10 oz. ***white bread,*** as described in the recipe for Boudins Blancs. In the processor or blender combine 1 lb. chilled ***stockpot chicken*** (or ***chicken and veal***), the *panada*, 6 oz. **butter,** 2 whole ***eggs, 6 egg yolks*** (reserve those whites and shells for other uses!), 2 tsp. salt, ⅓ tsp. ***white pepper,*** and ⅓ tsp. grated ***nutmeg.*** Process to a smooth consistency and shape the resultant "dough" into elongated ovals about two-thirds the length of Belgian endives. (This is best accomplished by using two large metal spoons.) Arrange the *quenelles* in a large buttered pan, leaving space between them, cover them with boiling salted water and poach 5 minutes at the gentlest possible simmer. Drain, pat *quenelles* dry and serve to 6, with either the sauce recommended above for *Boudins Blancs* or

• AURORA SAUCE •

Prepare an ounce or so of ordinary *roux,* well seasoned with fresh ground pepper and salt to taste. When all traces of flouriness have cooked out of the *roux,* beat in 1 cup rich hot ***white veal stock**** little by little over moderate heat, cooking until the blend reaches the consistency of heavy cream. Add ¼ cup thick ***tomato purée,*** blend well and finish with 2 tbs. ***butter.***

• CANNELLONI •

Prepare, cook, and drain 12 cannelloni wrappers as described on page 190, using fresh Egg Pasta* or Pasta Verdi.* Prepare a filling by blending ⅓ cup chopped leftover ***cooked spinach*** from which as much liquid as possible has been pressed, 1 cup minced ***stockpot chicken,*** ½ cup chopped leftover ***cooked ham,*** 1⅓ cups ***ricotta cheese,*** 1 tsp. chopped ***flatleaf parsley,*** 2 beaten medium ***eggs,*** ½ ***cup freshly grated Romano cheese,*** ⅓ ***tsp. grated nutmeg,*** and salt and pepper to taste. Divide filling into 12 parts and roll each into a four-inch-long cylinder. Place fillings on pasta squares, parallel with edges, and roll pasta around them to form well-packed tubes. Thinly cover the bottom of an ovenproof serving dish with marinara sauce* and arrange cannelloni side-by-side over sauce, seam-sides-down. Spoon more marinara sauce over cannelloni to cover, and cover *that* with a layer of Béchamel Sauce.* Sprinkle surface with chopped ***mozzarella cheese*** or dot with ***butter,*** cover with foil, and bake 20 minutes in a preheated 350° oven. Serve, with grated Parmesan on the side, to 6.

NOTE—Any Italian meat sauce may be substituted for marinara.

• CHICKEN HASH À LA RITZ •

French-born chef Louis Diat, who gussied up his *maman's* humble leek-and-potato soup and called it *vichyssoise,* was not above serving leftovers at the posh Ritz-Carlton Hotel when that establishment opened in Manhattan in 1910. His chicken hash remains a minor classic and this recipe departs from the original in no significant respect.

* * *

Mince 3 cups **stockpot chicken**, combine with 1½ cups ***light cream*** and cook over low heat until the cream reduces by half. Meanwhile, in a separate saucepan, melt 1½ tbs. ***butter,*** add 1½ tbs. ***flour*** and 1½ tsp. salt. Stir until smooth and cook a minute or two longer. Slowly add ¾ cup ***milk*** and stir constantly over low heat until mixture bubbles. Off heat, combine contents of both pans; pour the resultant mixture into a shallow baking dish and keep it warm.

In a saucepan heat without boiling 1 cup ***milk*** until a crinkly film forms on its surface; meanwhile, cook a *roux* of 2 tbs. ***butter*** and 2 tbs. ***flour*** in a separate pan. Skim the film from the hot milk and gradually add the latter to the *roux,* stirring constantly. Add 1 medium ***onion,*** sliced, and salt and pepper to taste and continue to cook over low heat for 15 minutes, stirring often. In a bowl beat 3 ***egg yolks*** lightly, reserving the whites for other uses, and add the hot white sauce very slowly, stirring constantly. Successively stir into the sauce 2 tbs. ***butter*** and 3 tbs. ***grated Parmesan cheese.*** Spoon the finished sauce evenly over the chicken hash and broil 4 inches or so below flame until the surface is golden. Garnish with a border of puréed cooked peas and serve piping hot to 4.

• CAPITOLADE •

Although Thomas Jefferson breakfasted on this chicken hash at Monticello, it might be more appropriate today as a weekend brunch offering.

* * *

In a large saucepan wilt 3 tbs. chopped ***onion*** in 2 tbs. melted ***butter.*** Stir in 1 tbs. minced ***shallots,*** 1 ***clove garlic,*** mashed, and 1 cup sliced ***mushrooms.*** Cook 5 minutes over low heat and stir in 1 tbs. ***flour.*** Add ⅓ cup ***white wine*** and 1 cup ***white chicken stock**** and cook over moderate heat until sauce bubbles. Reduce heat, simmer gently 10 minutes and stir in 2 cups cubed ***stockpot chicken***. Transfer mixture to a heated serving dish, garnish with ***chopped parsley*** and serve to 4.

Variation

Substitute sherry for half the white wine and add 1 oz. red pimiento, cut in thin strips.

• PAPAS RELLENAS •

A good many Mexican dishes are ideally suited to the use of stockpot solids. These savory stuffed potatoes may be served as a light luncheon entrée or as an adjunct to a more ambitious meal.

* * *

Cut 4 large baked ***Idaho potatoes*** in half lengthwise and scoop out about ¾ of the pulp, leaving a fairly even coating on the inner walls of the jackets. By hand or machine, mash the excised potato pulp until quite smooth, then beat in ⅔ stick (2⅔ oz.) ***butter*** and 4 oz. ***milk or cream.*** Reserve potato mixture and shells and prepare 1¼ cups thick ***Béchamel Sauce*** (1¼ cups hot milk thickened with a *roux* composed of 2 tbs. each butter and flour, seasoned to taste). While the Béchamel is still hot, stir in ⅔ cup grated ***Parmesan cheese,*** blending thoroughly, then fold in the following: ⅔ cup chopped leftover ***cooked ham;*** ⅔ cup ***chopped stockpot chicken;*** ½ cup fine-diced or ***puréed cooked carrots;*** ½ cup firm-cooked ***small peas;*** ½ tsp. chopped fresh ***coriander*** (optional); 1 canned ***chipotle chili,*** minced. Adjust seasonings and spoon the mixture into potato shells. Slather reserved mashed potato evenly over the top of each stuffed potato and bake about 15 minutes in a preheated 325°F oven, until the tops are lightly browned. Serves 4 as a main course, 8 as a side dish.

• TACOS DE POLLO •

Mexican cooks make extensive use of finely shredded meats and poultry as fillings for variously prepared tortillas. Unless you intend to make equally extensive use of the latter, it's questionable whether, in this case, making them from scratch is worth the time, practice and special equipment entailed. Should you wish to do so anyway, innumerable Mexican cookbooks will provide detailed procedural instructions. If not, reasonably decent products are stocked by most supermarkets. These tacos—inspired junk food—shouldn't be taken too seriously but make a tasty informal lunch or late supper.

* * *

Separate 1 lb. ***stockpot chicken*** into thin strands and set aside. In a blender or processor purée together 4 ***ancho chilis,*** 2 ripe ***tomatoes,*** peeled and seeded, 1 ***clove garlic*** and 1 medium ***onion.*** In a sauté pan or skillet heat ¾ tbs. ***vegetable oil,*** add the purée and cook 6 or 7 minutes over moderate heat, stirring constantly. Off heat, stir in 1 tsp. chopped ***parsley*** and season to taste. When sauce cools stir in 2 tbs. ***olive oil*** and 1 tbs. ***mild vinegar.*** Finally, blend in reserved ***chicken,*** grated ***Parmesan cheese*** to taste and ¼ head ***iceberg*** (yes, iceberg) ***lettuce,*** shredded. Fill 12 folded 4-inch *tacos* with the mixture and serve to 6 with shredded Monterey Jack cheese on the side.

Variations

Stockpot beef or leftover cooked turkey, lamb, pork, etc., may be substituted for the chicken.

• STOCKPOT CROQUETTES •

A good use for stockpot poultry, these croquettes may be augmented with veal from the same pot and enlivened with leftover cooked ham.

* * *

Prepare and keep hot 1 cup thick Béchamel Sauce.* In a large saucepan lightly beat 2 ***egg yolks,*** reserving the whites for other uses. Stir hot Béchamel a little at a time into egg yolks, then add 2 cups fine-chopped ***stockpot chicken*** (or a blend of ***chicken, veal and ham***), 2 tbs. ***chopped parsley,*** 1 tsp. ***grated onion,*** ⅓ tsp. ***grated nutmeg,*** and 1 tsp. ***Worcestershire sauce*** (optional). Blend all ingredients well, transfer to a shallow baking dish, and refrigerate. When mixture is well chilled, divide it into 12 parts and shape them into balls or cones. Successively coat croquettes with seasoned ***flour,*** beaten ***egg,*** and ***dry bread crumbs*** and fry a few at a time in 380° deep fat until golden (2 or 3 minutes). Drain croquettes on paper towels and serve hot to 4 with Mushroom Sauce.

• MUSHROOM SAUCE •

Over moderate heat sauté ¼ lb. thin-sliced ***mushrooms*** 5 minutes in 2 tbs. ***butter.*** Sprinkle with salt and white pepper to taste and 2 tbs. ***flour,*** stirring until mixture is smooth. Add 1 cup ***light cream*** and continue to cook, stirring constantly, until sauce bubbles and thickens.

Simmer 5 minutes longer, adding a splash of ***dry sherry*** a minute or so before removing sauce from heat. Adjust seasonings and serve.

Uses of Liquid Stock

There is little point in making stock in small batches, for it freezes extremely well, keeps for months in portion-controlled containers and may be thawed for use in minutes over low heat. The cook with a quantity of stock and stockpot solids on hand is never at a loss when an impromptu meal is called for. These materials are money in the culinary bank and may be drawn upon as needed, without standing in lines or filling out forms.

For thick opaque soups, stock can be used more or less as it comes from the pot and requires no clarification. For the thinner but nonetheless viscous and sapid consommés—the most elegant members of the soup family—however, and for sauces distinguished by their sheen and intensity, perfect clarification of your stock is the *summum bonum* and final transmogrification of dross into liquid gold.

CLARIFICATION OF STOCK

Clarification, the result of a truly miraculous culinary transubstantiation, is to the pragmatically minded a simple enough process whereby kitchen trash acts upon kitchen trash to produce gastronomic treasure. Having lifted the fat from your refrigerated stockpot, examine the content of the latter. What you will find is a dispiriting jelly of dishwater-gray coloration, with a thin layer of sediment at its bottom. What we have here is Cinderella before the intervention of her Fairy Godmother.

The clarifying agent is beaten egg white, a substance the frugal cook presumably has husbanded, along with a few eggshells, after putting the separated yolks of eggs to other good uses. Allow two whites per gallon of stock and add them to the pot, along with a few crushed eggshells, after the stock has been warmed sufficiently to liquefy it, but no more. Turn the heat up high and, stirring gently to prevent sticking at the bottom, bring the stock just to the verge of a boil. At this juncture, discontinue stirring immediately, turn the heat down to the point where it maintains a barely perceptible simmer, and slide the pot partially off the burner.

Now observe what transpires, for here is where the sorcery comes in. After a few moments a single pale mote will rise from the depths of the murk to the surface, there to be joined a moment or two later by one or more of its fellows, rising like angels to the light. In pairs and quartets, then octets and flocks, and finally as a mighty host, these ascending flecks of albumen will foregather on the surface, each bringing with it captive impurities, to form a loose fluffy mantle. Gradually this mantle will cover the entire surface, cohering as it does so. Let it cook for a while, occasionally giving the pot a quarter-turn and taking care to allow no impetuous bubbling-up of the now-obscured liquid to disturb its tranquility.

According to most authorities the clarification process requires an hour or more of cooking once a gentle simmer has been attained. Their concern, however, is with a costlier product, made from a standing start and enriched with substantial quantities of raw meat. For our purposes three-quarters of an hour or less will do the job, whose progress may be checked by inserting the point of a knife at some juncture between the outer edge of the egg-white mantle and the side of the pot. If what you see through the opening gleams darkly like a polished gemstone, clarification has been completed and the stock may be strained. Straining is best accomplished by lining a sieve or colander with a clean damp cloth of porous weave, such as a dish towel, with the device sturdily mounted on a second pot, and pouring the liquid through it. If all has gone according to plan (and there is no reason why it shouldn't have), your stock has been transmuted to an amber substance of absolute limpidity; if you have never clarified stock before you will be as awed by what you have accomplished as Jan van Eyck must have been when he stepped back to view his completed depiction of *The Arnolfini Marriage*.

You are now the possessor of a quantity of consommé, which can be used as is or cooked down further for greater concentration of its gelatinous properties and flavor. In its least concentrated form the clarified stock is eminently suitable for use as *brodo*, the Italian version of consommé, which is usually somewhat less full-bodied and viscous than the French and less satisfying unless used in conjunction with such relatively substantial garnishes as pasta, rice, dumplings, spinach, eggs and the like. Cooked down to an appreciably glutinous consistency, it becomes consommé in the classic French style and will jell more firmly when chilled. Cooked down still further it will jell still more stiffly, for use as aspic in garnishes and such molded preparations as *boeuf à la mode en gelée* and *oeufs en gelée*. Finally, reduced to a thick syrupy consistency, the stock becomes meat glaze (*glace de viande*), an invaluable culinary resource with a multiplicity of refined uses.

At every stage of concentration, then, stock is adaptable to a near-infinitude of dishes and sauces. To examine just a sampling at each stage, let's start with a few light soups made with a simple unreduced consommé.

• ZUPPA PAVESE •

According to legend this soup was devised by a Lombard peasant girl assigned to the feeding of François I, who was being held prisoner after losing the Battle of Pavia in 1525. Apparently nonplussed by the idea of serving plain broth and bread to a king, the maidservant combined them and added an egg.

* * *

In a little ***butter*** or ***olive oil*** sauté 4 thin slices of ***Italian white bread*** on both sides until golden, sprinkle liberally with grated ***Parmesan cheese*** and set in the bottoms of 4 soup plates. In a deep skillet bring 1 qt. ***clarified stock**** to an active simmer. Break an ***egg*** into a saucer, gently slide it thence into the stock and poach just until set. With a slotted spoon or skimmer remove egg from stock and slide it atop one of the bread slices. Repeat this process individually with 3 more eggs, transferring each to its own plate. Bring stock briefly to boil, remove from heat and strain into soup plates. Sprinkle with additional Parmesan cheese to taste and serve piping hot to 4.

• GNOCCHETTI IN BRODO •

This recipe was adapted slightly from one included in Edward Giobbi's excellent book *Italian Family Cooking*. Since it makes use of both stockpot solids and leftover cooked potatoes, it is ideally suited to our purposes. The Giobbi recipe calls for chicken stock and cooked chicken in the same proportions as those given here for mixed stock and mixed meats.

* * *

In a bowl blend 2 cups fine-chopped ***stockpot white meats*** (chicken or chicken and veal), 2 cups ***mashed cooked potatoes***, 2 whole ***eggs*** and 1 ***yolk***, 2 tbs. ***grated lemon rind***, ½ tsp. ***grated nutmeg***, and salt and fresh-ground pepper to taste. Shape mixture into 1-inch cylindrical dumplings, and roll them lightly in ***flour***, shaking off any excess. Bring 3 qts. ***clarified stock**** to boil and add dumplings a few at a time. Reduce heat, cover and cook at a gentle boil 5 minutes. Add ***juice*** of ½ ***lemon*** and continue to cook 5 more minutes. Distribute dumplings in soup plates with consommé to cover and serve with grated Parmesan cheese to 8–10.

• TORTELLINI IN BRODO •

Cook 24–32 fresh or frozen ***Stockpot Tortellini**** in 1 qt. rapidly boiling ***clarified stock**** for 5–6 minutes until al dente (7 or 8 minutes if frozen *tortellini* is used). Distribute *tortellini* and stock evenly in deep soup plates or bowls and serve, with a sprinkling of chopped ***parsley***, if desired, and grated ***Parmesan*** on the side, to 4.

• MINESTRA DEL PARADISO •

In the orthodox reading the stock for this Florentine creation is made with a preponderance of beef, but a good robust mixed stock will do nicely.

* * *

Separate 4 ***eggs***, reserving shells for future stock clarification. In a bowl beat whites until stiff. (In this case the stiffness refers to the condition of the egg whites and, in all probability, one's arm.) Beat yolks lightly in a separate bowl and fold into egg whites, along with 4 tsp. fine ***dry breadcrumbs***, 4 tsp. fine-grated ***Parmesan cheese*** and a light dusting of ***nutmeg.*** (The questionable hygiene of the procedure notwithstanding, the best way of accomplishing that last is to blow a pinch of the spice from the palm of the hand.) Bring 1½ qts. ***clarified stock**** to boil and drop egg batter into it from a small spoon or melon baller to form tiny puffs. When batter is used up remove pot from heat, cover, and let stand 7–8 minutes until dumplings are well puffed. Serve immediately to 6–8.

• POTAGE CRÈME DE CAPUCINE NANCY •
(Original recipe)

Why the French for this lovely peppery color-spangled manna? Only because it sounds prettier than "nasturtium soup." The "Nancy" of the title does not honor the manufacturing city on the Meurthe River, but a lady who no longer goes by that name.

* * *

Pick enough nasturtium leaves and variegated blossoms, in roughly equal proportions, to fill a loosely packed quart basket. In a processor or blender combine flowers and leaves with ⅓ cup ***cold clarified stock***,* 1 cup leftover ***boiled, baked or mashed potatoes***, and salt to taste. Run machine until nasturtiums are reduced to small flecks of color, then stir mixture into 1 qt. cool stock until thoroughly dissolved. Gradually warm mixture until just on the verge of a lively simmer. The consistency, which should be that of heavy cream, may be adjusted with additional stock if necessary. Serve hot to 4–6.

• AVGOLEMONO •

Stock made primarily with chicken would be best for this venerable Greek classic, but any stock not emphatically beefy or redolent of smoked meats will do reasonably well.

* * *

Heat 1 cup leftover ***cooked rice*** in 2 qts. ***clarified stock**** or, alternatively, cook ⅓ cup ***raw rice*** in the stock until tender. Remove pot from heat and slowly pour 1 cup of the liquid into a bowl containing 4 beaten ***eggs,*** beating constantly. Slowly pour this mixture back into remaining stock, again beating constantly. Heat soup over low flame, taking care not to bring to boil. Stir in juice of 2 ***lemons,*** 3 tbs. ***minced dill,*** and salt and white pepper to taste. Serve moderately hot to 4–6.

• SOPA CASTILLA LA VIEJA •
(Spanish cookery)

In an ungreased skillet heat 1 cup sliced ***blanched almonds*** over moderately high flame, tossing constantly until golden-brown. Lower heat, add 2 tbs. ***melted butter*** and allow its complete absorption by the almonds. Pour 6 cups ***boiling clarified stock**** over almonds, bring to a second boil, add 1 oz. ***cognac*** and simmer 6–8 minutes. Place 1 thin round of leftover ***dry bread*** in each of 6 large serving bowls. Pour soup over bread, distributing almonds evenly, and serve to 6.

• SOPA DE FLOR DE CALABAZA •
(Mexican cookery)

> The fecundity of members of the squash family never ceases to amaze home gardeners. If the question of what to do with all that zucchini (or pumpkin or whatever) arises in season, one way to nip the problem in the bud is by harvesting and eating the blossoms. Moreover, if your garden hasn't been impeccably tended, this fine soup also makes use of a common weed.

* * *

Harvest as many ***blossoms*** as you can of a summer's morning from your ***zucchini, yellow squash and pumpkin patches,*** adding a few ***day lilies*** if you so choose. Remove the stems, rinse blossoms clean of any resident insect life and chop them roughly. In a skillet sauté 1 chopped ***onion*** in 2 oz. ***butter*** until limp. Add blossoms and sauté 2 or 3 minutes longer. Meanwhile, heat 2 qts. ***clarified stock**** to which you have added a few leaves of ***pigweed*** (lamb's quarter). Add ***onion*** and blossoms to stock, simmer gently 5 minutes, remove and discard pigweed and serve soup to 6.

• DRAGON SOUP •
(Peking cookery)

Chicken stock is preferable here, but a light mixed stock may be substituted.

* * *

Heat 2 cups ***peanut oil*** in a deep fryer. Beat 1 ***egg white*** with 2 tbs. cold water until frothy, and reserve. Salt and pepper 1½ qts. ***clarified stock**** to taste and bring to boil. Add ½ cup ***diced stockpot chicken,*** cover and simmer 30 seconds. Add ½ cup ***diced crabmeat*** and ⅓ cup fresh or frozen ***peas.*** Add 3 tbs. ***cornstarch*** dissolved in an equal amount of cold water and stir 60 seconds until soup thickens. Add reserved egg white slowly, stirring constantly. Add 2 tsp. ***dry sherry*** and remove soup from heat. In heated peanut oil fry ½ oz. ***cellophane noodles,*** broken into 2-inch lengths, until puffed, turning once. Remove noodles with tongs, float them on soup and serve immediately to 6.

• PORK, SHRIMP AND BEAN CURD SOUP •
(Peking cookery)

This light but hearty cold-weather dish makes good use of the remains of last week's pork roast.

* * *

Soak 4 large dried ***black Chinese mushrooms*** in warm water until soft. Remove and discard tough stem stumps and quarter mushroom caps. Divide 3 squares ***bean curd*** into 8 pieces each. Place mushrooms and bean curd in a 2 qt. casserole, along with ¾ cup precooked (or canned) ***bamboo shoots,*** cut into bite-sized pieces, and 4 cups ***clarified stock.**** Bring to boil, lower heat and simmer, covered, 30 minutes. One minute before serving add ¼ cup diagonally shredded ***leek*** (some green top included), 2 or 3 oz. shelled and deveined ***raw shrimp*** and 3 oz. thin-sliced leftover ***roast pork loin,*** cut in pieces about 1½″ × ¾″. Serve, as soon as shrimp color, to 6.

More Intense Consommés

In general, greater concentration and viscosity distinguish the consommés of France from most eaten elsewhere. This is what the Victorian literary critic Eneas Sweetland Dallas had to say on the subject of consommé:

> This is a fine word and worthy to rank with the "mobled queen" in Hamlet. "That's good," says Polonius; "mobled queen is good." So is consommé. To the innocent English mind it suggests something consummate. It really means broth, which by boiling has been consumed away till it has become very strong. The best English rendering of it is Double Broth.

To produce a shimmering, full-bodied consommé in the French style it is necessary, then, only to boil away a fair proportion of the water from a well-made clarified stock. The degree to which the stock is to be reduced for consommé is best left to the individual cook, whose moral dilemma will arise when he tries to strike a practical compromise between the richness of his soup and the concomitant loss of its volume. Will he, in short, serve a fine soup to six or a great soup to four?

As Dallas went on to note in *Kettner's Book of the Table* (a work he ghosted for a prominent London restaurateur of the day), there are at bottom only two distinct kinds of consommé, of which one is based on a stock made predominantly with veal and veal bones and which is almost never served undiluted as soup. All other distinctions, Dallas observed, are

> mere thimble-rigging. The fact is, that there is no such broth as consommé of fowl distinct from ordinary consommé. A little more or less fowl cannot constitute a difference of kind; and the difference of name only perplexes cooks, who, if they work out a consommé in the proper way, are fairly entitled to some freedom in the choice of quantities.

The inherent character of any consommé resides, then, in the richness of its aroma and the sapidity of its mingled elements. Its identity, on the other hand, is conferred by its garniture. While by no means exhausting the number of possibilities, *Larousse Gastronomique* identifies and provides recipes for upward of a hundred consommés, while the august Auguste Escoffier chips in with just over ninety, a goodly proportion of which are unlisted in *Larousse*. Once again Dallas is instructive on the subject:

> It has been reckoned that there are about five hundred kinds of soup [in 1877, when the cuisines of the Orient and many other parts of the globe were relatively unknown in England]; but this number is reached by giving the dignity of a separate receipt to every little variation. Thus there are a dozen sorts of Italian paste—vermicelli, macaroni, nouilles, lasagnes, and the rest. Each of these put into a clear gravy gives rise to a different soup. If we put into the very same fluid sago or tapioca, bread or rice or barley, a purée of potatoes or peas, carrots or turnips, tomatoes, or Jerusalem artichokes—we are supposed instantly to create a new soup. It would be a waste of time to enumerate all the possible combinations of solids and liquids that may be called soup. The solids are innumerable. . . .

The dignity of a separate receipt shall not be given here to every little variation. Suffice it for our present purposes to set forth a few general observations on the subject, to enumerate a small sampling of fairly diversified possibilities and to add that any cook worth his salt should be able to serve a good soup every day of the year without inducing boredom.

The variety of consommé garnishes is limitless, with just about every known vegetable and many pastas eligible for inclusion and with stockpot solids eminently suitable for use in many forms closely based on standard recipes made up of raw ingredients. As a rule vegetables are cut in fine dice or julienne strips, shredded or, in the case of green leafy varieties, often rolled, with or without a filling of some sort. Meat and poultry garnishes usually take the form of *quenelles* or dumplings, small forcemeat balls, dice, bite-sized slices or julienne strips. Croutons of one sort or another—from humble crusts of stale bread to small pastry puffs—may be used to add belly-filling bulk or frou-frou, as the case may be, and the rolled sliced crêpes of *consommé célestine* and the various cereal grains serve much the same purposes. The inclusion of old dried-out domestic mushrooms always will add more flavor and character to a consommé than will the fresh product specified by most standard recipes, and eggs always can be counted on to enrich a consommé and enhance its visual appeal, whether they be poached, strung out in fine golden threads (*oeufs filés*) or beaten and stirred into the liquid to form the yellow-white ribbons of Chinese egg drop soup or the "little rags" of the Italian *straciatelle*. It hardly need be added that many consommés, like life itself, seem just a bit better when laced with a belt of brandy or fortified wine.

The classic French consommés are exhaustively explored in the aforementioned *Larousse* and Escoffier, among other more-or-less encyclopedic sources, many of whose recipes are readily adaptable to the stockpot solids and other leftovers of Connective Cookery. The recipes that follow are less formally codified and are included as examples of what can be done by the frugal, reasonably imaginative connective cook.

• POTLUCK CONSOMMÉ •
(Original recipe)

This soup originated on the spur of the moment, when guests arrived unexpectedly on the evening of a stock-making day in high summer, when there was a profusion of squash blossoms in the garden. Improvisatory as it may have been, it was enthusiastically received.

* * *

Fine-chop 3 oz. ***stockpot chicken*** and blend thoroughly with finely minced white of 1 ***scallion*** (reserving green top), a scant pinch of ***nutmeg***, salt and pepper to taste and ½ beaten ***egg***. Wet hands with cold water, form mixture into balls the size of hazelnuts and set aside. Slice reserved scallion top laterally in rings and set aside. Slice 6–8 rinsed ***zucchini blossoms*** laterally and set aside. Break 2 oz. ***vermicelli*** or ***angel's hair pasta*** into 1" lengths and set aside. In a 2-qt. pot bring 1½ qts. ***rich consommé**** to boil with a sprig or two of fresh ***rosemary*** submerged in the liquid in a metal teaball. Add pasta, stirring to separate strands, and lower heat after 2 minutes, to maintain a brisk simmer. Add the forcemeat dumplings and simmer until they rise to surface. Remove rosemary, add remaining ingredients, cook 2 minutes longer and serve very hot to 6.

• CRAB BAIT CONSOMMÉ •
(Original recipe)

> Chicken neckers was a term I was to hear often in the next twenty-four hours. Lester was talking about outsiders and rank amateurs, since there is a widespread belief among dilettante crabbers that chicken necks are the best crab bait.
>
> —William W. Warner,
> *Beautiful Swimmers*

A mess of chicken necks had been removed from the freezer to thaw in anticipation of an afternoon's dilettante crabbing, but the game was called on account of rain and the necks were tossed into the stockpot. Hence the name of the soup, a sort of minimalist's Gumbo.

* * *

Remove, separate into strands and set aside the flesh from 4–6 ***stockpot chicken necks***, taking care to winnow out bits of vertebra. Bring 1½ qts. ***rich consommé**** to a gentle boil and add ½ lb. sliced ***okra*** to pot. Cook 10–12 minutes until okra is tender, add ½ cup leftover ***cooked rice*** and reserved neck meat. Cook 2 minutes longer, adjust seasonings and serve to 6.

• CONSOMMÉ AU ROQUETTE •
(Original recipe)

Although the herb *arugula*, or rocket *(Eruca sativa)*, is used almost exclusively as a salad green, its virtues as a soup garnish shouldn't be overlooked, for it contributes to a light appetite-stimulating consommé with an intriguing nutlike flavor.

* * *

Bring 1½ qts. ***consommé**** to a lively simmer, add 1 bunch ***arugula***, washed and stemmed, and cook just until greens wilt. Serve, with grated ***Parmesan*** or ***Romano cheese***, to 6.

• CONSOMMÉS AUX FLEURS •

Just put some roses
in a soup and put
some dandelions in it too
and if you really want
to make it good add
some daisies in the soup
invite your friend over if you can
and when your friend
says "boy that smells
as good as flowers" laugh
your petals off.

—Jin Hwa (age 9), *Flower Soup*, 1978

* * *

As has been noted earlier, garden flowers merit more culinary attention than they usually receive. In season, singly or in combination, the petals of violets, roses, nasturtiums, day lilies and tiger lilies make colorful, often hauntingly aromatic, sometimes surprisingly pungent consommé garnishes. Because of their extreme delicacy and, in some cases, the fugitive nature of their colors, flower petals should be added to consommés at the very last moment before serving, with some stirred into the soup and a few floated on the surface. If nasturtiums are used, hold the pepper.

• CONSOMMÉ AUX AILERONS FARCIS •

A classic of the French repertory, this delectable consommé can be made almost entirely of stockpot gleanings and leftovers—if the cook exercises a little foresight by clipping and accumulating the wingtips of uncooked poultry.

* * *

Thaw 12 husbanded ***wingtips of chicken or ducks***, or 6 of ***turkeys or geese*** Strip them of their skins, keeping the latter intact, and stuff skins with a forcemeat made of ***stockpot poultry*** as described in the recipe for Stockpot Quenelles.* Poach stuffed wingtips 10 minutes in 1½ qts. actively simmering ***consommé***,* then remove them with a slotted spoon or skimmer and set aside. Strain consommé through a damp cloth if necessary and return to simmer. Add ½ cup rinsed leftover ***cooked rice*** and stuffed wingtips and simmer 5 minutes longer. Serve, lightly garnished with chopped ***parsley*** or ***chives,*** to 6.

• WON TON SOUP •
(Cantonese cookery)

This perennially popular offering usually is made with a rather thin chicken broth, but takes on real resonance if a good strong well-colored consommé is used.

* * *

Cut 6 water-softened dried ***black Chinese mushrooms*** (stem butts removed) into thin shreds and set aside. In a processor blend 1 cup ***flour,*** 1 whole ***egg*** and a pinch of salt, using the steel blade and adding cold water a few drops at a time until dough forms a soft elastic ball. Turn dough out onto a lightly floured surface and knead by hand for a minute or two until a velvety consistency is reached. Cover dough with a damp cloth and let it rest 15–20 minutes. While dough rests, prepare a filling by blending ½ lb. ground lean leftover ***roast pork,*** ¼ cup minced ***onion,*** 2 tbs. fine-***minced celery,*** 1 beaten ***egg,*** 1 tbs. ***soy sauce,*** ½ tsp. ***dry sherry*** and ½ tsp. ***cornstarch.***

On a floured surface roll out dough as thin as possible and cut into 3″ squares. To fill won tons, moisten each dough square on one side with water and place 1 scant tsp. filling slightly off-center on dough. Fold dough over filling so that edges meet, pressing unfilled areas firmly together. Fold back two corners of each won ton, so that they just overlap at tips. Moisten tips with water and press them firmly together.

Bring 1½ qts. ***rich consommé*** to boil. Add 24 ***won tons*** while gently stirring soup and boil 5 minutes until dough is *al dente.* Lower heat to simmer, add reserved ***mushrooms*** and ¼ lb. ***spinach,*** cleaned and trimmed, and cook 2 minutes longer. Garnish off heat with laterally chopped ***scallion green*** and ***lean leftover roast pork*** cut in julienne strips. Serve to 6.

NOTE—Excess won ton skins or filled dumplings will freeze well for future use. Conversely, any previously frozen pasta dough may be thawed and rolled out for use as won ton skins.

To lay the shade of E. S. Dallas to rest, let's refrain from any further detailed examination of the innumerable little variations that have been sedulously catalogued and anatomized as consommé-this and consommé-that. Almost any combination or permutation of garnishes will produce an acceptable consommé, if not a magnificent one. Let your ingenuity be your guide or consult the standard recipes to see how they can be adapted to Connective Cookery. Always bear in mind, however, that stockpot solids substituted for raw ingredients usually will require less cooking time, and often more emphatic seasoning, than the latter.

The Pot Thickens 4

WE HAVE by no means exhausted the uses to which clarified stock can be put. When chilled, a good intense consommé will jell to a firm consistency, for use in such cold soups as Consommé Madrilène and as a glaze or chopped garnish for cold meats and vegetables. Further reduction of the stock, and the concomitant concentration of its gelatinous properties, produces a stiffer aspic jelly for use in molded dishes. Still further reduction produces sauce bases of notable intensity, culminating in the *glace de viande* mentioned earlier. Let's begin with a few jellied soups.

A WORD ABOUT JELLING CONSOMMÉS

Packaged gelatine will of course stiffen any consommé to the desired consistency and is looked upon benignly by many a respected authority on culinary technique. The view from this quarter, however, is that a well-made consommé, like a well-made woman, requires no adventitious support.

• CONSOMMÉ MADRILÈNE •

Chicken stock or a mixed stock with chicken dominant should be used for this traditional hot-weather favorite, which is found far more often on French menus than in Madrid, its putative city of origin.

* * *

Warm together 4 cups ***consommé***,* ⅔ cup concentrated ***tomato purée*** and a pinch of ***cayenne***, stirring well. Pour mixture into individual serving cups and chill until firmly jelled. Stir soup loosely with a fork, garnish with ***lemon wedges*** and serve to 4.

NOTE—Alternatively tomato purée may be added to stock before clarification. For either version diced ***sweet pimientos,*** simmered briefly in stock, may be added to the soup.

• JELLIED BULLSHOT •
(Original recipe)

A solution of sorts to the problem of getting happily through lunch or dinner with your maiden aunt Millicent, a strict tee-totaler by whom you hope to be remembered when she goes to her reward.

* * *

Pour 1 cup strong ***beef consommé**** into one of two serving cups, ⅔ cup of same into the other. To smaller portion add 2 oz. ***vodka*** (or ***gin***) and a dash each of ***Worcestershire sauce*** and ***Tabasco.*** To both portions add 1 tsp. fresh ***lemon juice.*** Stir well, chill until jelled, stir lightly with a fork and serve, taking care to avoid any who-gets-which confusion.

On second thought Aunt Millicent may do better by you, when the time comes, if *she* receives the spiked cup.

• JELLIED MUSHROOM CONSOMMÉ •

Simmer 2 cups chopped ***mushroom stems*** 30 minutes in 3½ cups strong ***consommé.**** Strain mixture through a damp cloth, pressing mush-rooms to express as much liquid as possible and reserving them for other uses. Add 2 tbs. ***dry sherry*** and salt and pepper to taste. Pour soup into individual serving cups, chill until jelled, stir lightly with a fork and top each portion with a dollop of ***sour cream.*** Serves 4.

• JELLIED CUCUMBER CONSOMMÉ •

Peel, halve lengthwise, seed and grate 1 good-sized ***cucumber*** and set aside. Grate ⅓ medium ***onion*** and add to grated cuke. Fine-chop ¼ cup ***fresh mint*** (loosely packed) and add to foregoing mixture. Stir the mixture into 4 cups lukewarm ***consommé**** (chicken by preference) with ***juice*** of ½ ***lemon.*** Adjust seasonings, pour soup into individual serving cups and chill until firmly jelled. Stir lightly and serve to 4.

• R.I.P. AUNT MILLICENT •
(Original recipe)

A glorified, soupified variant on the bloody mary with which to toast your late, temperate relative, who presumably made generous provision for your future solvency before meeting her Maker.

* * *

Fine-dice (1/16″ × 1/16″) 2 oz. ***stockpot beef*** and 1 oz. each ***stockpot carrot*** and ***celery*** and set aside. Prepare 1 qt. ***Consommé Madrilène,**** using a very concentrated ***clarified stock**** and doubling the normal amount of ***tomato purée.*** Allow mixture to cool to room temperature (assuming you don't live in an igloo) and stir in 9 oz. ***vodka, juice*** of 1 ***lemon,*** 1 tsp. ***Worcestershire sauce,*** a good zap of ***Tabasco*** and salt and pepper to taste. Pour into 4 large serving cups, chill until jelled, stir lightly with a fork and serve to 4.

NOTE—Vodka in quantity may act somewhat like antifreeze and prevent the soup from jelling stiffly. Nobody will mind.

• JELLIED TARRAGON CONSOMMÉ •

Bring 5 cups full-bodied ***consommé**** to simmer and remove from heat. Stir in 3 or 4 sprigs ***fresh tarragon*** (the equivalent of 3 tsp. picked leaves) and allow to steep 6–8 minutes. Strain consommé into individual serving cups, discarding tarragon. Chill soup until jelled, stir lightly and serve to 4.

• JELLIED WINE CONSOMMÉS •

Fortified wines such as port, sherry, Madeira and Marsala have a particularly felicitous effect on many hot and cold consommés. For the jellied wine consommé of your choice add ½ cup of any of the aforementioned to each quart of strong consommé* while the latter is still liquid. Stir well, chill and serve as for the recipes given above.

Aspics

> **As•pic** (as' pik) **n.** 1. A cold dish of meat, fish, vegetables, or fruit combined and set in a gelatin mold. 2. A jellied garnish of meat or fish stock and gelatin [French (*sauce*) or (*ragout*) *à l'aspic*, from *aspic*, ASPIC (snake), from the different colors of the jelly, as compared with those of the snake.]
>
> —*The American Heritage Dictionary* (1969)

> And now it may be asked, Why is it called aspic? There is upon this point the most curious ignorance, although the explanation lies upon the surface. Most Englishmen think it must have to do with the asp, and the more readily since they remember the question of Cleopatra, bitten by the snake—"Have I the aspic in my lips?" Even Frenchmen, who ought to be better informed, make a similar mistake. The great lexicographer, M. Littré . . . says that aspic is so called because it is cold as a snake, which is proverbially cold! . . . It has nothing to do with anything so venomous. It means lavender—in old French, espic or spic; in good old English, spike, lavender-spike, and spikenard.
>
> —E. S. Dallas, *Kettner's Book of the Table* (1877)

The invaluable Dallas goes on to explain that lavender-spike is to be found in the sauces of classical Rome and in French and English herbal recipes of the fourteenth century, but that lavender, being an inferior seasoning, "dropped out of account while still the name remained," and

> in the course of time it has come about that aspic belongs to the long list of things which, like houses dispossessed of their first owners, retain names no longer their own—cervelas without brains, orgeate without barley, blancmanger without fowl, galantine without galingale, cheesecakes without curd, pomatum without apple, Julienne without wood-sorrel, bisque

without wood-pigeon, marmalade without quince, vinegar without wine.

The virtues of aspics are threefold: They stimulate the palate by delighting the eye; they preserve cooked foods from the debilitating effects of exposure to air; they are the only meat-based sauces appropriate to many cold dishes. In the pompous Carême-derived cookery of another era, aspics were cut into decorative shapes (*croutons en gelée*) as embellishments to various dishes but the practice—overly showy and essentially purposeless—has been largely dispensed with since. Today's aspics take three primary forms: They are chopped for use as a garnish with cold hors d'oeuvre and buffet offerings, applied as a coating to cold meats, fish and fowl, or molded in combination with various cold ingredients. Skillfully and imaginatively constructed, a fine aspic adds a visual dimension to dining unlike anything else cookery has to offer; outstanding examples of the molded genre are to the culinary arts what vintage St. Louis, Clichy and Baccarat paperweights are to the decorative arts.

• OEUFS EN GELÉE •

A poached egg suspended in an artfully decorated aspic requires a bit of fussing with, but if you *have* to show off to the neighbors it's worth the effort. The elegance of the shimmering finished product notwithstanding, no special molds or equipment are needed, as can be seen from the improvisatory gear described below.

Equipment

1 8-oz. mustard jar or any similar circular container with a bottom about 2½ inches in diameter

1 4″ × 4″ square of aluminum foil for each serving

1 straight-sided bar glass (lowball type), 3 inches in diameter, for each serving

For each *Oeuf en Gelée* make a mold by centering mustard jar on foil and drawing up foil edges around sides of jar. Smooth foil against sides of jar and remove and grease resultant mold thoroughly with

soft butter (a forefinger will do the job nicely). Break one ***egg*** into each mold. In a large shallow pan bring ½″ water to boil, place molds in water, poach eggs, covered, just until whites are set and plunge molds into cold water to arrest cooking process.

Over very low heat warm to a syrupy consistency ½ cup ***Jellied Tarragon Consommé***,* preferably of a fairly pale color, for each serving. Using bar glasses as aspic molds pour about ¼″ warmed consommé into each and refrigerate until aspic sets, meanwhile keeping remaining consommé in a semi-solid state. When aspic in molds has set firmly, arrange one pair blanched ***tarragon leaves*** top-side-down on each surface. Moisten surfaces with a thin film of reserved consommé and return molds to the refrigerator for a few minutes.

Strip foil from poached eggs, place one egg top-side-down in the center of each mold, add reserved semi-set consommé to cover and refrigerate once more until aspic sets. Meanwhile cut 2 oz. leftover ***cooked ham*** or ***beef tongue*** into julienne strips. When aspic in molds has set, arrange equal portions of ham or tongue on surfaces, cover with remaining reserved consommé and chill once more until thoroughly stiffened. To unmold aspic, dip glasses briefly in very hot water to level of aspic, wipe dry and invert onto serving dishes. Serve one egg per portion as a first course.

> **NOTE**—For added pizzazz add a dash of ***lemon juice*** to the consommé while it is still liquid, and for added visual appeal add a few bits of ***black olive*** to the decorative scheme, bearing in mind that what goes into the mold first ultimately will be its crowning glory. Thin slices of ***truffle*** or ***foie gras***, cut in interesting shapes, would of course be the *ne plus ultra*.

• PETIT ASPIC DE VOLAILLE •

The procedure for this very attractive first-course offering is essentially the same as for *Oeufs en Gelée** but the ingredients derive almost entirely from the stockpot. For each serving decorate the bottom layer of aspic (ultimately the top) as desired, with thin rounds of ***cooked carrot*** cut into fancy shapes (a set of truffle cutters comes in handy here, as it does for decorating pastry crusts, cold poached fowl, etc.), ***tarragon leaves,*** bits of ***black olive,*** cutouts of ***hard-boiled egg white,*** dice of ***pimiento,*** etc. Then shape a few ounces of ***Moussé de Raton Laveur*** (alternative version)* into a squat cylinder slightly smaller in diameter than your mold, place it atop the first layer of aspic, add semi-solid ***consommé**** to cover and chill until set. Any full-bodied consommé may be used for the aspic, either as is or variously flavored with ***tarragon, celery, mushrooms, fortified wine,*** etc., as described in the pertinent recipes for Jellied Consommés.*

• BOEUF À LA MODE EN GELÉE •

If evidence were required that leftovers need not be dreary this revered French standby might be submitted as Exhibit A.

* * *

For individual servings trim leftover roast ***tenderloin of beef,*** leftover ***pot roast*** or the like, slice in rounds about ⅛″ thick and set aside, figuring on about 4 oz. per serving. In separate salted waters cook until tender a handful of shelled ***peas*** and a slender ***carrot.*** Slice narrower end of carrot in thin rounds and remainder on the bias, to produce thin ovals. Add ***port wine*** to cooled ***consommé**** in proportion given for Jellied Wine Consommés* and stir well. Pour about ⅛″ of consommé into each of the desired number of individual molds (short straight-sided bar glasses or custard cups will do) and chill until semi-set. Arrange a few ***peas*** in a circle on the aspic surface, leaving a little space between them and the inner wall of the mold. Add semi-set consommé to cover and chill until stiff. Arrange carrot ovals on aspic surface with a carrot round at their center, to produce a flower shape. Add consommé to cover and again chill until set. Following the same procedure alternate slices of beef with consommé to cover, ending up with a ⅛″ layer of consommé. Chill until aspic is well set, unmold onto serving dishes and surround molds with cold julienne ***string beans*** vinaigrette or a salad of mixed vegetables. Serve with ***Mayonnaise*** on side.

Variations
As they do with consommés the French meticulously differentiate among minor variations on a single theme, describing what is essentially the same dish as *"à la niçoise," "à la parisienne," "à la strasbourgeoise,"* etc., if a mere substitution of a single element of garniture is made. As a certain young Capulet put it, "What's in a name?" Beef in aspic may be constructed in a variety of ways to be served individually or portioned out at table. The meat may be sliced, diced, cut in julienne strips or molded in one large piece. Vegetable salads may be served on the side or incorporated into the aspic. Molds may be shallow (a soup dish will do, with the beef arranged in overlapping slices) or deep, round or oval or rectangular. Aspics may be unmolded onto lettuce or cold rice beds or large shaped croutons. Accompaniments and garnishes may run a virtually inexhaustible gamut so long as they are reasonably compatible. Let your imagination be your guide.

• DUCKLING IN ASPIC •

This regal hot-weather offering is, in Robert Farrar Capon's terminology, a festal dish but it makes splendid use of ferial components. Needless to say the remains are to be put to good use when the initial feast is no more than a happy memory.

* * *

Rub the body cavities of 2 good-sized ***ducklings*** with halved ***lemons,*** squeezing the latter as you rub, to extract the juice. Fill the same cavities with sliced ***oranges,*** adding a couple of ***whole cloves*** to each. Roast birds breast-side-up for 2 hours in a 350°F oven, basting every 20 minutes or so with a blend of the pan juices and 1½ cups leftover ***dry white wine.*** Allow birds to cool, tidy them up with paper towels and refrigerate until well chilled, reserving pan juices and fats for future splendors. To 4 cups rich ***consommé**** add ¼ cup ***Grand Marnier.*** Stir well and chill, stirring occasionally, until mixture is well thickened but not set. Spoon semi-set aspic over ducklings and return them to the refrigerator. Chill remaining consommé in shallow pans until stiffened, turn resultant aspic out onto wax paper and chop into fine glittering dice. Arrange ducklings on a chilled serving platter (preferably silver) and surround them with chopped aspic. Serves 6.

• DUCKLING MOUSSE IN ASPIC •
(Original recipe)

Blend Grand Marnier and cooled strong ***consommé**** in the same proportions as above, add 1 tsp. strained ***lemon juice*** and stir well. Proceed as for *Petit Aspic de Volaille,** substituting an equal amount of *Mousse de Raton Laveur* (first version minus the rabbit)* for the chicken mousse.

• TERRINE OF DUCK LIVERS •

Having roasted a couple of birds for Duckling in Aspic,* you may find yourself wondering what to do with the livers (assuming they weren't excised at the source of supply). Combine them with any others previously stashed in the freezer and make this simple, refined hors d'oeuvre of them.

* * *

Over low heat sauté until transparent ⅓ large ***yellow onion*** and ½ ***clove garlic,*** both sliced, in 1 tbs. ***butter*** or ***duck fat.*** Increase heat, add 6 oz. ***duck livers*** and sear them on all sides. Reduce heat and sauté until livers are cooked on outside, pink within. Empty contents of pan into a blender or processor, using a rubber spatula to scrape up bits and drippings. Add 1 tsp. ***Cognac,*** 1 generous pat ***butter,*** 1½ oz. ***heavy cream*** and salt and pepper to taste. Purée until a smooth creamy consistency is reached, adding more cream a few drops at a time if necessary. Pour mixture into 4 small individual serving terrines or crocks and cover each with ⅛″ semi-liquid Port-Flavored Consommé* (see Jellied Wine Consommés*). Chill thoroughly and serve in molds with toast points on the side.

NOTE—If your concept of Connective Cooking doesn't exclude the use of items as costly as truffles (and there is no reason it should in principle), a thin round or fancy cutout, pressed into the surface of the terrine before the aspic is added, would not be amiss. On the other hand it's highly questionable whether a microchip of the black fungus will add perceptible flavor or aroma, so you may be as well off gastronomically—and better off financially—by settling for a sliver of black olive.

• TURKEY IN ASPIC •

Cut ***breast*** of leftover ***roast turkey*** into uniform thin slices and set aside. Cover bottom of a deep platter with cooled liquid ***consommé**** (spiked, if you wish, with a jolt of ***cherry brandy)*** and chill until set. Arrange turkey slices in an overlapping pattern and garnish with ***blanched pitted cherries.*** Coat turkey and fruit with consommé to cover and chill until resultant aspic is quite stiff. Surround with a well-spiced border of cold leftover ***turkey dressing*** and/or chopped aspic. Number of portions will vary according to amount of meat used.

• POULARDE À L'ESTRAGON EN GELÉE •

Truss a plump 4–5 lb. ***chicken*** and poach 1 hour in very gently simmering ***white stock**** to which a half-handful of fresh ***tarragon*** has been added. Allow fowl to rest in the poaching liquid off heat until cooled to room temperature. Remove fowl from stock, allowing liquid to drain back into pot from body cavity and reserving stock for future re-use. Pat bird dry, remove trussing, place on a serving platter and chill, lightly covered, in the refrigerator. Thaw 2 cups frozen ***Jellied Tarragon Consommé**** (or warm an equal amount of the same refrigerated preparation) and stir in 1 cup ***Madeira.*** Allow consommé to thicken to a heavy syrupy consistency and paint it lightly onto the surface of the chilled chicken. Decorate chicken breasts with fan-shaped arrangements of blanched tarragon leaves and refrigerate again until aspic coating sets firmly. Apply a second, somewhat thicker coating of aspic to chicken and refrigerate until it sets firmly, meanwhile refrigerating remaining consommé in a shallow pan until it too has firmly set. Chop the latter as for Duckling in Aspic,* surround the chicken with it and serve to 4.

• SUPRÊMES DE VOLAILLE JEANNETTE •

A poor man's adaptation of a luxurious French classic that conventionally incorporates *foie gras,* this is no mean dish in its own right.

* * *

Remove ***breasts*** from 3 ***chickens,*** reserving remainder of birds for other uses. Poach breasts (the *chicken* breasts, for heaven's sake!) in simmering salted water just until cooked through. Allow flesh to cool, remove skin and trim flesh to form 6 uniform ovals. Cover each piece with 1 rounded tbs. ***Mousse de Raton Laveur*** (either version)* and mound the mixture evenly to cover chicken breasts. Place pieces on a rack and coat evenly with ***Chaud-froid Blanc*** (recipe below). Top each piece with a decorative ***truffle*** (or ***black olive***) cutout and spoon concentrated light-colored ***consommé,*** chilled to a syrupy consistency, over each piece. Arrange pieces in a radiating pattern, like flower petals, on a serving platter and refrigerate 20 minutes or more. Fill uncovered surfaces of platter to its border with ***chopped aspic*** of good color and serve to 6.

• CHAUD-FROID BLANC •

In a small saucepan over low heat blend 1 tbs. each ***flour*** and ***butter*** to make a smooth *roux*. Gradually add ½ cup very gelatinous ***chicken consommé**** and ½ cup ***milk,*** stirring constantly until mixture just begins to boil. Add ½ cup ***heavy cream,*** place saucepan in a bowl of cracked ice and stir sauce until very cold and just on the verge of jelling. Immediately pour sauce over meat, coating the latter evenly and smoothly. (If sauce over-thickens and won't pour, warm it gently until the desired consistency is reached.)

• VEGETABLE SALAD IN ASPIC •

In a pan of cracked ice chill a 1-qt. decorative mold and line it with a good thick coating of strong blond ***consommé**** cooled to the syrupy stage. (Tilting the mold this way and that will facilitate matters.) When aspic has set, decorate the bottom and inner walls of the mold with leftover ***cooked chicken, cooked vegetables, whites of hard-boiled eggs,*** etc., all cut into ornamental shapes and dipped in semi-thickened consommé to ensure adhesion. When decorations have set firmly cover bottom and sides of mold with a ⅜″ layer of semi-set ***consommé*** and chill until stiffly jelled. Blend 2½ cups mixed ***cooked vegetables*** (whole

peas, and dice of ***green beans, artichoke*** bottoms, ***carrots, asparagus, celeriac,*** etc.) and ***raw vegetables (celery, avocado, onion, yellow squash, cucumber,*** etc.) with ¾ cup ***Mayonnaise Colée*** (recipe below). Fill mold nearly to the top with the mixture; fill remaining space with semi-set consommé and refrigerate 2 or 3 hours. Unmold salad onto a chilled serving platter lined with ***lettuce leaves*** and garnish with ***hard-boiled egg*** wedges, ***cherry tomatoes,*** scoops of cole slaw, etc. Portions will vary according to use.

• MAYONNAISE COLÉE •

Soften very stiff aspic* to syrupy consistency and blend thoroughly with an equal amount of Mayonnaise.*

The foregoing examples represent only a fraction of the combinations and permutations to which cold foods lend themselves in liaison with aspic. The stuff is an invaluable resource, especially where party buffets are concerned, for there is nothing so dispiriting as a tray or sideboard laden with erstwhile temptations that have begun to dry up, curl and discolor even before the majority of the guests have arrived. On the other hand a gleaming array of offerings set like jewels in a glittering bed of edible ruby, amber or topaz chips lends panache to any occasion. Needless to say any of the few festal preparations cited easily can be adapted to the needs of the ferial cook. For example, whole fowl need not be sacrificed to such dishes as Duckling in Aspic* or *Poularde à l'Estragon en Gelée.** In either case trimmed cooked leftovers will take a new lease on life if treated in the same manner as the unmutilated birds. Similarly sliced leftover ***roast leg of lamb*** (rare, please) may be prepared as for *Suprêmes de Volaille Jeannette** if *Mayonnaise Colée** is substituted for *Chaud-froid Blanc,** and cold sliced leftover ***cooked ham*** may be successively glazed with *Chaud-froid Blanc** and ***Port-Flavored Aspic*** (see Jellied Wine Consommés*) to produce a simplified but eminently palatable variant of the French classic *Jambon Glacé Reine Pedauque.* Larger pieces of ***stockpot meats,*** leftover ***cooked ham, tongue, pork, veal*** or whatever may be roughly cubed and combined, suspended in a stiff aspic flavored according to preference and served in slices like headcheese. But why go on? A reasonable sense of the fitness of things will enable you to produce a near-infinitude of adapted classics and autograph creations.

Meat Glaze (Glace de Viande)

> Our forefathers knew how to make meat extracts. They compressed them into cubes and used them when required in the preparation of soups and sauces.
>
> . . . Here is a recipe for cubes of meat extract, "easy to carry, and which will keep for a year or more." It is taken from *Les secrets de la nature et de l'art concernant les aliments* (1769).
>
> "Take a quarter of large beef carcase, a whole calf (or part of it only according to size), two sheep, two dozen old hens and cocks, or a dozen turkeys, plucked and drawn . . ."
>
> —*Larousse Gastronomique* (English edition, 1961)

> The various glazes of meat, fowl, game and fish are merely stock reduced to the point of glutinous consistency. Their uses are legion. Occasionally they serve in decorating dishes with a brilliant and smooth coating which makes them appetizing; at other times they may help to strengthen the consistency of a sauce or other culinary preparation, while again they may be used as sauces proper after they have been correctly creamed or buttered.
>
> —Auguste Escoffier, *The Escoffier Cook Book*

The eighteenth-century recipe quoted in *Larousse* reads like the culinary equivalent of a cosmic Black Hole. Fortunately for budget-minded modern cooks it isn't absolutely necessary to combine a quarter of beef, a whole calf, a couple of sheep and a flock of poultry in order to produce a bouillon cube. Even so, considered in terms of its volume alone, *glace de viande,* the ultimate concentration of stock, may leave the impression that the mountain has labored to bring forth a mouse, for gallons of soup must be consumed away to produce a few ounces of the stuff. The impression is deceptive: All that has been lost is water and the addition of water is all that is necessary to reverse the process and make consommé of meat glaze. (Pointless as that inversion may seem it has a practical application today that Escoffier, who died in 1935, could not have foreseen during his lifetime: It saves enormous amounts of space in the modern home freezer.)

Glace de Viande is ready for use when the stock has evaporated to the point at which it will evenly coat the back of a spoon. As that point is approached the heat should be steadily reduced to prevent the thickening syrup from scorching. The finished product keeps almost indefinitely in the freezer, where it maintains a caramel-candy consistency and is always ready for instant use. As Escoffier put it, those uses are legion. *Glace de Viande* will add intensity and luster to any standard sauce based on brown stock, an appetizing patina to grilled or roasted red meats, game, duck, etc. It will also do wonders as a sugarless glazing medium for carrots and, in most cases, it cuts down appreciably on working time.

Without going into the legion uses to which Meat Glaze can be put (a treatise in itself), it may prove instructive to reproduce two *Larousse Gastronomique* recipes for Chateaubriand Sauce (used with grilled meats), one based on *Glace de Viande,* one not.

> Chateaubriand sauce I (for grilled meat). SAUCE CHATEAUBRIAND—Cook down by two-thirds ½ cup (1 decilitre) of ***white wine*** with a tablespoon of **chopped shallot.**
>
> Add ¾ cup (1½ decilitres) of *Demi-glace sauce* [the preparation of which entails the cooking down of still another, "mother" sauce, *Espagnole,* which itself requires a mere six hours of cooking not including the making of its stock base]; cook down by half.
>
> Add, away from the fire, 6 tablespoons (100 grams) of fresh ***butter*** and a tablespoon of chopped ***tarragon.*** Season with a little ***cayenne*** and a few drops of ***lemon juice.***
>
> Mix well; do not strain.
>
> Chateaubriand sauce II. SAUCE CHATEAUBRIAND—Heat 2 tablespoons of ***meat glaze*** (or extract), mixed with a tablespoon of ***white stock*** (or water). Add 8 tablespoons (¼ pound) (125 grams) of fresh ***butter*** divided into tiny fragments, a tablespoon

of chopped ***parsley*** and a few drops of ***lemon juice.*** Season with a little cayenne. Mix well.

NOTE—Because *Glace de Viande* concentrates natural salts, it is advisable to refrain from salting stocks that are to be subjected to ultimate reduction.

A Fine Kettle of Fish 5

MEAT, POULTRY and mixed stocks seldom are appropriate to fish cookery. For this the poaching and saucing mediums are mostly court-bouillon and fish stock respectively. This is what our informative friend Dallas has to say on the subject of the former:

> This is a favourite term of the French kitchen for which we have no corresponding term in English. More than two hundred years ago [i.e., in 1653] an English cook tried to translate it, and he rendered it *short broth!* . . . It would be better in English after the analogy of small beer to say "small broth." But anyway the phrase has an odd sound. It really means the thin liquor in which fish is boiled, made up of water, vinegar or white wine, which has been seasoned with pepper, salt, onions, carrots, and a faggot of herbs. But the term is by no means exact. There is a Court-Bouillon called after the town of Nantes—à la Nantaise—which is half water, half milk, with pepper and salt. And often to cook fish in a Court-Bouillon means no more than to cook it *au bleu* [with vinegar and water].

The term is indeed by no means exact. *Court-bouillon à l'eau salée,* for example, which *Larousse Gastronomique* recommends for the poaching of certain marine fish, is nothing but salted water, whereas Fish Court-Bouillon, according to *Gourmet's Menu Cookbook,* is to all intents and purposes not only a fish *stock* but a fish stock cooked longer than most.

Dallas, a notorious philanderer whom his friend Dickens accurately described as "a gentleman of great attainments and erudition, much distinguished as the writer of the best critical literary pieces in *The Times,*" may have been a more exacting connoisseur of womanflesh than the flesh of fish. Steeped in the venerable tradition of wretched British cooking, he naturally wrote "boiled" where any Frenchman would have written "poached." Here again, though, the terminology is by no means exact, for most dictionaries define the verb "to poach" as to cook in "boiling or simmering liquid." The finer points of lexicology aside, with such rare exceptions as a trout cooked *au bleu* (which must be done to death in rapidly boiling acidulated water), fish poached in Court-bouillon should be gently simmered, for their flesh is far too fragile for rougher treatment.

The function of court-bouillon vis-à-vis fish is that of perfume vis-à-vis women: subtle accentuation of inherent desiderata. Therefore a proper poaching broth should be a mild decoction of delicate essences and not so strongly flavored a bath as to upstage the production's principal actor.

• COURT-BOUILLON FOR POACHING FISH •

As is their inveterate wont the French have developed numerous variations on the theme of court-bouillon, with sundry, elements included or omitted according to the particular type of fish to be poached, braised, steamed or boiled. This recipe—a compromise—is for general-purpose use.

* * *

To 1 qt. water add an equal amount of accumulated ***white wine heeltaps,*** 2 small ***carrots,*** 2 sliced medium ***onions, juice*** of 1 ***lemon*** and a ***bouquet garni*** made up of a few ***celery*** tops and ***parsley*** stems, a ***bay leaf*** and a dozen ***peppercorns.*** Bring to boil, cook 15 minutes and strain.

Having poached your fish you'll want to sauce it. *Beurre blanc* is all the rage these days, particularly at *nouvelle cuisine* restaurants where the cooking is done by erstwhile lawyers and chorus dancers, but its undeniable appeal may begin to pall with unrelieved exposure to what is after all nothing more than butter beaten to a froth with a shallot- and parsley-scented reduction of vinegar. On the other hand stock-based sauces offer great versatility, in most cases at appreciably less expense, and constitute one of the strongest links in the chain of Connective Cookery. Moreover a good supply of fish stock will produce all the piscatorial equivalents of the basic meat-stock compounds, *glace de viande* excepted, and enable you to draw upon a whole repertory of soups at negligible cost.

Even more so than others, fish stock is a scavenger's delight. Its salient components often may be had for the asking at the fishmonger's or salvaged from good dinners at far less cost than those of other stocks. Finally, a first-rate fish stock can be produced in a fraction of the time required by others. As is the case with meat, game and poultry stocks, precisely itemized and measured recipes for fish stock abound. Again there is no good reason to take them literally or follow them slavishly. The single unvarying requirement is that the main ingredients be irreproachably fresh or have been frozen in that condition.

• A NON-RECIPE FOR FISH STOCK •

Figuring on a pound or so of solid matter for every quart of liquid, collect and roughly chop a good mess of ***fish bones*** and ***trimmings***. Spread the bottom of a large pot or kettle with minced ***onion*** (allowing about one medium-sized bulb for each half-gallon of liquid), a handful of ***parsley sprigs***, a ***bay leaf*** and a sprig or two of ***fresh thyme***. (If you lack a garden there is no excuse for not having a pot or two of thyme growing on the kitchen windowsill.) If you've saved the leftover ***stems of mushrooms*** after stuffing or otherwise using the caps, chuck them into the pot too (or substitute water previously used for softening dried mushrooms). Cover this assortment with your fish trash, including one or more whole ***fish heads*** if you have them, gills and blood removed. Add the desired amount of liquid to the pot, using water and/or ***court-bouillon**** and/or leftover lees of ***white wine***, singly or in any convenient combination. For added richness toss in any or all of the following substances salvaged from previous efforts: ***oyster liquor, scallop liquor, clam broth, mussel broth, pan gelatine from baked or braised fish dinners***, etc. Add a squirt of ***lemon juice*** (maybe 10 drops per gallon of liquid) and a teaspoonful of salt per gallon of stock (or none if substantial quantities of clam broth are used). Bring the pot to a rolling boil, reduce heat, simmer gently for half an hour and strain the resultant stock through a damp cloth.

Your stock is now ready for use in most sauces and any thick or highly colored soup. (Fish consommé, although highly esteemed in many parts of the world, enjoys limited appeal hereabouts. Consequently the stock need not be clarified in these parts unless it is to be used as aspic.)

• CLARIFIED FISH STOCK •

Mercifully for himself and us, Auguste Escoffier was laid to rest nearly half a century ago, when a very different economy allowed the master chef blandly to assert that a half-pound of "good caviar" was the proper clarifying agent for a gallon or so of fish stock, and to concede that pressed caviar would do in a pinch. Should you decide to abide by Escoffier's formula the suggestion here is that you refrain from using the finished product for culinary purposes and instead bottle it in tiny vials and market it under some such label as "Passion de Poisson." For the purposes at hand, hens' eggs may be substituted for those of Caspian sturgeon.

* * *

Without folding them in add the stiffly beaten ***whites*** and ***crushed shells*** of 3 ***eggs*** to each half-gallon of ***fish stock**** to be clarified. Slowly bring liquid to a full boil, meanwhile constantly sweeping a wire whisk across surface of stock. Remove pan from heat and let it stand undisturbed 30 minutes. Strain clarified stock through a damp cloth and refrigerate.

Variations

For enhanced color and bouquet, add a pinch of ***saffron*** or ***curry*** to the stock before clarification. Backtracking a bit, the substitution of red for white wine at an earlier stage will do the same. A red-wine stock to be used as aspic, however, should be colored no more deeply than a pale rose.

A properly gelatinous Clarified Fish Stock will set stiffly enough when chilled for use in molded aspics, as a binder for various fish mousses or as an aspic glaze and chopped garnish for such cold buffet dishes as poached whole striped bass or salmon, poached or smoked trout, etc. A few examples:

• ANGUILLE AU CHABLIS EN GELÉE •

Cut young ***eels*** into 1½″ lengths and poach in a ***Chablis-based Clarified Fish Stock**** 15 minutes until tender. Line a mold with the cooled poaching stock and chill until aspic is well set. Arrange eels and semi-set stock in alternating layers, refrigerating each layer of stock in turn until set and finishing with a ⅜″ layer of stock. Refrigerate until aspic has set thoroughly. Unmold and serve as an hors d'oeuvre. (The number of servings will depend on quantities used, figuring on about 6 pieces of eel to a portion.)

• COLD SALMON MOUSSE •

Whip ¼ cup unflavored ***heavy cream*** until it forms peaks and set aside in refrigerator. Roughly break up 2 cups cold ***poached fresh salmon*** and purée smoothly in a blender or processor with 2 tbs. ***lemon juice,*** 1 tsp. salt, a pinch of ***cayenne*** (optional) and ½ cup very gelatinous ***Clarified Fish Stock.**** Transfer mixture to a bowl and fold in 3 tbs. ***Mayonnaise**** and reserved ***whipped cream.*** Pour mixture into a 1-qt. mold and chill several hours, loosely covered with an absorbent cloth, until firm. Unmold onto a chilled serving platter, garnish with deviled or curried ***eggs*** and serve as a first course to 4.

Variations

Either ***smoked salmon*** or ***gravlax**** may be substituted for fresh salmon in whole or part. If significant amounts of either are used, the dish almost cries out for Champagne as an accompaniment. Sea or bay ***scallops*** also may be used in lieu of salmon, as may any leftover scraps of non-oily cooked fish or shellfish. A saffron- or curry-tinctured stock will add a pleasing tint and a touch of pizzazz to mousses of white-fleshed fish and a few bits of ***pimiento,*** added to the purée ingredients, will do the same for a salmon mousse.

• PICKLED JELLIED FISH •

Almost every European culture has its own version of this venerable preparation. A frugal but perfectly creditable reading can be put together by using uncooked bits and pieces put by during the preparation of earlier meals—cheeks of striped bass or cod, a caudal section lopped from a fish that turned out to be too long for the pan, the fillet of red snapper that went into the freezer when one member of a foursome couldn't make it for dinner, etc.

* * *

Cut into bite-sized morsels 2 lbs. non-oily ***fish***, scaled but unskinned and unboned. Rub them with coarse salt and refrigerate 2 hours. Cook 1 sliced ***onion*** and 1 small thin-sliced ***carrot*** 15 minutes in 2 cups very gelatinous ***Clarified Fish Stock***.* Add ⅓ cup mild ***white vinegar*** and a ***bouquet garni*** of ***mixed pickling spices***. Bring to boil, add reserved fish (rinsed free of salt), reduce heat and simmer, covered, 15 minutes. Remove fish with a slotted spoon and transfer to an earthenware crock or bowl. Discard *bouquet garni*, arrange carrots and onions atop fish and pour cooking stock into crock to cover solids by ⅜". Chill for 24 hours or more and serve as a first course to 6–8.

• GEFILTE FISH •
(Jewish cookery)

The proverbial Jewish mother may look askance at this recipe but the adaptation departs in no significant way from the traditional formula.

* * *

Break 3 ***eggs*** into the work bowl of a processor, add 1 large quartered ***onion*** and run machine, using the steel blade, until onion is finely minced. With machine turned off add 1¾ lbs. each ***whitefish*** and ***pike*** and ½ lb. ***carp***, using fillets and including any ***raw boneless trimmings*** on hand. Add 2 tbs. ***matzo meal***, salt and pepper to taste and 3½ tbs. cold water. Run machine until fish is chopped fine and ingredients are well blended. Shape mixture into balls and drop them one by one into 1½ qts. gently simmering ***Clarified Fish Stock**** of good gelatinous character to which 1 or 2 sliced ***carrots***, 1 ***celery stalk*** and 2 sliced ***onions*** have been added. Cover and cook 2 hours at a very slow simmer, then allow stock and forcemeat balls to cool together. Transfer fish balls to a serving platter, cover loosely with a damp cloth and keep in a cool place. Strain stock, reserving carrots, and refrigerate until jelled. Stir jelly loosely with a fork and serve with fish balls and a garnish of the reserved carrots. Yields 6–8 first-course servings.

Fish Soups

With a good supply of stock in the freezer there is virtually no limit to the number of fine economical fish soups that Connective Cookery is capable of producing. The selection that follows represents only the proverbial tip of the iceberg.

• SOUPE DE POISSON À LA MARSEILLAISE •
(Provençal cookery)

In a processor purée together ⅓ lb. leftover ***cooked fish*** (stockpot solids, table scraps, etc., minus skin and bones), ¼ cup diced cooked ***fennel bulb*** (if unavailable add a splash of ***Ricard*** or ***Pernod*** to the soup as it cooks), 2 tbs. leftover ***sautéed sliced onion,*** ¼ cup ***tomato purée,*** 1 ripe ***tomato*** (peeled, seeded and quartered), 2 crushed ***garlic cloves*** and, if you like, 1 leftover ***cooked carrot***. Stir mixture into 2 qts. warmed ***unclarified fish stock,**** add a pinch of crumbled saffron, bring to simmer and cook 15 minutes, adding ½ cup leftover ***cooked elbow macaroni*** or ***vermicelli,*** if desired, at the last minute. (If used, vermicelli should be cut into short lengths.) Serve in crocks or deep bowls to 6.

NOTE—If uncooked pasta is used, add to soup 10 minutes before the latter is done.

Variation

Omit pasta and serve soup with lightly toasted rounds of leftover ***French bread,*** shredded Gruyère cheese and *Rouille* (recipe below) on the side.

• ROUILLE •

In a processor or blender combine 2 oz. ***pimientos,*** 1 small ***hot red chili pepper*** (or a healthy dash of ***Tabasco***), 3 crushed ***cloves garlic*** and 1 ***egg yolk,*** reserving white for other uses. With machine running add ⅓ cup ***olive oil*** in a thin stream to produce a fairly thick mayonnaise. Keep at room temperature and just before serving beat in ⅙ cup hot ***fish stock.****

NOTE—The accepted procedure is to slather a crouton liberally with *Rouille,* float it on the soup and top it with cheese.

• BOURRIDE •
(Provençal cookery)

To 6 cups unclarified ***fish stock**** add 1 cup ***dry white wine*** and 1 strip ***dried orange peel***. Bring to a gentle simmer and add ¾ lb. assorted non-oily leftover ***fish fillets*** or ***pieces***, cooking them just until opaque. Remove fish and keep warm, meanwhile gradually combining 1 cup ***Aioli*** with 1 cup of the hot stock, beating constantly with a wire whisk. When this mixture is well blended, gradually add it to remaining stock, beating constantly. Cook mixture over low heat, stirring constantly, until it is thick enough to coat a wooden spoon. Line soup bowls with thin rounds of fried leftover ***French bread***, top croutons with fish and add *Aioli*-thickened stock. Serve to 6 with any remaining *Aioli* on the side.

• AIOLI •

The Provençal *aïoli* and Spanish *ali-oli* derive from the *alium oleum* of ancient Rome, and ultimately from Egypt, where mashed garlic was combined with oil to sauce fish and meats. Today's *aïoli* is a pungent mayonnaise.

* * *

In a blender or processor combine 3 ***cloves garlic,*** lightly crushed with the side of a knife, 2 ***egg yolks,*** and salt and ***lemon juice*** to taste. With machine running, gradually add 1 cup unchilled ***olive oil*** in a thin continuous stream, blending until mixture is the consistency of ordinary mayonnaise. Yields about 1¼ cups.

• BOUILLABAISSE •
(Provencal cookery)

A street there is in Paris famous,
For which no rhyme our language yields,
Rue Neuve des Petits Champs its name is—
The New Street of the Little Fields.
And here's an inn, not rich and splendid,
But still in comfortable case;
To which in youth I oft attended,
To eat a bowl of Bouillabaise.

This Bouillabaisse a noble dish is—
A sort of soup, or broth, or brew,
Or hotchpotch of all sorts of fishes,
That Greenwich never could outdo:
Green herbs, red peppers, mussels, saffron,
Soles, onions, garlic, roach, and dace:
All these you eat at Terré's tavern
In that one dish of Bouillabaise. . . .

—Thackeray,
The Ballad of Bouillabaise (1855)

. . . no mussels or other such molluscs should be added [to Bouillabaise], as is the wont of many Paris restaurants.

—*Larousse Gastronomique*

Had the author of *Vanity Fair* and *Henry Esmond* (who once remarked that eating an American oyster was like swallowing a baby) eaten his Bouillabaisse in its home town, Marseilles, instead of in some Paris tourist trap, he might have revised his verses somewhat. Mussels and other molluscs are not included in an authentic Bouillabaisse for the simple reason that this most magnificent of soups traditionally has been the product of Mediterranean trash fish brought to port, along with more desirable items, by the city's offshore fishermen, who took the former home for dinner after profitably disposing of the better stuff when they tied their boats up in the Vieux Port. Atlantic lobster, a commonplace component of today's Bouillabaisse, also would have been an anomaly in Marseilles, where the critters were not indigenous, and the red pepper referred to by Thackeray could only have been added by a restaurateur with a better feeling for color then authenticity. As served in this country the dish bears little resemblance to the real McCoy. It is still a regal affair, however, and one of the very best of the bastardized versions is the one served in New York at the Tout Va Bien restaurant, from which this recipe was adapted.

Prepare 2 qts. unclarified ***fish stock**** as for *Soupe de Poisson à la Marseillaise,** omitting the fennel bulb, doubling the amount of ***tomato purée*** and leftover ***cooked fish***, and tripling amounts of fresh ***tomato*** and ***crushed garlic.*** Add a strip of dried ***orange peel*** and while stock gently simmers hack a live ***lobster*** into serving pieces and cut into thick slices 1½ lbs. each striped ***bass*** and ***red snapper*** or ***grouper.*** Add lobster to stock, along with ***Pernod*** to taste (don't overpower the soup) and 24–30 cleaned mussels in their shells, and cook 10 minutes. Add fish and cook 8 minutes longer. Add 24 shelled small shrimp and cook another 2 minutes. Remove fish and seafoods from stock, bed them in serving plates on large rounds of hard leftover ***French bread***, pour soup over fish and sprinkle with chopped ***parsley*** to taste. Serve with *Rouille** on the side to 6–8.

NOTE—Two or three tablespoons of ***olive oil,*** added to the soup halfway through the cooking process, won't detract from the enterprise. As an old Provençal saw has it, fish born in water are destined to die in oil. Broth and solids may be served in separate courses in that order.

• WATERZOÏ •
(Flemish cookery)

In a kettle melt 2 oz. ***butter.*** Add 1 cup roughly diced ***celery*** (preferably from the lower parts of the stalks), chopped whites of 3 ***fat leeks,*** 2 chopped ***onions*** and, if available, 2 whole ***parsley roots.*** Sauté vegetables 5 minutes over low heat without browning them. Add 3 lbs. assorted (preferably freshwater) fish cut into chunks of uniform size. Add 1 cup leftover dry ***white wine*** and 2 qts. hot unclarified ***fish stock***.* Bring to a hard boil, reduce heat and simmer 10–12 minutes until fish is cooked through but still firm. Discard parsley roots, garnish with chopped parsley and serve immediately, over toast or with buttered bread on the side, to 6–8.

Variations

For a thicker soup stir in either powdered ***melba toast*** or a half-and-half blend of ***egg yolk*** and ***heavy cream.*** In either case add the thickener off heat just before serving.

• SOPA DE AJO AL PESCADO •
(Malagueñan cookery)

Bring 6 cups unclarified ***fish stock**** to boil. In a large skillet or earthenware casserole gently sauté 8 lightly crushed ***garlic cloves*** in 6 tbs. ***olive oil*** until browned on all sides. Discard garlic and fry 6 thin slices ***whole wheat bread*** in ***oil*** until browned on each side. Off heat stir 1 tsp. ***paprika*** into the oil, add boiling stock and break up bread with the edge of a spoon. Add salt to taste and cook, covered, 18 minutes over low heat. About 2 minutes before serving, garnish soup with salvaged bits of ***cooked white fish*** and assorted leftover ***cooked shellfish***. Serve in large bowls to 4–6.

• SOPA DE MARISCOS •
(Filipino cookery)

This hearty catchall is an excellent excuse for clearing the freezer of all those surplus fish and seafoods squirreled away in small quantities over the course of several weeks.

* * *

Cut ⅓ lb. leftover raw ***white-fleshed fish*** into chunks and set aside. Pick meat from 2 steamed ***blue-claw crabs*** (or equivalent amount of any other crab) and set aside. Steam 24–30 hard clams just until shells open; extract meats and set them aside, reserving expressed broth. Clean ¼ lb. ***squid,*** hack body sacs into thin ringlets and set aside, reserving tentacles for other uses. Shell, devein and set aside ¼ lb.

small shrimp. In a heavy pan simmer together 1 sliced ***onion,*** 1 cup ***tomato purée*** and ¼ cup ***olive oil*** until onion wilts, adding 1 tsp. ***sugar*** and salt and pepper to taste after about two minutes. In a heavy pot brown 2 lightly crushed ***garlic cloves*** in 3 tbs. ***olive oil.*** Discard garlic and fry 2 cups cubed ***white bread*** in same oil until crisp on all sides. Remove bread and set aside to drain on paper towels. Add 2 tbs. ***raw rice*** and reserved squid to the same oil, sauté 1 minute, then add 6 cups boiling unclarified ***fish stock**** and cook until rice is tender. Add fish, clams, crabmeat and tomato sauce. Cook 3 or 4 minutes and add shrimp, along with salt, pepper and reserved clam broth to taste. Stir well, remove from heat and before serving garnish with reserved croutons, 1 tbs. chopped ***parsley*** and 2 sliced ***hard-boiled eggs.*** Serves 6.

• SAKANA OSHIOJIRU •
(Japanese cookery)

To 4½ cups clarified ***Fish Stock**** add 2 tbs. ***sake*** (Japanese rice wine), 1½ tbs. ***light soy sauce*** and salt to taste (the finished soup should be a bit saltier than most). Bring to boil, meanwhile distributing ¾ cup finely chopped ***whole scallions*** among serving bowls. Ladle boiling soup over scallions in fairly small portions and serve to 8–10.

• FISH CHOWDER •
(Original recipe)

During the early history of the New World, French cod fishermen on the Grand Banks subsisted largely on *chaudrées,* or fish soups, cooked in a kettle called a *chaudière,* or hot-pot. It is from the latter that the American term "chowder" derives but there is a good deal more agreement about *that* than about the proper composition of a chowder. The view here is that the milk or cream on which most chowders are based no more belongs in a fish soup than in a dry martini, traditional notions to the contrary notwithstanding. To carry the idiosyncratic nature of this recipe a bit further, the salt pork is not first browned, as it is in most others.

* * *

In a heavy pot combine 2 oz. ***salt pork*** cut in fine dice, 2½ cups diced ***raw potato,*** 3 lbs. leftover ***cooked fish*** (preferably ***cod, haddock*** or something similar), boned and flaked, ⅓ stick ***butter*** and 1 large ***yellow onion,*** sliced and sautéed until limp. Add 5 cups unclarified ***fish stock,**** 1 tsp. fresh ***thyme leaves,*** 1 ***bay leaf*** and salt and fresh-ground white pepper to taste. Bring to boil and cook 10 minutes, stirring occasionally. Reduce heat and simmer gently 15 minutes longer. If chowder needs thickening, remove and mash a few of the potato cubes and stir back into the mixture. Remove bay leaf if you like and serve piping hot, with plain crackers, to 6. (The crackers may be eaten as an accompaniment or broken up and mucked into the soup.)

• STUFFED CLAMS IN CONSOMMÉ (Taiwanese cookery) •

Traditionally this festive soup is based on clam broth diluted with water. The substitution of fish stock, though unconventional, adds richness to the dish.

* * *

Steam 2 dozen scrubbed ***cherrystone clams*** in a covered pot with a heeltap of ***white wine*** just until clamshells open, shaking pot occasionally. Remove clams from shells, reserving half the latter, along with ***clam broth.*** Fine-chop clams and blend well with the following: 4 oz. chopped lean raw ***pork trimmings***; 2 oz. ***minced shrimp;*** 1 rounded tbs. minced ***water chestnuts;*** 1 tsp. ***Chinese rice wine*** or ***sake;*** ½ tsp. ***sesame oil;*** 1 large ***presoftened Chinese black mushroom,*** minced; 1 oz. fine-chopped leftover ***cooked ham***; and 1 tbs. ***cornstarch.*** Fill reserved shells with resultant mixture, mounding fillings firmly with a spoon. Steam stuffed clams in a covered vessel 6–8 minutes, using some of the reserved clam broth as the steaming medium. Place 4 stuffed clams in each of 6 serving bowls. Strain 1 cup reserved clam broth through a damp cloth (reserving remainder for other uses) and combine with 4 cups ***Clarified Fish Stock.**** Bring to boil, season to taste, pour hot soup over stuffed clams and garnish with shredded fresh ***ginger root.*** Serves 6.

NOTE—Leftover clam broth has multitudinous uses. To itemize just a few, it can be drunk as is, does wonders for bloody marys and can be used as a stock for Velouté Sauce in appropriate instances or as a cooking medium for *risotti* or pastas to be sauced with seafoods. It freezes very well.

• BRODO DI PESCE (Italian cookery) •

In a heavy pot combine 2 qts. unclarified ***fish stock***,* 2 ***whole cloves garlic***, ½ cup each diced ***celery*** and ***carrot***, 1 diced ***onion***, 1 medium ***tomato***, seeded and chopped, and 2 ***bay leaves***. Bring to simmer and cook 15 minutes. Add ½ cup ***raw rice*** and continue to cook. When rice is about half-cooked add 1½ lbs. leftover ***poached fish***, salvaged ***stockpot fish***, unbrowned portions of leftover ***broiled, baked, fried fish***, etc. Cook until rice is *al dente* and serve, after removing garlic and bay leaves, to 6.

NOTE—If it is reasonably glutinous, 1¾ cups leftover ***cooked rice*** may be substituted for raw rice, in which case it should be stirred into the soup a minute or two before serving.

• LOBSTER BISQUE •

Few of nature's critters are treated as wastefully or brutalized as egregiously as the noble *Homarus americanus*, the lobster native to the northeastern seaboard of North America. With the combined U.S. and Canadian catch running upward of 70 million pounds annually—a paltry figure alongside the 130 million pounds taken, with the heroic abetment of Diamond Jim Brady, in the record year of 1885—it safely can be said that tens of millions of pounds of eminently usable material are thoughtlessly discarded in this country every year. The reason is that most Americans know little about eating, and less about cooking, the beasts. Typically we go to steakhouses for our big lobster blowouts (which makes much the same sense as going to fish houses for steaks and chops). There we disburse unconscionable amounts of pelf for mammoth specimens which are desiccated under the broiler and borne to the table smelling like a conflagration in a plastics factory. We dig out whatever tail-meat that exposure to dry heat hasn't inextricably fused to the shell, drench it with more butter than we can safely ingest in an attempt to restore it to some semblance of palatability and, if we're persistent enough, we gag down the parched meat of the claws too, often turning as green in the act as the object of our putative affection was in its natural state. Twenty minutes and forty dollars later the busboy more often than not lugs off to the trash bin enough unconsumed meat, coral and tomalley, along with potentially useful shell, to provide a hungry couple with a week's good eating had it all not been ruined in the kitchen. In the home most lobsters, though they may be smaller and more sensibly cooked, are similarly eaten—or, to be more precise, partially eaten. Years of close observation have led to the inescapable conclusion that nineteen diners out of twenty don't trouble to extract anything near to all that is edible, or much that is delectable, even from a one-pound chicken lobster.

Any standard recipe for Lobster Bisque will specify that whole live lobsters be used. That this is arrant nonsense may be deduced from a visit to the kitchen of any restaurant that serves the soup. No restaurateur in his right mind would use an unabridged crustacean to produce four servings of bisque at, say, four dollars per copy when he can peddle the same decapod as a single entrée for, say, twenty bucks. Professional chefs do not use whole lobsters for bisque. Instead they buy up in bulk and for relative pittances stripped-down lobster carcasses, after the purveyors have removed the fancier appendages for sale at premium prices. Be guided in principle by their sagacity.

* * *

Assemble as many ***lobster carcasses*** as have come one way or another into your possession. (Presumably you haven't hesitated to demand that the remains of any restaurant dinner be packaged for your later use, that your fishmonger save for your use what *doesn't* go into the containers of lobster meat that he puts up for sale at fancy prices, or that your friends and neighbors make a garbage-disposal unit of your home freezer.) Pick out the body meat, coral (roe), tomalley (liver: the greenish slime) and fat and set aside, also setting aside the shells, body fluids and any other detritus that looks interesting or repulsive, possibly excepting the sac and intestinal vein.

In a heavy pot bring the desired quantity of unclarified ***fish stock**** to boil with reserved lobster hardware tossed in, figuring on 1 qt. stock for each cup of meat you will use. Reduce heat and simmer 20 minutes. Meanwhile sauté equal amounts of finely chopped ***onion, celery*** and ***red bell pepper*** in a little ***peanut oil,*** allowing about ½ cup in aggregate for each qt. of stock. Strain stock, discarding solids, and return it to rinsed pot. Add sautéed ***vegetables*** and 1 tbs. ***raw rice*** per qt. of stock. Lace the soup with a healthy belt of ***Cognac*** and simmer until rice and vegetables are soft. Strain soup once more, reserving rice and vegetables, and return liquid to pot. In a blender or processor combine and purée reserved rice, vegetables and reserved lobster meat, assorted software and juices. Stir the puréed mixture into the soup, add ½ cup ***heavy cream*** for each qt. of stock and season to taste with salt and ***cayenne.*** Cook a few minutes longer, stirring occasionally, and swirl in a few small pieces of butter just before serving.

Variations

With the addition of ***curry powder*** and omission of butter, Lobster Bisque may be served cold. ***Shrimp, crawfish, crab*** or any ***other crustacean*** may be substituted for lobster in the proportions given above. A garnish of the appropriate leftover ***cooked fish,*** cut in dice, will in no way detract from the finished product.

As was remarked earlier, many fish sauces are based on fish stock or court-bouillon. There would be little point in giving recipes here that can be found in any reasonably comprehensive standard French cookbook, such as Larousse Gastronomique or *The Escoffier Cookbook*. To list a few possibilities:

Allemande Sauce
Aurora Sauce
Bercy Sauce
Bonnefoy Sauce
Breton Sauce
Burgundy Sauce
Cardinal Sauce
Chaud-froid Sauce
Chivry Sauce
Crevettes, Sauce au
Curry Sauce
French Sauce
Greque, Sauce à la
Sauce Hongroise
Joinville Sauce
Mornay Sauce
Nantua Sauce
Newburg Sauce
Sauce Normande
Sauce Régence
St.-Malo Sauce
Velouté Sauce
Sauce Vin Blanc

What's Your Beef? 6

THE AVERAGE American snaffles up more than his own weight in beef each year, mostly in the form of hamburgers, hot dogs, steaks and roasts. As most nutritionists will agree, this is far more than our systems can safely tolerate. As most home economists will agree, it is far more than most of us can afford. And as most serious students of gastronomy will agree, it deprives us of a diet of interest, variety and refinement. Any way you look at it, it's a dumb way to eat.

As stated earlier, it isn't the purpose here to banish steak from the American table: Obviously, most of us are not prepared to give up *that* carnivorous pleasure, for the frequent rending of bloody flesh seems to be regarded as a status symbol by the population in general, and by American males in particular as a flattering reflection on their virility. Beef, ingested in quantities deemed obscene elsewhere in the world, is the stuff on which the Homeric heroes fed (at least, according to Homer, who himself probably ate far more fish than meat), and beef, by God, is the stuff that still distinguishes the he-men from the pansies.

Perhaps it does, but are we so insecure about our masculinity that we must indulge in extravagant overkill? Is a full pound of red meat, consumed at a single sitting, the only form of reassurance whereby the American male (often rendered so torpid by his gluttony that he can't perform in the post-prandial bed) can dispel his self-doubts? It little matters that the notoriously amorous Latins or the incredibly fecund Chinese eat very little beef: Its ostentatious consumption—at the expense of the inordinate quantities of edible grain that its production entails—is the badge of American manhood.

Beef is an undeniably toothsome substance, at least as perceived in a beef-oriented society. Still, the view here is that it is best enjoyed, and provides its broadest range of satisfactions, when cooked and eaten in moderation. Succulent as those sixteen ounces of fat-saturated sirloin may be when broiled to perfection and plunked on a plate, they remain sixteen ounces of broiled sirloin—at least twice as many as any of us need at one go; anywhere from thirty-two to forty-eight mouthfuls of seared flesh that grow progressively more monotonous as each is ingested, until finally the last few bites are either gagged down or left untouched on the table.

Contrary to prevailing American notions of French eating habits, an unsauced steak, a stack of fries and a simple salad—the quintessential "American" meal—constitute the most popular menu in France by far. A French steak, however, bears little resemblance to its American counterpart. Differences of cut, quality, flavor and marbling aside, the average French *biftek* is smaller by at least half than what most Americans consider essential to survival. Indeed, according to *Larousse Gastronomique,* "In France, a steak taken from the ribs of beef, or a *contre-filet* (sirloin), of a pound . . . or a little less is considered sufficient for 4 persons." Curiously, the most dedicated feeders in the Western world find such portions not only adequate but enjoyable, while their only serious competitors, the Italians, notwithstanding an occasional hefty *bistecca alla fiorentina,* get along quite happily on much less.

The problem in this country is that beef—originally a more-or-less despised by-product of the leather industry—has come to be regarded as essential to both our physical well-being (dubious at best) and to the maintenance of our self-esteem. Our overriding gastronomic desideratum (at least insofar as white Americans are concerned) is a primeval hunk of red meat, festally conceived and consumed. When times are hard, we adamantly refuse to entertain sensible alternatives but resort instead, in our benighted efforts to economize, to the lowly, trashy frankfurter and the "extended" hamburger. "Well," sighs the homemaker on the evening news, whose husband has been laid off as sales of domestic cars plummet, "I guess we'll be eating a lot more hot dogs." And, she adds wistfully, a lot more meat loaf, shepherd's pie and like abominations.

Our abruptly impoverished homemaker could do a lot better. There is nothing economical about the use of hot dogs or ground chuck, padded and extended as they may be. Nor is it necessary to buy the most expensive cuts of beef to enjoy the stuff to the utmost. Consider, for example, the uses of beef shoulder, usually packaged as "London broil" and priced appreciably below the choicer cuts. At a Manhattan supermarket at the time of this writing, beef shoulder with no bone and very little fat sold for $2.59 per pound, whereas chuck fillet was $.40 more, top sirloin and rib steaks were $3.99 and short-loin shell steaks were tagged at $5.39. Of these cuts, shoulder is not only the most versatile but yields a higher ratio of meat to fat and/or bone than any of the others. Broiled and sliced on the bias, beef shoulder yields a fine steak dinner, but its uses hardly end there. The connective cook engaged in the wholesale and deliberate manufacture of leftovers can provide himself and another with an eminently satisfactory meal of grilled meat while judiciously husbanding enough on which to base several subsequent dishes of at least as much interest as the first. Split lengthwise along one of its natural dividing lines, half (the fat-edged half) of the steak may be broiled and sliced, to be served as is or with a Mushroom Sauce,* potatoes and a green vegetable or salad. The remainder can be put to a multiplicity of interesting, elastic uses.

The Japanese, who pay prohibitively high prices for their beef, have learned to get as much mileage from it as any cooks on earth. Take, for example . . .

• NEGIMAYAKI •

Versatile enough to be served as a first course, main dish or cocktail accompaniment, depending on the quantities used, these simple rollups are savory and satisfying, whatever the use to which they are put.

* * *

Semi-freeze a ¼-lb. broad, thick piece of uncooked husbanded ***beef shoulder*** (to facilitate slicing). In a cup blend 4 oz. ***soy sauce,*** 1½ oz. ***sake*** and 5 oz. ***mirin*** and set aside. Working across the grain, cut semi-frozen meat into very thin uniform slices about 3″ long. Cut 1 bunch ***scallions*** into 3″ lengths and lay two pieces, one white and one green, lengthwise on each slice of meat. Roll beef tightly around scallions and press overlap against roll to prevent unrolling. Repeat process until meat is used up; chop and reserve any remaining scallion for garnish. Preheat broiler, arrange beef rolls on a shallow pan and broil 4–5 minutes, turning once. Arrange *Negimayaki* on serving dishes, pour reserved sauce over them and serve with lightly sautéed ***bean sprouts.*** Serves 2 as a main dish.

NOTE—*Sake* and *mirin,* dry and sweetened rice wines, respectively, can be found in Japanese food shops and many non-Japanese liquor stores.

Variation

Substitute lightly steamed young ***asparagus stalks*** for scallions, reserving tips for other uses.

• GYŪNIKU NO YAWATAMAKI • (Japanese cookery)

Constructed along the same lines as *Negimayaki,* these beef rolls are a forager's delight, for they make good use of a common weed that may be had for the pulling.

* * *

Proceed as for *Negimayaki,** substituting ***burdock root*** (scraped, cut into ¼″-thick batons and boiled 3 minutes with 1 tbs. ***vinegar*** in water to cover) for scallions. Secure beef rolls with wooden picks and skillet-brown them in 2–3 tbs. ***corn*** or ***peanut oil,*** turning until all surfaces are well colored. To the pan add a blend of 4 tbs. ***soy sauce,*** 1 tbs. each *mirin* and *sake* and 1 tsp. ***sugar*** (optional). Cook 6–8 minutes over moderate heat, turning beef rolls occasionally, until meat is thoroughly impregnated with sauce. Drain off sauce, remove picks and serve hot or cold.

• **BEEF KAKUNI (Japanese cookery)** •

As remarked earlier, the enjoyment of beef needn't be an exercise in overkill. With side dishes of rice, sautéed bean sprouts and the like, a half-pound of meat will suffice for two as a main course or may be served to four as one of a sequence of small dishes. The concern here is not with saturation but what the Franch call *dégustation*.

* * *

Cut ½ lb. lean, gristle-trimmed husbanded raw ***beef shoulder*** into 1″ cubes, place them in a pot and add water to cover. Bring to boil and cook meat through, skimming all risen scum from the surface. Add ¾ cup ***soy sauce,*** 2 tbs. ***sake,*** 2 tbs. ***mirin*** and 1 small piece fresh ***ginger root,*** slivered. Reduce heat and simmer until meat is tender. Serve meat and pot liquor together in small bowls to 4.

Conventional culinary wisdom specifies that certain beef dishes be prepared with cuts of illogically high quality. When raw meat is sliced petal-thin, as it is, for example, for Carpaccio,* not one palate in a thousand could discriminate between the beef usually used and a much cheaper cut. Similarly, when distinguishing textures are broken down, as for Tartar Steak,* it would be an unnecessary extravagance to use filet when the differences between it and equally tasty beef shoulder (or any other comparable lean "inferior" cut) are virtually undetectable in the finished product. Even in the case of *Shabu-shabu* the discernible distinctions, if any, between the traditionally insisted-upon prime sirloin and the normally spurned choice shoulder, when each is sliced as thinly as possible, are hardly worth the price differential.

• **SHABU-SHABU (Japanese cookery)** •

The actual cooking begins when this hot-pot is brought to the table. The real work (hardly an exhausting business) is the advance preparation. The name, incidentally, is supposed to be an onomatopoetic rendering of the sound of broth as it boils.

* * *

Preparation

Semi-freeze ¾ lb. trimmed husbanded ***beef shoulder***, slice it very thin (about 1/16″) and arrange on a large serving platter along with the following: 1 medium ***carrot,*** scraped, halved crosswise and sliced as thinly as possible; 4 small ***mushrooms*** sliced into ⅛″ vertical sections; 4 oz. ***watercress;*** 1 cake ***tofu*** (bean curd) cut into 1″ cubes; ⅓ head ***Chinese cabbage*** cut into 1½″ pieces; 2 large ***onions*** cut into ½″-wide strips; 8 ***scallions*** cut into 1½″ lengths; 2 ***bamboo shoots*** cut in ½″-thick slices (parboiled if the fresh article is used, as is if tinned); 4 oz. each ***shirataki*** (yam noodles) and ***udon*** (wheat noodles), lightly cooked, refreshed and drained.

In separate serving bowls prepare ***Gomadare*** and ***Ponzu,*** the two dipping sauces that will accompany the meal.

Gomare: Blend together 2 oz. each ground toasted ***sesame seed*** and ***ground walnuts,*** 2 tsp. ***mirin,*** 3 oz. ***soy sauce,*** 1 tsp. ***sake.***

Ponzu: Blend together juice of ¼ ***lemon*** and 2 oz. each ***soy sauce*** and ***su*** (Japanese rice vinegar) or other mild ***white vinegar***.

In a deep serving pot or casserole add four 2″ × 4″ pieces of ***kombu*** (dried kelp), washed under running water, to 1 qt. water and bring to boil.

Service

Over a table heater (or, outdoors, a hibachi) keep the *kombu* broth at a gentle simmer and the pot within easy reach of the diners, each of whom should be equipped with wooden or bamboo (*not* plastic or metal) chopsticks. Pass the serving platter as often as need be, allowing each member of the assembled company to pluck a few items from it on each go-round, as his fancy dictates. From here on in, each participant is on his own and dips a morsel at a time into the simmering broth, swishing it about until it is cooked to taste, then dipping it in the sauce of choice and ingesting it. Needless to say, at least a modicum of decorum must be observed during the ritual, with participants refraining from any last-one-in-is-a-rotten-egg unseemliness. Traditionally, each diner dips a slice of beef first, on the dubious proposition that its immersion enhances the flavor of the broth to a detectable degree. Serves 4.

• QUICK-BRAISED BEEF (Szechuanese cookery) •

Cut ½ lb. trimmed semi-frozen husbanded ***raw beef shoulder*** into the thinnest slices possible, about 1″ × 2″. (Very rare leftover ***London broil*** may be substituted for raw beef.) Arrange meat in a shallow dish and sprinkle with ¼ tsp. salt, 2 tsp. ***soy sauce*** and 1 tsp. ***flour.*** Toss ingredients thoroughly and let stand 1 hour at room temperature (assuming once again that you don't live in an igloo). In a wok, paella pan or large skillet heat 2 tbs. ***peanut*** or ***vegetable oil.*** Add 2 tbs. ***chopped onion,*** ⅓ tsp. minced fresh ***ginger root*** and 1 tsp. chopped fermented ***black beans.*** Stir-fry mixture 20 seconds over moderate heat. Quickly add stalks of 3 ***asparagus,*** hacked diagonally into 1½″ lengths, and 1 tbs. ***hoisin*** sauce and continue to stir-fry another 30 seconds. Add ¾ cup ***chicken stock,**** 1 tbs. each ***dry sherry*** and ***soy sauce.*** Bring to boil, reduce heat and simmer gently 10 minutes. Turn heat up high and add reserved sliced beef and 2 scallions cut in inch-long sections. Distribute all ingredients evenly in pan and after 90 seconds add 1 tbs. ***flour*** dissolved in 4 tbs. water. Stir until sauce thickens and serve immediately in a heated casserole or other deep dish. As is usually the case with Chinese foods, the number of servings will depend on the orchestration of the entire meal. As a single entrée accompanied by ***boiled rice,*** the dish should be adequate for 2.

NOTE—*Hoisin* sauce and fermented black beans are compounds that even Chinese cooks and chefs rarely prepare themselves. Both can be found in any Chinese grocery.

• QUICK-FRIED BEEF WITH ONION • (Chinese cookery)

A fine use for all those odds and ends of beef, trimmed from larger cuts, that presumably have accumulated in the freezer, this dish, like export porcelain, is perhaps better known in the West than in its country of origin.

* * *

Slice ¾ lb. lean ***beef trimmings*** into 1½″ julienne strips. In a bowl sprinkle the meat with ½ tsp. salt, 1½ tsp. ***sugar,*** 2 tsp. ***flour*** and a few twists of ***fresh black pepper.*** Toss meat thoroughly for even distribution of dry ingredients. Add 2 tbs. ***soy sauce*** and 1 tbs. ***dry sherry,*** toss meat and allow to marinate 20 minutes. Meanwhile dissolve 2 tbs. ***flour*** in ⅓ cup very concentrated ***chicken stock,**** stir in 1 tbs. ***dry sherry*** and set aside. In a wok or large skillet heat 2 tbs. ***vegetable*** or ***peanut oil;*** add 1 large ***yellow onion,*** cut vertically into very thin slices, and 1 tsp. shredded fresh ***ginger root.*** Stir-fry 2 minutes over high heat, drain oil from pan and set onion mixture aside in a bowl. Return pan to burner, add 2 tbs. ***fresh oil,*** heat thoroughly and add reserved beef with its marinade. Distribute meat evenly, return onion mixture to pan and stir-fry 30 seconds. Add reserved stock-flour mixture, stir-fry until beef is coated with thickened sauce and serve at once in a heated dish. Serves 4, with rice and vegetable accompaniments, as an entrée.

• CARPACCIO (Venetian cookery) •

Why name a modern dish for a sixteenth-century painter of the Venetian school? Because the dish originated at Venice's Hotel Cipriani during an exhibition of Vittore Carpaccio's paintings in that city. This simple refined first-course offering provides all the taste sensations of good red meat without dulling the appetite for whatever is to follow.

* * *

Figuring on 2 oz. of meat per serving, trim a thick semi-frozen strip of husbanded ***beef shoulder*** into a uniform rectangle about 1½″ wide, working between lines of connective tissue and excising all fat. Slice the meat as thinly as possible and arrange it in an overlapping circular pattern around the edges of each serving dish. Allow beef to thaw thoroughly to room temperature and serve with a generous splodge of ***Salsa Verde*** in the center of each plate, and with freshly grated ***Parmesan cheese*** on the side.

NOTE—This dish should not be prepared longer in advance than it takes the meat to thaw (a matter of minutes), lest it discolor.

• SALSA VERDE •

In a blender or processor blend together ½ cup ***parsley,*** 2 tbs. drained ***pickled capers,*** ½ clove ***garlic,*** 2 ***cornichon pickles,*** pulp of ¼ leftover ***baked potato*** (or ½ ***boiled potato),*** 2 ***anchovy fillets*** and 1 tbs. ***olive oil.***

• TARTAR STEAK •

This preparation supposedly traces its name back to the times of Genghis Khan's cavalry, when warriors in the field subsisted on raw meat, which they tenderized by stowing it beneath their saddles. In one of the more absurd nomenclatural extrapolations of recent times, some *nouvelle cuisine* practitioners have taken to calling raw chopped fish *poisson tartare,* which conjures up some fairly squishy, not to say smelly, visions of life among the Mongol hordes. As is the case with most beef dishes, Tartar Steak usually is served in needlessly gross portions in this country, where it isn't uncommon to find a pound of the stuff on a single dinner plate. A good Tartar Steak is a fine flavorsome dish but, with the appropriate garnishes, it is far too rich for large-scale ingestion and begins to cloy about halfway through a "normal" portion. The suggestion here is that it be served sparingly as an hors d'oeuvre. In Connective Cookery it's a cart-before-the-horse sort of preparation, which is to say that the "leftovers" should be used first, while they are freshest and their color is at its best. The ideal moment would be a day or two in advance of London Broil for a large group.

* * *

After trimming beef shoulder for later use as broiled steaks, strip the spare parts of all fat, sinew, connective tissue and the like. Allowing ¼ lb. ***lean meat*** per serving as an appetizer (and about half that for cocktail canapés), fine-grind it (or, better, chop it by hand) and, using two forks, thoroughly fold in the following: yolk of 1 ***large egg;*** 3 minced ***anchovy fillets*** (or 1 tbs. ***anchovy paste***); 1 tbs. drained and chopped ***pickled capers;*** 1 tsp. ***Worcestershire sauce;*** and salt and fresh pepper to taste. (Since anchovy fillets are used, make allowance for their salt content.) Serve on toast points.

NOTE—A food processor will produce a creditable piece of work if the machine is not run overlong, thereby reducing the meat to mush. In France, incidentally, the egg yolk is omitted from the preparation called *biftek à la tartare.* When egg *is* included, the dish is called *biftek à l'américaine.*

Variations
Serve ***ground beef*** plain, with a whole ***egg yolk*** nested in a well at its center and with the above-listed garnishes and condiments on the side, or form finished Tartar Steak into small balls, roll them in finely chopped walnuts, chill well and serve on picks as cocktail accompaniments. A lacing of ***Cognac*** or ***sour mash whiskey*** won't do any appreciable damage to Tartar Steak, and some aficionados include chopped ***onion*** among the garnishes.

• BEEF SATAY (Thai cookery) •

Cut ½ lb. trimmed beef ***shoulder scraps*** or other lean beef trimmings (very rare leftover ***roast beef*** will do nicely, too) into ½" cubes and marinate meat 3 hours in an earthenware bowl with ½ cup ***soy sauce,*** 3 oz. ***peanut oil,*** 1 large ***onion,*** finely chopped, 1 ***clove garlic,*** minced, and 1½ tbs. lightly toasted ***sesame seeds.*** Drain off and reserve marinade. Thread beef cubes onto thin wooden skewers and brush meat with a blend of 1 tsp. ***cumin,*** 1 tsp. ***lemon juice*** and a pinch of finely minced ***coriander leaves*** ("Chinese parsley"). Broil beef, occasionally turning and basting with reserved marinade, about 5 minutes. Season with salt and pepper to taste and serve on skewers to 4 as an appetizer.

• BEEF BIRDS IN WHITE WINE •

> [For] those whose Purses cannot reach the Cost of Rich Dishes, I have descended to their meaner expenses.
>
> —Robert May, *The Accomplisht Cook* (1660)

Beef and veal "birds"—the poor man's small game—are common to most European cuisines and are prepared in endless variations, including one of Belgian origin called *alouettes sans têtes (headless larks).*

* * *

Working with three or four at a time, place twelve ¼" slices of trimmed husbanded raw ***beef shoulder*** or other ***lean beef oddments*** between sheets of wax paper and pound them very thin. Center a slightly smaller thin slice of leftover ***cooked ham*** on each slice of beef. Prepare a filling of 1 cup ***minced parsley,*** ¼ cup each ***chopped pine nuts*** and ***white seedless raisins,*** and 3 tbs. grated ***Parmesan cheese*** and distribute the mixture evenly among the incipient "birds," centering each portion lengthwise over the ham. Roll up beef slices so as to form the longest possible cylinders and tie each roll at ½" intervals with light string. In a skillet brown rolls on all sides in 2 tbs. ***oil,*** then add ¾ cup husbanded heeltaps of ***dry white wine*** and simmer, covered, for 30 minutes. Remove strings and serve to 4 with ***rice pilaf*** and a ***leafy green vegetable.***

Variations

Beef Birds may be filled with the egg-bound forcemeat of ***stockpot veal, beef, chicken,*** etc., and broiled. Thin-sliced ***mozzarella cheese*** and/or Italian ***Salsiccie Dolce**** (uncased and crumbled or left in the case and very thinly sliced) also may be used, and the birds may be alternated on skewers with cubes of leftover ***stale bread,*** brushed with ***olive oil*** and broiled about 6–8 minutes, until browned on all sides.

Filled with 1 chopped sautéed ***onion,*** 1 stalk ***celery*** similarly treated, 1¼ cup toasted ***breadcrumbs*** and a pinch of ***marjoram,*** a dozen beef birds may be dredged in seasoned ***flour,*** browned in a little ***butter*** and then braised in the same pan for 30 minutes, covered, with 1½ cups leftover ***red wine.***

Second Comings

The transformations to which cooked beef lends itself are well-nigh innumerable and many are more interesting in their own right than the dishes from which they sprang. Let's examine a few examples.

• ÉMINCÉ DE BOEUF EN MIROTON •
(French cookery)

Mince 2 medium ***onions*** very fine and brown them well in 1 tbs. ***butter.*** Sprinkle with ½ tsp. ***flour*** and cook over low heat, stirring, for a few moments, then add ⅔ cup ***consommé,**** ⅓ cup wine vinegar, ⅓ cup leftover ***white wine*** and a generous twist of ***fresh black pepper.*** Bring to boil, reduce heat, simmer gently 7–8 minutes and set aside. Sauté 2 medium ***onions*** in 2 tbs. ***butter*** until transparent and make a bed of them in a long ovenproof dish. Cut 1 lb. leftover ***roast or braised beef*** into very thin slices, or the same amount of leftover ***boiled beef*** into somewhat thicker slices, and arrange the meat over the onions in an overlapping pattern. Pour reserved sauce evenly over meat and sprinkle the surface with melted butter or leftover ***pan drippings***. Broil under moderate flame until heated through and brown on top. Serve to 4, garnished with ***chopped parsley.***

• FRICANDELLES DE BOEUF AVEC VIANDE CUITE (French cookery) •

Mince 1 lb. leftover ***boiled or braised beef*** and blend well with 1⅓ cups puréed leftover ***boiled, baked, or mashed potato,*** ½ cup chopped ***onion,*** 2 lightly beaten ***eggs,*** a pinch of grated ***nutmeg*** and salt and pepper to taste. Divide mixture into 8 parts, shape them into balls and, on a lightly floured board, roll them out to form thick flat cakes. Heat 2 oz. ***butter*** or ***rendered beef fat*** in a large skillet and brown *fricandelles* on both sides. Arrange *fricandelles* on a fireproof sheet and bake 25 minutes in a preheated 350°F oven. Serve to 4 with ***Sauce Piquante, Deviled Butter Sauce*** or ***Sauce Robert.***

• SAUCE PIQUANTE •

In a large saucepan combine ¾ cup leftover ***white wine,*** 1 tbs. ***vinegar,*** 1 tbs. ***chopped shallot,*** freshly ground pepper to taste and a ***bouquet garni*** of 1 ***sprig thyme*** and half a ***bay leaf.*** Bring to boil and cook until liquid is reduced by two-thirds. Remove *bouquet garni,* stir in 2 tbs. ***Meat Glaze,**** add ¼ cup ***Madeira*** and cook, stirring, 3 or 4 minutes longer. Just before serving stir in 1 tbs. ***chopped parsley, cayenne pepper*** to taste and, if desired, a few small pieces of ***butter.***

• DEVILED BUTTER SAUCE •

To 6 tbs. melted ***butter*** add 2 tbs. ***Dijon mustard,*** 3 tbs. each ***lemon juice*** and ***Worcestershire sauce*** and salt and pepper to taste. Heat sauce through, stirring, and serve.

• SAUCE ROBERT •

Cook 2 tbs. minced ***onion*** in 1 tbs. ***butter*** until soft. Sprinkle the mixture with 1 tbs. ***flour*** and cook, stirring, over moderate heat until flour browns lightly. Add ½ cup leftover ***white wine*** and 1½ tsp. ***Dijon mustard*** and cook, stirring, until sauce thickens. (If overthick, add a little ***Stock***.*) Strain or serve as is, according to preference.

• LÜBECK-STYLE HASH •
(German-American cookery)

The trouble with most sorts of hash
Is, they're nothing but warmed-over trash;
Though they cut down on waste,
Most lack verve and taste,
But this one has much more panache.

Roll out enough rich unsweetened ***pie dough*** to line and cover a 1-qt. casserole; line the vessel tightly, allowing a little of the pastry to overhang the rim, and reserve the remainder. In a bowl mix together 3½ cups fine dice of leftover ***roast beef*** and/or ***rare steak,*** 3 beaten ***eggs,*** 4 chopped ***anchovy fillets,*** 2 tsp. ***drained and chopped pickled capers,*** 1 small ***onion,*** chopped and lightly sautéed, 3 tbs. ***breadcrumbs,*** ¼ tsp. ***grated nutmeg*** and salt and pepper to taste. (The mixture should be smooth and somewhat moist. If needed, add another beaten egg.) Pour mixture into pastry-lined casserole and cover with rolled-out reserved pastry dough. Press pastry all around rim of casserole, crimping top and lining together to form a decorative border; slash top decoratively to allow steam to escape. Bake 45 minutes in a preheated 350°F oven, or until crust is golden. Serve to 6 with Caper Sauce on the side.

• CAPER SAUCE •

In a saucepan prepare a *roux* of 1½ tbs. each ***butter*** and ***flour.*** Add ⅓ tsp. ***Worcestershire sauce*** and salt to taste. Gradually add 1 cup ***consommé,**** stirring until sauce is smooth and thickened, then stir in 1 tbs. chopped (or very small whole) drained ***pickled capers.***

Variations

Lightly cooked leftover ***carrots***, cut into fine dice, may be added to the hash and ***chopped anchovy fillets*** may be substituted for capers in the sauce.

• DEVILED ROAST BEEF BONES •

One of the best ways of amortizing the high cost of a festal meal, this secondary preparation is considered by true buffs to be more delectable than its primary source. That the dish traditionally has been a staple of hotel menus shouldn't be held against it, for it's the stuff of Neanderthal feeding at its ultimate. The tactic here is to excise the bones (well padded with meat) from your rib roast after it has come out of the oven but before it is borne to the table, where what your guests don't see won't be missed. Alternatively, you can dispense with the roast altogether if you're on friendly terms with a butcher who will reserve an occasional mess of rib bones for your use (in which case the bones should be lightly baked before they are deviled and broiled).

* * *

Figuring on 2 big meaty pieces per serving, liberally pepper and salt to taste leftover ***roast beef rib bones*** and coat them well with ***Dijon*** or ***English mustard***, according to preference, laced, if you like, with a few drops of ***Tabasco***. Roll each rib in ***breadcrumbs***, covering it thoroughly. Arrange ribs on an oven rack and broil, turning once, under moderate heat until lightly browned. Serve very hot with mustard sauce.

• MUSTARD SAUCE •

In a saucepan prepare a *roux* of 1 tbs. each ***flour*** and ***butter***. Add 1 tbs. finely minced, lightly sautéed ***onion***, stir, and gradually add a blend of ¼ cup leftover ***dry white wine*** and ¾ cup ***stock**** (preferably veal), stirring. Simmer gently 10 minutes, stirring frequently, and stir in 2 tsp. ***Dijon*** or ***English mustard*** and, if desired, a dash of ***Tabasco*** just before removing sauce from heat.

Leftover boiled beef has been converted to regal fare at least since the days of Louis XV, who is supposed to have doted on *Boeuf bouilli au pauvre homme* (poor man's boiled beef):

> When you have any boiled beef left over, cut it into slices, arrange on a dish, sprinkle with salt, pepper, chopped spring onions and parsley, add a little dripping or fat skimmed off the stockpot, a pinch of garlic, a glass of stock or water, a little breadcrumbs and leave to simmer for a quarter of an hour on hot ashes. (*Larousse Gastronomique*)

• BOEUF BOUILLI À LA DIABLE (French cookery) •

Allowing 2 good-sized pieces per serving, cut cold leftover ***boiled beef or stockpot beef*** into fairly thick slices and coat them evenly on all surfaces with Dijon mustard. Sprinkle one side of each slice with ***olive oil,*** melted ***butter*** or good rendered ***beef fat*** and cover with ***breadcrumbs***. Turn meat over and repeat process, making sure edges are thoroughly covered with crumbs. Shake off excess crumbs, broil as for Deviled Roast Beef Bones (above) and serve with ***Diable Sauce.***

• DIABLE SAUCE •

Boil down by two-thirds ¾ cup leftover ***white wine*** and 1 tbs. ***vinegar*** to which have been added 1 tbs. ***minced shallot,*** a pinch each ***thyme*** and pepper, and a scant ***pinch cayenne.*** Add ½ cup ***dark meat stock**** and 1 tsp. ***Meat Glaze**** and cook, stirring, over moderate heat until sauce coats spoon lightly. If desired, swirl in a small piece of butter off heat.

• BOEUF BOUILLI SAUTÉ À LA LYONNAISE (French cookery) •

Sauté 1⅓ cups sliced ***onion*** in 2 tbs. ***butter*** until translucent and set aside. Cut 1 lb. cold leftover ***boiled beef or stockpot beef*** into fairly small, thin slices and sauté in 2 tbs. ***butter*** until lightly browned on both sides. Add reserved onions to pan along with salt and pepper to taste and heat mixture through, tossing thoroughly. Transfer to a heated serving platter and heat 2 tbs. tarragon vinegar in the emptied sauté pan. Drizzle beef-onion mixture with vinegar, sprinkle with ***chopped parsley*** and serve immediately to 4.

• DRUNKARD'S BEEF (Original recipe) •

This dish was born when a pleasant sufficiency of bloody marys led its creator to the fridge in search of an antidote. What he found there was a thick hunk of stockpot beef and little else. A fifth drink, virtually untouched, was reluctantly pressed into service as a braising medium. The finished product seemed magnificent to its author, whose critical faculties may or may not have been somewhat skewed by then.

* * *

For each serving prepare but don't imbibe a good spicy ***bloody mary*** with plenty of freshly grated horseradish. Figuring on ⅓ to ½ lb. meat per portion, place leftover ***boiled beef or stockpot beef*** in a casserole or Dutch oven (preferably in one piece) and pour the libation over it. Simmer half-covered until the liquid is reduced to a creamy consistency, basting the meat occasionally with the sauce. Serve sprinkled liberally with chopped parsley.

• BOEUF BOUILLI À LA HONGROIS •
(Hungarian-derived French cookery)

Cut 1 to 1½ lbs. leftover ***boiled beef or stockpot beef*** into large dice. In a large pan lightly sauté ¾ cup roughly ***chopped onion.*** Add beef to pan and sauté, tossing until meat and onions are lightly browned. Season to taste with ***paprika*** and just before serving stir in ¾ cup ***Cream Sauce.*** Serves 2.

• CREAM SAUCE •

Prepare a *roux* of 2 tbs. each ***butter*** and ***flour.*** Gradually stir in ¼ cup ***boiling milk,*** stirring. Still stirring, gradually add ½ cup ***heavy cream*** and finish with salt and pepper to taste.

• SUBRICS DE BOEUF À LA MÉNAGÈRE •
(French cookery)

These miniature patties, usually served as an hors d'oeuvre or light luncheon entrée, derive from preparations originally baked on bricks *(sur briques)*. Hence the name.

* * *

Cut 1½ cups leftover ***boiled beef or stockpot beef*** into very small dice and combine in a bowl with ½ cup ***grated Gruyère*** or similar cheese, 2 ***eggs*** beaten with 1 tbs. ***flour*** and salt and pepper to taste. In a large skillet (or, preferably, two large skillets) heat a half-and-half mixture of ***butter*** and leftover ***rendered duck, chicken or beef fat*** sufficient to coat the bottom of the pan to a depth of about ⅛″. When fat mixture is quite hot, add beef mixture to the pan a spoonful at a time, keeping the blobs well separated, and shape each into a patty with the back of the spoon. Fry, turning once, until browned on both sides, transferring ***subrics*** to a heated serving platter as they are done. Serve with ***tomato sauce*** or ***Sauce Piquante**** on the side. Portions will vary according to use. Freshly fried ***potato chips*** make an ideal accompaniment to *subrics* served as a main course.

Variations

Substitute for the beef an equal quantity of diced leftover ***cooked veal, chicken, ham, pork, tongue, fish, shellfish, various innards, cooked vegetables,*** etc.

To enumerate the multitudinous uses to which excess raw beef and variously cooked beef leftovers lend themselves would require a book without end. With a little imagination and a decent grasp of culinary principles, the dedicated connective cook should be able to adapt innumerable standard recipes to the economical use of calculated leftovers both cooked and raw. Numerous versions of chili con carne may be produced from various hand-me-downs, as may the sundry regional *picadillos* and *empanadas* of Latin American cookery; and even as complex and festive a production as the Brazilian national dish, *Feijoada,* is largely concoctable from the remnants of earlier meals.

• FEIJOADA •

One of the great catchall dishes of world cookery, a really good *Feijoada* is an amalgam of soul-stirring resonances derived from the cuisines of Portugal, various Amerindian cultures and Black Africa. Ordinarily the dish requires several hours of preparation but the foresighted connective cook can assemble a first-rate version in a fraction of the time by cannibalizing the remains of several earlier meals.

Preliminary procedures

Condiments: Peel, slice and seed 3 ***oranges.*** Lightly toast ½ cup ***farofa*** (***manioc flour,*** available in Latin American food shops). Thinly slice 4 ***onions.*** Set all the foregoing aside in separate serving dishes.

Sauce: In a blender or processor purée 2 ripe medium ***tomatoes,*** peeled and seeded, with 3 ***hot chili peppers*** (fresh or pickled, seeds removed) and 2 cloves ***garlic.*** Transfer mixture to a sauce boat and stir in ⅓ cup ***wine vinegar;*** juice of 2 ***lemons;*** 2 cloves ***garlic,*** 2 small ***onions*** and 3 ***scallions,*** all minced; 1 tbs. chopped ***parsley;*** ¾ cup ***consommé****; and salt, white pepper and ***cayenne*** or ***Tabasco*** to taste. (The sauce should be hellaciously spicy.)

Set aside 4 cups leftover ***Coach House Black Bean Soup**** or ***Black Bean Soup Another Way,**** having allowed the soup to thaw thoroughly if frozen. (Purists doubtless will shudder at the substitution of a thick soup for the orthodox whole cooked beans. If rigorous authenticity is desired, you will have reserved the requisite amount of whole cooked beans *before* puréeing your last batch of beans for soup. To cook the beans from a standing start specifically for a *Feijoada* is a waste of time.)

Slice and set aside up to 1 lb. leftover ***cooked smoked beef tongue***. Thinly slice and set aside ½ lb. or so of any leftover cooked ***Chorizo**** and/or ***Italian sausage (Salsiccie Dolce**** or ***Salsiccie Piccante****) that may be lying around. Thickly slice 1 lb. or thereabouts of leftover ***pot roast, braised beef or rare broiled steak*** and set aside.

In salted water to cover simmer 1 medium ***green cabbage,*** 8–12 small ***white onions,*** 1 lb. ***collard greens*** and, if desired, a double handful of baby ***carrots*** until vegetables are tender. Drain, cut cabbage into 8–12 chunks and keep vegetables warm.

While veggies are cooking melt 2 tbs. ***butter*** in a skillet; add 2 large ***onions,*** chopped, and 2 ***cloves garlic,*** minced. Sauté until translucent. In a saucepan combine 1 cup of the reserved ***bean soup*** with the onion-garlic mixture, ¼ cup of the ***sausage meat*** and 3 small ***hot chili peppers,*** seeded and diced. Add ½ cup ***mixed meat stock**** or leftover ***braising liquid*** from ***smoked ham*** or ***tongue*** and cook 20 minutes over low heat, stirring frequently and adding liquid as needed to prevent sticking. Roughly purée mixture in a blender or processor and return to the saucepan to keep hot.

Arrange meats and vegetables on a heated serving platter and warm them through in a preheated 250°F oven, meanwhile steaming 6 cups leftover ***cooked rice*** and separately heating remainder of reserved bean soup (or ***whole beans;*** if soup is used it should be quite thick). Just before serving pour soup-sausage purée over meats and serve the *Feijoada* forth immediately to 8–12, passing all other components around the table.

> NOTE—A hunk of ***salt pork*** or ***slab bacon***, salvaged from an incompletely consumed ***choucroute garni*** or some such dish and sliced into serving pieces, may be included with the meats, as may some leftover ***grilled blood sausage***, if any is on hand.

· INTERLUDE ·

Do Your Wurst

SPEAKING of sausage, as we were a moment ago, this is as good a place as any to go into the subject in some detail. As remarked earlier, sausages are not culinary elements but compounds. Their history is long, intimately involved with Connective Cookery and mostly honorable, going back in the West at least to Roman and early Gallic times. *Mostly* honorable because to buy sausage is—more often than not quite literally—to buy pigs in pokes, and various forms of fraud and adulteration have been practiced through the ages. As a venerable French story has it, a *charcutier* accused in court of mixing horsemeat with rabbit first denies the charge flat out, then confesses under stern questioning that, well, yes, there may be just a *little* equine flesh in his products. Pressed by the judge for a more precise accounting, he admits that the proportions are "half and half." Pressed still further and warned that his goods have been subjected to laboratory analysis, he finally concedes that the "halves" are one rabbit and one horse.

Whether or not the seller is suspect, there really is no good reason for using store-bought sausage, except possibly in the case of smoked varieties when home smoking is impractical. Particularly where fresh sausage is concerned, the home product is cheaper, easy and enjoyable to make, and free of questionable commercial preservatives, fillers and colorants. Moreover, the cook who makes her own sausage can make it precisely to her taste, originate her own blends and recipes and take honest satisfaction from her work.

The varieties of sausage—considerably augmented by the

recent *nouvelle cuisine* vogue for stuffing all manner of seafoods, and even meatless vegetable mixtures, into gut casing—are countless. As a consequence, no attempt will be made here to treat the subject exhaustively. Rather, it is hoped that the sampling to follow will serve as a spur to original creativity guided by culinary commonsense.

A Few General Observations

It should be noted that the joys of eating most varieties of sausage are largely the joys of eating fat. The ratio of lean meat to plain fat usually is no higher than two-to-one and more often than not significantly lower. The conflict to be resolved, if conventional medical wisdom can be credited, is between the abuse of the arteries and the satisfactions of the palate. The choice is yours.

Although the work is more tedious, hand-chopped meat generally produces a better pork sausage than meat put through a grinder, and grinders do better than processors.

Pork sausage does not freeze well but will keep for several weeks, even without refrigeration, if it is first cooked and then stored in sterilized crocks or glass jars, with melted lard to cover by a depth of half an inch, under an airtight cover.

In lieu of a mechanical device with a sausage-filling attachment, the simple funnel procedure described under *Boudins Blancs* (page 46) will do quite nicely for stuffing pork casing with any sort of filling.

Fresh sausage should not be packed as tightly as possible, lest it burst when cooked.

Any air pockets or bubbles should be pricked with a needle before sausage is cooked.

• HERBED PORK SAUSAGES •
(American cookery)

Finely chop, grind or process together ¾ lb. each lean chilled ***fresh pork shoulder*** or ***butt*** and fresh chilled ***pork fat.*** In a bowl blend mixture thoroughly with 2 tbs. each ***minced parsley*** and ***snipped chives***, 1 tsp. each ***white pepper***, crumbled dried ***sage*** and cold water, ¾ tsp. dried ***summer savory***, a generous pinch each of ***sugar***, dried ***thyme*** and dried ***marjoram*** and a scant pinch of ***fresh-grated nutmeg***. Fill casing, as prepared for *Boudins Blancs*,* with the mixture, tying off sausages in 5″ links. Prick sausages lightly with a needle, arrange them in a skillet and add water to a depth of ¼″. Bring water to a lively simmer and cook sausages, covered, 10 minutes. Uncover pan and cook over high heat until water has evaporated, then sauté sausages, turning from time to time, until golden brown. Serves 6–8 in combination with ***eggs***, ***pancakes***, ***waffles***, ***grits***, etc.

• SALSICCIE DOLCE (Italian cookery) •

This basic recipe for plain sweet sausage lends itself to innumerable variations and modifications. The finished product may be pan-sautéed or broiled and combines particularly well with such vegetables as onions, peppers, dried beans, cauliflower, cabbage and potatoes. Sliced leftover cooked sausage makes a fine antipasto component and a splendid addition to open-face omelets *(frittati)*, hearty peasant-style soups, potato salads and dishes based on veal and chicken. In this case hand-chopped forcemeat is preferable by far to ground meat, but if the meat must be ground (or processed), its texture should be quite coarse. This recipe yields a fairly lean product, but fresh chilled pork fat may be added to taste.

* * *

Coarsely chop boneless ***pork butt*** or ***shoulder*** and blend thoroughly with ½ tsp. salt and ¾ tsp. ground fresh pepper per pound of meat. Fill prepared casing, tying off sausages at 3″ intervals.

Variations

• SALSICCIE CON SEME DI FINOCCHI •

To the foregoing add ½ tsp. lightly crushed ***fennel seeds*** per pound of meat before filling casing.

• SALSICCIE ALLA SICILIANA •

Proceeding as for *Salsiccie Dolce,* add ¼ cup fine dice of ***Provolone cheese,*** 4 tbs. chopped ***Italian (flat) parsley,*** ¼ tsp. ***whole fennel seeds*** and ¼ cup leftover ***dry white wine*** to each pound of meat before filling casing.

• SALSICCIE PICCANTE •

Proceeding as for **Salsiccie Dolce**, add 1 clove ***garlic,*** minced, and ⅓ tsp. crumbled dried ***hot red chili peppers*** (seeds removed) or ***hot pepper flakes*** to each pound of meat before filling casing.

• SALSICCIE DI PEGATO DI MAIALE •
(Italian cookery)

Pick over 2 lbs. very fresh ***pork liver,*** discarding membranes and other inappetent anatomical features. Chop the stuff coarsely by hand and combine it in a bowl with ¾ lb. chopped ***caul fat,*** 2 cloves ***garlic,*** chopped, ¾ cup fine-chopped leftover ***orange rind*** and salt and hot pepper flakes to taste. Stuff prepared casing with the mixture, tying sausages off at 3½" intervals. Lightly coat the bottom of a skillet with ***olive oil,*** sauté ***sausages*** over moderately high heat until lightly browned on all sides, turn down heat and cook about 12 minutes, turning occasionally and squirting sausages with a little ***lemon juice*** 2 minutes before they are done. Serve, moistened with pan juices, to 6.

> **NOTE**—Before use, caul fat should be soaked for a few minutes in lukewarm water to cover with a tablespoon of ***vinegar*** added, then drained and patted dry.

Variation

Wrap pairs of uncooked sausages in water-softened ***caul fat*** after inserting a ***bay leaf*** between each pair. Tie bundles with string as for Beef Birds in White Wine* and broil 10 minutes, preferably over coals, turning as parcels brown and basting occasionally with ***lemon juice.*** Discard caul and serve 1 pair of sausages per portion.

• CERVELAS (French cookery) •

The term *cervelas* is a culinary mutant, like the aspic discussed earlier. Originally any sausage so called was made with a significant proportion of brain (Italian *cervello*), the organ of intellect in question usually being that of the pig. At some point between its Italian origin and French adaptation the sausage lost its wits but retained its name, except for the substitution of an *s* for the terminal *t* of early orthography. Later, the British anglicized it, meaninglessly rendering it "saveloy." Brainless or not, and by any name you choose to apply to it, it's a superior sausage for boiling and is particularly felicitous with a hot potato salad made from leftover boiled spuds or, in the Alsatian style, with sauerkraut.

* * *

Grind together 2 parts ***lean pork,*** preferably from the neck or shoulder, and 1 part ***lean beef trimmings***. For each ¾ lb. of combined meats add and thoroughly blend together ¼ lb. ***fat bacon,*** cut into fine dice, ½ tbs. salt, 1 scant tsp. ground fresh black pepper, ½ ***clove garlic,*** mashed, 2 finely ***chopped shallots*** and 1 small pinch ***saltpeter*** (optional; a color-enhancer only, of no nutritional or palatal value, the substance, obtainable at most druggists, will be looked at askance by any former servicemen, although its alleged antiaphrodisiacal properties are wholly mythical). Fill prepared casing (preferably beef gut) with mixture and tie at both ends. Soak in brine (recipe below) to cover 48–72 hours, drain, prick here and there with a needle and simmer gently for 1 hour in water, leftover ***red wine*** or any combination of the two, to cover. Number of servings will depend on quantities used.

• BRINE FOR SAUSAGES •

To 2 cups boiling water add 1 lb. ***sea salt or kosher salt,*** 1 tbs. ***saltpeter*** and 1 tsp. ***bicarbonate of soda.*** Return to boil, stir in 3 cups leftover ***dry white wine*** and a small ***bouquet garni*** of ***peppercorns,*** stick ***cinnamon*** and ***cloves,*** and remove immediately from heat. Allow brine to cool thoroughly and discard bouquet garni before use.

• CRÉPINETTES (French cookery) •

Chop or grind ¼ lb. each lean uncooked ***pork trimmings*** and ***veal scraps,*** together with ½ lb. each hard ***fatback*** and leftover cooked ***chicken, duck, rabbit,*** or something similar. Season mixture evenly with a handful of ***chopped parsley,*** 1 tsp. ***quatre épices*** (***ground pepper, nutmeg, cloves*** and ***cinnamon*** in equal proportions) and salt to taste. Divide mixture into golf-ball-sized portions and wrap each snugly in a 4″-square piece of ***caul fat*** (presoftened in ***vinegar***-laced lukewarm water and patted dry), pressing corners of each square against covering for adhesion and indenting the *crépinettes* here and there with a thumb. Brush *crépinettes* liberally with ***melted butter,*** roll in ***breadcrumbs*** and broil under very low flame, turning occasionally, until cooked through and golden on all sides. Serve with puréed ***potatoes*** to 4, or skewer with picks and pass around with cocktails.

Variations

Crépinette fillings, bound with various thick sauces, may be made with any leftover ***hashed cooked meats*** in combination with leftover ***sautéed mushrooms***. Variations on the basic theme are boundless and such additions as ***pistachios, pine nuts*** and the like make for interesting textural contrasts. ***Pork liver,*** in combination with ***sausage meat*** and such economical oddments as lung and spleen, also makes a fine filling, and the addition, in almost any context, of a little leftover ***cooked ham or tongue*** will enliven the end product appreciably. In cases where raw pork is not used in the filling, *Crépinettes* may be rolled successively in beaten ***egg*** and ***flour*** and deep-fried. In almost all cases these versatile little preparations may be sliced and eaten cold. Let your ingenuity be your guide.

• SPIEDINI DI FEGATO ALLA RETICELLA (Italian cookery) •

The kinship between these brochettes and the French *crépinettes* is obvious.

* * *

Cut 1 lb. trimmed fresh ***pork liver*** into 1½″ cubes. Marinate liver ½ hour in a blend of 2 tbs. ***minced rosemary,*** 4 cloves ***garlic,*** sliced, juice of 2 ***lemons*** and salt and pepper to taste. (The operation is best accomplished in a sealed plastic bag, which should be shaken well once or twice during the marination.) Drain liver, reserving marinade, and pat dry. Wrap each cube of liver, together with a small ***bay leaf,*** in a 3″ square of ***caul fat*** softened as for *crépinettes.** Align packets on metal skewers and broil 10 minutes under moderate flame or over coals, basting occasionally with the reserved marinade and turning from time to time. Serve hot as a first course to 4–6.

• HÁZI KOLBÁSZ (Hungarian cookery) •

Simple and savory, this sausage is not tied off in links but coiled and baked whole.

* * *

Using a heavy chef's knife or Chinese cleaver (that's *Hungarian?*), fine-chop 2 lbs. ***boneless pork butt*** or ***shoulder,*** all fat included, or grind the meat coarsely. In a bowl mix the pork thoroughly with ½ tbs. ***Hungarian paprika*** (supermarket paprika just won't do), 1½ ***cloves garlic,*** minced, grated rind of ½ ***lemon,*** 1 pinch ***ground cloves,*** 1 tbs. salt and ½ tsp. freshly ground black pepper. Prepare 1½ yards ***sausage casing,*** tie one end, fill with pork mixture and tie off other end, discarding any excess casing. Arrange sausage in a loose coil on the bottom of a greased round iron pan or ovenproof dish and bake in a preheated 350°F oven 20–25 minutes, or until sausage is bright red. Serve to 6 as a main dish or cut into thick slices and spear with wooden picks as cocktail hors d'oeuvres for 18–20.

Variation

Before its final rising, divide a batch of ***French*** or ***Italian bread*** dough into halves. Beat one half down into a large greased black-iron skillet, arrange the sausage atop the dough in a loose coil, as above, and beat the remaining dough down over the sausage. Allow dough to rise, covered with a cloth; brush top lightly with ***olive oil*** and bake according to the bread recipe you are using. Cut the finished loaf into pie-like wedges and serve to 8, with a tossed salad, as an informal luncheon or late supper.

• MAJÁS HURKA (Hungarian cookery) •

Plenty of nutrition here at very little cost, and your guests needn't be told precisely what it was that they put away so enthusiastically.

* * *

Gently cook 1 lb. ***pork lung*** in ¼ lb. ***lard*** until tender. Remove lung from pan with a slotted spoon and set aside to drain in paper towels. In the same pan cook 1 large ***onion,*** minced, until limp but not colored. Add to pan 1 lb. very ***fresh pork liver,*** picked over and cut into small pieces, and cook 10 minutes over low heat without allowing onions to brown. Drain lard from pan and reserve for other uses. When liver mixture has cooled, fine-grind it together with reserved pork lung and ¼ lb. leftover ***cooked fatty pork*** or ***cooked fatty fresh ham***. Heat 2½ cups leftover ***cooked rice*** in ⅔ cup ***beef or mixed stock***,* cooking until liquid is absorbed. In a bowl thoroughly mix meats and rice together with 1½ tsp. pepper, a small pinch of ***marjoram*** and 1½ tsp. salt (or to taste). Prepare 1½ yards ***sausage casing*** (preferably 1½" in diameter), tie one end, and stuff with filling. Tie off sausage at its other end, discarding any excess casing. Prick sausage all over with a needle and poach 15 minutes in gently simmering water. Drain sausage, pan-broil or bake it slowly until well browned and serve to 6–8 with ***mashed potatoes*** and ***stewed prunes.***

• KIELBASA (Polish cookery) •

Eaten in various forms throughout central Europe and in some parts of Russia, this garlicky sausage is characterized by a denser texture than most and hence may be successfully prepared with a processor.

* * *

Process together ½ lb. each ***boneless beef shin*** (reserving the bone and its marrow for other uses), ***fresh pork fat*** and lean ***pork trimmings***, all chilled, together with 2 tbs. ice water, 2 tsp. coarse salt (or less to taste), 1½ tsp. ***sweet paprika*** (preferably Hungarian), 1 tsp. ***ground fresh pepper,*** ½ tsp. ***crumbled dried marjoram,*** 1 pinch ***dried summer savory*** and 1½ tsp. ***finely minced garlic,*** allowing the machine to run until the meats are reduced to a fine paste. Fill prepared casing with the mixture, tying off only both ends, and tie ends together to form a long loop. In cool weather, hang the sausage in a dry, airy space for several hours before use, or, in warm weather, refrigerate it, uncovered, 12–18 hours. To cook the *kielbasa,* lay it flat in a large pan, immersed to half its depth in water. Bring to simmer and poach 15 minutes, turning sausage once. Drain, return to pan and brown well over moderate heat. Serves 4–6.

• CHORIZOS (Spanish cookery) •

These peppery, extremely versatile sausages are seldom served whole. Sliced and pan-fried they are served ubiquitously as appetizers in Spanish restaurants in this country and are used in various bean dishes, tripe stews and some versions of *Caldo Gallego.** Most English-language recipes for *Chorizos* are so wildly divergent that reading any three chosen at random is something like sitting through a filming of *Rashōmon.* While no more definitive than any other, the one that follows—an attempt to reconcile extremes by compromise—produces a very tasty item.

* * *

Combine and run through a grinder, processor or food mill 1 sweet ***red bell pepper,*** seeded and deribbed, 1 small ***hot red chili pepper,*** ditto, and 4 fat ***cloves of garlic.*** Chop or grind ¾ lb. ***lean pork shoulder*** or ***butt,*** ¾ lb. ***hard fatback*** and ½ lb. ***lean uncooked beef trimmings,*** all chilled. In a bowl thoroughly blend all the foregoing, together with ¼ cup left-over ***red wine,*** 1 tbs. ***wine vinegar,*** 1 tbs. each ***paprika*** and salt, ½ tsp. ***sugar*** and 1 pinch each ***cayenne pepper*** and ***ground cumin.*** Fill prepared pork casing with mixture, tying off sausages at 5″ or 6″ intervals.

NOTE—*Chorizos* shouldn't be used immediately, but hung to dry overnight at a temperature between 60° and 70°F, or refrigerated on an uncovered rack for two or three days. Alternatively, they may be lightly smoked before use.

• BRATWURST (German cookery) •

Combine and finely grind ½ lb. ***lean tissue-free veal*** and 1 lb. ***pork loin.*** Blend meats thoroughly with 1½ tsp. salt, ½ tsp. each ***ground mace*** and ***nutmeg,*** 1 tsp. ***white pepper*** and salt to taste. (Easy on the salt.) Fill prepared pork casing with the mixture, tying off sausages at 5″ intervals. To cook, place sausages in a deep pan and cover with hot water. Bring to boil, remove pan from heat immediately and leave sausages in water for several minutes, until firm. Drain sausages, pat dry and dip in ***milk.*** Broil under low flame, turning occasionally, until golden-brown. Serve hot to 4 with ***mashed*** or ***mousseline potatoes.***

Creature Comforts 7

When he arrived, he had a large cardboard box under each arm. One box contained a fresh-killed chicken (he never bought "dead" chickens), a gallon of his own wine and a large loaf of Italian bread. The other box contained a jar of home-canned wild mushrooms, a quart of my mother's spaghetti sauce, a pound of imported Italian pasta, pecorino cheese his brother had made in Italy, some salami, homemade biscotti, and home-canned tomatoes.

. . . After lunch . . . I tried to think of something to do that would please Pop. Knowing his love for animals, I thought he would enjoy the zoo at Central Park. We first went to see the big animals—the lions and tigers, etc. My father seemed bored and I began to worry that the excursion had not been a good idea after all. But at that moment, we got to the area where the small North American mammals are kept. To my surprise, my father's face lit up. When we came to the cage with the raccoons, he said, "You know, you would have to marinate them in wine for about four hours before you cook them." Then we walked up to the cage of an opossum and he said, "That one looks tough. I think I would marinate him in vinegar and water overnight." At the next cage he said, "I'd cook that one in a nice tight sauce with wild mushrooms."

—Edward Giobbi, *Italian Family Cooking*

LIKE HIS FATHER before him, Ed Giobbi is a superb cook who usually spurns the flesh of large beasts. So do most Italians and so, out of economic necessity, natural scarcity, religious or moral conviction, or palatal preference, do the overwhelming majority of the world's cooks. And yet, above the level of mere subsistence, most of the world gets along just fine without regaling itself with beef, elephant steaks or eland chops. Of the earth's creatures great and small, the smaller are by far more available, more economical, probably more healthful and, to most of the world's human feeders, tastier and more interesting. Because of their smaller size they are less likely to lend themselves to the deliberate and wholesale manufacture of leftovers than the larger ruminants, but the frugal connective cook has only to observe, say, the multiple uses to which a Chinese chef puts a relatively flesh-poor duck to know that there is more good eating in most smaller critters than seems apparent at first blush. Borrowing and adapting from the Chinese and other cuisines, our friend J—he of the famous raccoon mousse—had better luck with a single bird when he prepared this five-course dinner for two couples: Crisped Duck Skin; *Crostini di Fegatini di Anitra;* Duck Consommé; *Magret de Caneton aux Olives;* Duck Soong. As redundant as five dishes extracted from a single web-footed friend may sound, it was a fine, well-varied and well-received meal produced at a cost of well under two dollars per person.

One Duck Five Ways

Preliminary procedures

Draw the point of a knife along the breastbone of a 4-to-4½-lb. ***duckling,*** splitting the skin from stem to stern. Again working with the point of the knife, make circular incisions around the thighs and wings where they meet the body. Disjoint all four of these appendages, set wings aside and strip skins off legs intact, as though rolling down a pair of stockings. (These may be reserved for future use; stuffed with a farce based on the ***giblets, neck meat*** and other oddments and sewn up at the ends, they'll make a delectable light lunch or dinner first course when pan-browned in a little of the bird's fat.) Working away from the breastbone, strip the bird of its body skin and subcutaneous fat, preferably in one whole sheet, taking care not to damage the flesh of the breast, and set the skin aside. Remove and reserve the two thick packets of fat from the arse end. Working as close to the bone as possible, remove breasts from bird and set aside. Remove as much meat as possible from the skinned legs and carcass and set it aside, too. Split the carcass, remove whatever squishy innards you find therein and set them aside, along with the bird's liver. Prepare a consommé,* using the carcass, reserved wings, neck and giblets. (In point of fact, this step—a waste of time on so small a scale—took a transactional form on the evening in question, when the ingredients were banked in the freezer for wholesale future use and an equivalent amount of previously banked Duck Consommé was withdrawn from the account.)

• CRISPED DUCK SKIN •

Cut reserved duck's body skin into strips about ½" × 2½". In a heavy skillet render reserved fat from the bird's rear end over low heat; add strips of skin, outer-side-down, and fry over moderate heat until cracklings are golden-brown and rendered of their fat. Remove skins from pan with a slotted spoon, drain on paper towels and serve hot with pre-dinner drinks, reserving pan fat for other uses.

> **NOTE**—The view here is that these cracklings should be served and eaten unseasoned, but *chacun à son goût*. In any event, they are very rich and so unconscionably addictive that prudence dictates that only a small quantity be cooked for a party of four. The uncooked excess will freeze well for future indulgences.

• CROSTINI DI FEGATINI DI ANITRA •
(Italian cookery)

Lightly sauté 1 small ***onion,*** chopped fine, in 1½ oz. reserved ***duck fat.*** When onion has wilted, push it to one side of the pan, tilting the vessel to allow fat to flow onto unoccupied surface. Keeping onion away from the flame, increase heat, sear reserved duck liver on all sides (along with ***giblets*** salvaged from the stockpot if you've troubled to make ***consommé*** for the occasion). Add a splash of ***Cognac, sherry,***

port or ***Marsala*** and sauté, stirring meat and onions together, until liquor evaporates. Transfer contents of pan to a blender or processor, add salt and freshly ground pepper to taste, 1 small piece of ***orange rind*** (inner white lining removed), ½ tsp. drained ***pickled capers*** and 1½ tsp. reserved ***duck fat,*** chilled. Blend ingredients to a pasty consistency and chill mixture lightly. Cut decrusted leftover ***Italian*** or ***white bread*** into 8 rectangles about ¼″ × 1″ × 2½″, fry in 2 oz. reserved ***duck fat,*** pressing pieces lightly with a spatula and turning once, until golden-brown. Drain fried bread on paper towels, spread evenly with liver mixture and run briefly under a moderate broiler. Serve immediately to 4.

NOTE—Fried leftover ***polenta*** or ***corn bread*** makes even better *Crostini* than the breads specified.

After the richness of the two foregoing offerings, a light clear soup, served in small portions, will clear the palate nicely. Hence . . .

• DUCK CONSOMMÉ •

To 2 cups strong reduced ***clarified stock**** (made, of course, with a preponderance of duck) add a handful of matchstick ***turnips.*** Bring to a gentle simmer, cook 5 minutes and serve in small bowls to 4, with turnips evenly distributed and with a garnish of chopped ***parsley*** or ***snipped chives.***

• MAGRET DE CANETON AUX OLIVES •

This, an adaptation based in equal parts on French *nouvelle cuisine* and an old bourgeoise classic, *Caneton aux Olives,* may or may not be an original recipe, but who really cares?

* * *

Trim both halves of duck's breast and set aside. Halve 16 pitted ***green olives*** lengthwise, blanch 2 minutes in boiling water, refresh under cold running water, and set aside. In a saucepan heat together ½ cup reduced ***brown stock**** and ⅓ tsp. ***Meat Glaze***.* Add 12 ***green peppercorns*** and cook, stirring, until glaze is dissolved and sauce coats a spoon lightly. Turn heat very low and add ***olives.***

In 1 tbs. ***butter*** heated in an iron skillet briefly sauté duck breasts over moderately high heat, turning once, just until lightly seared on both sides (the interiors should be very rare). Transfer duck breasts to a heated serving dish, carve them laterally in ¼"-thick slices, pour sauce over them, and serve immediately to 4.

• DUCK SOONG •
(Adapted from Chinese cookery)

Wash, dry and set aside 4 large outer leaves of ***iceberg lettuce*** (in good condition, without blemishes). Gather all remaining reserved ***duck meat,*** including trimmings from breast ends left from the proceding recipe. Using a sharp knife or Chinese cleaver, cut meat into thin slices. Stack slices and cut lengthwise into thin shreds and then crosswise to form tiny dice. Place meat in a bowl and, using the fingers, blend it thoroughly with ½ tsp. salt, 1 beaten ***egg white*** and 1 scant ***tsp. cornstarch.*** Cut 10 ***water chestnuts*** into tiny dice, as you did the duck meat, and in a second bowl combine them with ½ cup finely ***diced celery,*** 3 tbs. finely ***diced carrot*** and 1 tsp. ***minced fresh ginger root.*** In a third bowl combine 2 tbs. ***minced garlic*** and 3 tbs. ***finely chopped scallions*** (whites and green tops). In a small deep dish blend 2 tbs. ***dry sherry,*** 1½ tsp. ***light soy sauce,*** 1 tsp. ***sugar,*** and 1 tsp. ***hot chili paste*** (optional). In a similar dish dissolve 1 tbs. ***cornstarch*** in 1½ tbs. water.

In a wok or skillet heat 1½ cups ***peanut oil*** over high flame. When oil is hot but not smoking add cubed duck and cook 60 seconds, stirring constantly. Immediately drain contents of pan through a colander mounted on a receptacle that will catch the oil. Return 2 tbs. oil to pan and add water chestnut mixture. Cook 30 seconds over high heat, stirring, and add scallion mixture. Cook, stirring, another 10 seconds and return duck cubes to pan. Continue to stir-fry 30 seconds and add sherry mixture and ½ tsp. ***sesame oil.*** Quickly stir cornstarch mixture, add it to the pan and stir rapidly for 30 seconds.

Transfer contents of pan to a heated platter and serve immediately to 4, with reserved lettuce leaves on the side.

NOTE—At this juncture the diners take matters into their own hands. Each centers his or her portion of the duck mixture on a lettuce leaf, folds the leaf into an envelope and eats the resultant package with the fingers.

Assiduous research and experimentation have yet to turn up a satisfactory dessert made with duck. Until this culinary breakthrough is achieved, the best alternative would seem to be a fresh fruit compote, macerated with orange and/or cherry liqueur.

As already noted, the Chinese cook gets an awful lot of mileage out of very little food. Take chickens, for example: In this country a fryer usually serves two, not including any dishes to be derived from innards, necks, carcasses and so forth. By extension, three such birds would serve six. According to the meticulously calibrated *Chinese Cuisine: Wei-chuan's Cookbook* (a Taiwanese publication), on the other hand, the same three birds will serve no fewer than thirty-six, again excepting dishes made from spare parts and by such other connective processes as the manufacture of stock and stockpot-derived preparations. To be sure, the disparity is not as striking as it may seem at first glance, for an elaborate Chinese meal usually consists of a series of abbreviated gastronomic sensations—what the French call a *menu de dégustation*—whereas we Americans usually mount a sustained assault on a single main course. Thus, while the Chinese gastronome is content to experience briefly the various sensory pleasures to be derived from a single leg of fried chicken, no less than half the bird will satisfy most Americans. Still, integrated with appropriate vegetable components in a series of dishes or meals, a chicken consumed by a Chinese has a far longer and more interesting life span than one eaten by most Occidentals. Let's see how far we can go with those three small birds by adapting a few recipes from the volume cited. In each case the suggested number of servings is six, presumably in conjunction with the service of two or three other dishes.

Three Stretched Chickens

Preliminary procedures
Remove ***legs, wings*** and ***breasts*** from 3 ***frying chickens,*** reserving remainder for other uses. Putting aside elements separately according to their nature as each operation is completed, bone 2 of the legs as follows: Make 2 cuts, parallel to the bones, on the inner side of each leg and work the meat from the bones, cutting through the cartilaginous joint when it is exposed; reserve bones for the stockpot. Spread meat skin-side-down on a work surface and pound it lightly with the blunt edge of a chef's knife or cleaver (to prevent curling when the meat cooks). Hack remaining legs laterally into inch-wide serving pieces, leaving skin on and bones in. Hack wings into thirds, cutting through bones. Skin chicken breasts. Lay breast of 1 bird on a counter and cut diagonally, as you would *gravlax,** into slices about ⅛" × 1½" × 2½". In the same manner, cut the second breast into translucently thin slices; stack slices, hack into shreds, and then hack shreds crosswise into bits about the size of pine nuts. Cube third breast.

• OIL-DRIPPED CHICKEN •
(Chekiang-Kiangsu cookery)

In a large bowl let ***boned chicken legs*** rest in a marinade made of 2 tbs. ***soy sauce,*** 1 tbs. ***rice wine,*** 2 ***minced scallions,*** ⅓ tsp. finely ***minced ginger root*** and 1 piece ***star anise.*** After 30 minutes remove chicken and pat dry with paper towels. Strain and reserve marinade. In a wok or large skillet heat 3 cups ***peanut oil*** to 275°F and add boned chicken legs skin-side-down, keeping them well separated. Fry 2 minutes over moderate heat, turn meat and fry 2 minutes longer. Remove chicken with a slotted spatula, drain on paper towels and turn up heat until oil reaches 375°F. Return chicken to pan and deep-fry until golden brown. Again using the slotted spatula, remove chicken and set on paper towels to drain. Cut drained legs crosswise into 6 pieces each, arrange on a heated serving dish and sprinkle with chopped white stalk and green top of 1 scallion. Empty pan of oil, reserving latter for other uses, and heat a mixture of 1½ tsp. ***sesame oil,*** ½ tsp. ***sugar*** and 1 chopped ***scallion*** just until oil begins to smoke. Drizzle contents of pan over chicken pieces, return pan to fire and add reserved marinade to it, along with 1½ tsp. ***sugar.*** Bring mixture to boil, drizzle it over chicken pieces, garnish with ***parsley sprigs*** and ***carved radishes*** and serve immediately.

• LEMON CHICKEN •
(Cantonese cookery)

In a bowl marinate reserved sliced ***chicken breast*** in a blend of 1 tsp. ***rice wine,*** 1½ tsp. ***soy sauce,*** lightly ***beaten yolk*** of 1 ***egg,*** ¼ tsp. salt and a generous pinch of black pepper. After 10 minutes remove chicken from marinade and dredge slices individually in a blend of 4 tbs. (¼ cup) ***cornstarch*** and 2 tbs. ***flour.*** In a wok or skillet heat 3 cups ***peanut oil*** to 375°F, add chicken and fry, stirring constantly, 30 seconds. Transfer chicken to a colander with a slotted spoon, increase heat to 400°F, return chicken to pan and stir-fry 10 seconds longer. Immediately pour contents of pan into a colander mounted on a receptacle to catch the oil. Return 1 tbs. oil to pan, reserving remainder for other uses. Add to pan a blend made up of 3 tbs. ***sugar,*** ¼ tsp. salt, 2 tbs. ***lemon juice,*** 3 tbs. water and ½ tsp. ***cornstarch.*** Bring to boil, stir in 1 more tbs. oil, pour over chicken and serve immediately, garnished with ***Chinese parsley*** (coriander) and thin slices of halved ***lemon*** twisted into decorative shapes.

• CRISP SAVORY CHICKEN WINGS •
(Taiwanese cookery)

Marinate reserved pieces of 6 ***chicken wings*** 20 minutes in a blend of 1½ tsp. ***rice wine,*** 1 tsp. salt and ¼ tsp. freshly ground black pepper. Remove chicken and dredge pieces individually in ***cornstarch,*** shaking off excess. In a wok or skillet heat 3 cups ***peanut oil*** to 375°F, add chicken pieces and deep-fry 15 seconds, stirring lightly to separate pieces. Lower heat to about 325°F and continue to fry 3 minutes, or until chicken is golden, with well-crisped skin. Remove chicken from pan, drain on paper towels and arrange on a heated serving dish. Sprinkle chicken to taste with a blend of ***ground sea salt and ground brown Szechuan peppercorns.*** Garnish with raw ***carrot,*** cut into decorative shapes, and serve immediately.

• SAUCY CHICKEN •
(Chekiang-Kiangsu cookery)

In a bowl tumble reserved pieces of ***unboned chicken legs*** in 1 tbs. ***soy sauce,*** moistening them thoroughly. Roughly hack ½ ***onion*** and 1 ***carrot*** into bite-sized pieces. In a wok or skillet heat 3 cups ***peanut oil*** to 375°F. Slide pieces of chicken down sides of pan into oil, increase heat to just short of the smoking point and deep-fry chicken 1 minute, or until golden. Pour contents of pan into a colander set on a receptacle to catch the oil (reserve it) and drain chicken on paper towels. In a bowl moisten chicken pieces with 1 tbs. ***rice wine*** and stir in a blend of 1 tbs. ***soy sauce,*** 1 cup water, 1½ tbs. ***tomato paste,*** 1 tbs. ***sugar*** and salt to taste. Return 2 tbs. oil to pan and heat well. Add onion and stir-fry until fragrant. Add carrot and continue to stir-fry 30 seconds. Return contents of chicken mixture bowl to pan and bring to boil as quickly as possible. Reduce heat and simmer gently about 15 minutes, or until liquid is reduced by half. Stir in 1½ tsp. ***cornstarch,*** dissolved in 1 tbs. water, and cook until sauce thickens enough to coat solid ingredients lightly. Drizzle with ½ tsp. sesame oil, toss briefly and serve immediately on a heated platter.

• STIR-FRIED CHICKEN WITH CASHEWS •
(Cantonese cookery)

In a bowl toss reserved ***cubed chicken breast*** with a mixture composed of 1 tsp. ***rice wine,*** ½ ***egg white,*** beaten to a froth, and 2 tsp. ***cornstarch,*** coating chicken well. Seed, de-rib and dice 1 ***green bell pepper*** and set aside. In a wok or skillet combine ¼ lb. ***raw cashews,*** washed and drained, with 1 cup water and ½ tsp. salt. Bring mixture to boil, decrease heat and simmer gently 5 minutes. Remove cashews and drain, disposing of liquid. Reheat pan and add 3 cups peanut oil. Heat oil to 275°F and deep-fry cashews 30 seconds, stirring occasionally. Reduce heat to low and continue to fry 5–6 minutes, or until golden. Remove cashews with a slotted spoon and drain on paper towels. Pour off all but 2 tbs. oil from pan, reserving it for future use, and reheat remainder until just shy of smoking. Add whites of 3–4 ***scallions,*** cut into ½″ lengths, and 12 thin ⅜″-square slices of fresh ***ginger root,*** and stir-fry until fragrant. Add green pepper and stir-fry for a few seconds. Add ½ tsp. rice wine, drained chicken, and a blend of 2 tbs. water, ½ tsp. ***sesame oil,*** 1 tsp. ***cornstarch*** and a generous pinch of ***fresh-ground black pepper.*** Toss lightly to combine all ingredients, remove from heat, add cashews and toss quickly. Serve immediately.

• CHICKEN "RICE" WITH PINE NUTS •
(Chekiang-Kiangsu cookery)

In a bowl marinate reserved minced ***chicken breast*** 20 minutes in a blend of 1½ tsp. ***rice wine,*** ½ tsp. beaten ***egg white,*** ½ tsp. salt and 1½ tsp. ***cornstarch.*** In a wok or skillet heat 3 cups ***peanut oil*** to about 300°F. Add a scant handful of ***pine nuts*** and fry about 4 minutes, or until golden. Remove pine nuts with a slotted spoon and drain on paper toweling. Reduce oil heat to about 275°F; add minced chicken and stir-fry just until it becomes opaque. Pour contents of pan into a colander mounted on a receptacle to catch the oil and drain chicken on paper towels. Return 1 tbs. oil to pan and bring to high heat. Add chopped whites of 2 ***scallions*** and stir-fry until transparent. Return chicken to pan with a blend of 1 tbs. ***cornstarch,*** 2 tsp. water and salt to taste. Stir-fry briefly until mixture is heated through, transfer to a heated serving dish and serve, tossed with the pine nuts, immediately.

As may have been noticed, none of the foregoing chicken dishes make use of such eminently edible parts as livers, gizzards, necks and hearts. Having already derived considerable good eating from the surface flesh, we still have much that is useful, nourishing and delicious to deal with. Naturally, the necks and carcasses go into the stockpot, ultimately to produce soups, sauces and various dishes such as those described in Chapter 3. Now let's examine just a few of the manifold good uses to which the innards and other oddments may be put.

Taking Wing

It was William Cowper, borrowing from earlier sources, who observed that "Riches have wings." Had Cowper's priorities been as well ordered as those of his compatriot Byron, he might have transposed the nouns, for there are riches aplenty to be gleaned from the pinions of fowl. Of wings and Byron, the magisterial Isabella Mary Beeton wrote, "The wings, breast, and merrythought [wishbone] are esteemed the prime parts of a fowl, and are usually served to the ladies of the company, to whom the legs, except as a matter of paramount necessity, should not be given. Byron gave it as one reason why he did not like dining with ladies, that they always had the wings of the fowl, which he himself preferred."

As we've already seen (recipe page 134), the Chinese esteem chicken wings highly enough to make individual dishes of them. So do connoisseurs and frugal cooks the world over. In this country, though, the culinary potential of these delicacies is overlooked far too often and all but a very few cookbooks are mum on the subject. Usually the wings are spurned when a whole bird is served—and usually for good reason, for they are apt to be overdone by the time the rest of the critter is ready for the table. For the same reason, they often are excluded from the pan when a chicken is cut up for one dish or another. There is no good reason, though, for not husbanding them, in the latter case, for future use as the chief components of first-course or main dishes. Moreover, they represent an exception to the rule against buying chicken in parts, for, thanks to the average American's baseless prejudice against them, they are often relatively cheap when sold in bulk.

• AILES DES VOLAILLES CHASSEUR •
(French cookery)

The French say *chasseur* and the Italians *cacciatore.* Either way, the dish is cooked hunter's style and will be essentially the same, give or take a subsidiary ingredient or two. The French, who are inclined toward standardization, might take a dim view of the matter if you decided to toss in a few slices of bell pepper or substitute olives for mushrooms or red or fortified wine for white. Regional differences persist in Italian cookery, though, and any such variations would be considered legitimate *somewhere* in Italy.

* * *

Cut the tips from 2 lbs. ***chicken wings,*** reserving them for stock. Dry the wings with paper towels, salt and pepper them to taste, and dredge lightly in ***flour,*** shaking off excess. In a large skillet heat 2 tbs. ***butter*** and 1 tbs. ***olive oil.*** Add wings and sauté 5 minutes over moderately high heat, turning until brown on all sides. With a slotted spoon transfer wings to a holding dish and add to skillet ⅓ cup chopped ***scallion,*** 3 tbs. ***chopped onion,*** and 1 ***clove garlic,*** minced. Sauté over moderate heat until onion wilts and add ⅔ cup ***sliced mushrooms,*** ½ tsp. ***thyme*** or, if you prefer, ***rosemary,*** 1 tbs. ***minced parsley,*** and salt and pepper to taste. Sauté 5 minutes longer, add ½ cup leftover ***dry white wine*** and cook over high heat until liquid has reduced by half. Add reserved wings to pan and stir in ½ cup ***chicken stock**** and ½ cup peeled, seeded, chopped ***ripe tomato.*** Adjust seasonings, bring to a boil and immediately reduce heat to moderately low. Cook, covered, 20 minutes longer, and another 10 minutes with pan uncovered. Sprinkle with minced parsley and serve immediately to 4.

• ALE DI POLLO CON POMODORI E CIPOLLE (Italian cookery) •

The recipe was supplied by the aforequoted Edward Giobbi, a noted painter concerned as much with his palate as with his palette.

* * *

Separate 8 ***chicken wings*** at the joints and sauté them over moderate heat in 3 tbs. ***olive oil,*** turning often. Salt and pepper to taste and when wings start to brown add 1 ***clove garlic,*** chopped, and ½ cup ***chopped onion.*** When onion is limp add ½ cup leftover ***dry white wine*** and 1 tsp. ***dried rosemary.*** Cover pan, simmer 5 minutes, and add ½ cup chopped ***ripe tomato.*** Re-cover and cook 15 minutes longer over moderate heat. Serve immediately, with rice, to 2.

• CHICKEN WING PAELLA (Spanish cookery) •

Clean and barber 1 dozen ***mussels.*** Clean, skin, and slice into rounds the body sacs of ½ lb. ***squid*** and cut off tentacles just below the eyes, discarding the latter if they give you the creeps. (Stout-hearted types have been known to ingest them with apparent satisfaction.) Cut the tips from 1½ lbs. ***chicken wings*** and reserve for stockpot use. Salt and pepper wings to taste. In a paella pan or large all-metal skillet brown wings over moderately high heat in a blend of 2 tbs. ***oil*** and 1 tbs. ***unsalted butter.*** Transfer wings to a holding dish with tongs or a slotted spoon.

Add 1 ***chorizo sausage,**** cut in ¼″ rounds, to pan. Sauté *chorizo,* tossing frequently, until lightly browned and transfer to holding dish with slotted spoon. Add to pan 1 chopped medium ***onion,*** 1 chopped ***bell pepper*** (seeded and de-ribbed), and 1 large ripe ***tomato,*** peeled, seeded, and chopped. Add 2–3 ***cloves garlic,*** minced, and salt and pepper to taste. (Easy on the salt with those mussels in the offing.) Cook over moderate heat, stirring, until all but a very little of the expressed liquids has evaporated; remove from heat.

In a large saucepan bring just to boil 2½ cups ***chicken stock,**** stir in ¼ tsp. ***turmeric,*** and transfer mixture to paella pan, along with 2 cups unconverted ***long-grain rice.*** Add reserved wings and *chorizo,* along with any accumulated juices therefrom, and squid and mussels. Bring to boil and transfer pan to the bottom rack of a preheated 350°F oven. Bake 25 minutes, add ½ cup fresh shelled ***peas,*** and bake 10 minutes longer, or until liquid has been absorbed and mussels have opened. Let pan stand outside oven 5 minutes, covered with a light towel, and serve to 4, garnished with ***pimiento*** strips.

• STUFFED CHICKEN WINGS (Chinese cookery) •

Divide 16 large, meaty ***chicken wings*** at the joints, reserving first and third segments of each for other uses. In a saucepan add middle segments of wings to 2 cups boiling ***chicken stock**** and cook 4 minutes over moderately high heat. With a slotted spoon transfer chicken to a holding dish; set stock aside to cool.

With a sharp knife cut ½″ from each end of wing segments and, using the fingers, extract the bones without tearing the skin. Cut to the same lengths as wing segments 16 thin strips each leftover ***cooked ham, bamboo shoot,*** and ***scallion,*** each about the width of a strand of fettucine. Stack strips in mixed groups of three and insert stacks, one apiece, into wings, filling the latter from end to end. Transfer stuffed wings to a dish and sprinkle them successively with 1 tbs. ***soy sauce*** and ½ tbs. salt. Marinate 20 minutes, turning wings once.

Cut into 1½″ × ¼″ strips ¼ lb. large ***mushroom stems,*** 1 ***green pepper,*** and ½ cup ***bamboo shoots,*** all sliced thin. Halve 2 ***scallions*** lengthwise and cut into 1½″ pieces. Mince enough peeled fresh ***ginger root*** to measure 2 tsp. In a wok or large skillet heat 3 tbs. ***peanut oil*** over high flame. When oil is very hot add chicken and ginger and sauté 3 minutes. Turn chicken and sauté 1 minute longer. Stir in mushrooms, pepper strips, and scallions and stir-fry 2 minutes. Add ***bamboo shoots,*** 2 tsp. ***soy sauce,*** and ½ tsp. ***sugar*** and stir-fry 1 minute. Stir in ¾ cup reserved ***chicken stock*** and cook 2 minutes. Add 2 tsp. ***cornstarch*** dissolved in 2 tbs. reserved stock and cook, stirring mixture, until sauce has thickened. Serve immediately to 4.

• SOUFFLÉ DE FOIE DE VOLAILLE •
(French cookery)

One of the most savory of soufflés, this dramatically puffed dish makes a regal offering of a few inexpensive elements.

* * *

Thoroughly ***butter*** the inside of a 1½-qt. soufflé dish and coat with fine ***breadcrumbs,*** shaking out and reserving excess crumbs for other uses. In a skillet melt 1 oz. (¼ stick) ***butter,*** add 2 cloves ***garlic,*** minced, and sauté over low heat until garlic softens. Add 6–8 husbanded ***chicken*** (or ***duck***) livers and sauté gently 5 minutes, without browning either livers or garlic, turning livers occasionally. In a blender or processor reduce liver mixture and 6 juniper berries (optional) to a coarse paste. Transfer mixture to a bowl and add 1 cup hot, fairly thick ***Béchamel Sauce*** (recipe below) and a scant handful of chopped ***parsley,*** mixing ingredients well. With a wire whisk whip in 4 ***egg yolks,*** one by one, whipping well after each is added. Whip the 4 separated ***whites,*** along with 2 husbanded ***egg whites,*** until they peak firmly, and whip ⅓ into the liver mixture. Gently fold remaining ⅔ of the egg whites into the mixture, fill the soufflé dish to within ½″ of its top and smooth surface with a rubber spatula. Bake 30 minutes in a preheated 375°F oven and serve immediately to 4.

NOTE—A splash of ***Cognac*** or ***Calvados,*** added when the livers are sautéeing, imparts fragrance and character to the soufflé.

• BÉCHAMEL SAUCE •

To a *roux* made up of 2 tbs. each ***butter*** and ***flour*** and cooked a few minutes over a low flame gradually add 1 cup ***hot milk,*** stirring, a pinch of ***nutmeg*** and salt and pepper to taste. (When using for soufflé, season generously, allowing for other unseasoned ingredients.) Cook, stirring, over moderate heat until the desired thickness is reached.

• FEGATINI CON CARCIOFI (Italian cookery) •

Remove stems, tough or blemished outer leaves, and chokes from 4 medium ***artichokes.*** Slice each artichoke vertically into 8 pieces, place them in a large bowl of ice water acidulated with 2 tbs. ***lemon juice*** and allow to stand 15 minutes before draining and drying them. In a large skillet (or two, if needed) brown artichoke slices on both sides in 3 tbs. ***olive oil,*** with salt and pepper to taste, adding a little water or ***stock**** from time to time if artichokes seem to be drying out. In another pan melt 2 oz. (½ stick) ***butter,*** add 1 lb. trimmed husbanded ***chicken livers*** and cook 5 minutes, turning occasionally. Add 2 slices ***prosciutto,*** cut into julienne shreds, stir briefly and transfer contents of pan to artichoke pan. Sprinkle with juice of ½ ***lemon*** and 1 tbs. ***chopped parsley*** and serve immediately, as a dinner first course or light luncheon entrée, to 4.

• FEGATINI PRIMAVERA (Italian cookery) •

Trim and halve 1 lb. husbanded ***chicken livers*** and set aside. In a skillet heat ¼ cup ***olive oil*** or an equal amount of mixed ***oil*** and ***butter.*** Add 2 finely chopped medium ***onions*** and cook over low heat just until wilted. Add 1 large ***ripe tomato,*** peeled, seeded and chopped. Increase heat and simmer gently until mixture starts to thicken. Add chicken livers and cook over high flame, turning livers occasionally, until their color changes. Add ¼ cup each ***chopped scallions*** and ***chopped Italian (flat-leaf) parsley,*** 1 tbs. ***chopped fresh basil*** (or 1 tsp. dried basil flakes), 1 tsp. ***dried oregano,*** 1 cup leftover ***dry white wine*** and salt and pepper to taste. Simmer, partially covered, 4–5 minutes, or until livers are done but slightly pink inside. Serve, with reheated leftover ***rice*** or ***mashed potatoes,*** to 4.

• CHICKEN LIVER AND WALNUT PÂTÉ •
(American cookery)

The Manhattan restaurant Mr. & Mrs. Foster's Place is, alas, no longer funct, but for those who knew and loved it this engaging first-course offering will revive happy memories. For those who didn't, it remains a toothsome little conceit.

* * *

Pick over and dice ½ lb. husbanded ***chicken livers,*** discarding any blemishes or other undesirable matter. In a broiler pan combine livers, 1 chopped medium ***onion*** and 2 tbs. melted ***butter.*** Season to taste with salt and pepper, dust lightly with ***paprika*** and toss ingredients to coat solids with butter. Distribute livers over pan bottom, leaving space between pieces, and broil close to high heat, turning with a spatula until golden on all sides. Set pan aside. In a measuring cup blend 2 oz. each ***Madeira*** and ***dry sherry.*** Pour half the wine mixture into the work bowl of a blender or processor and, with the machine running, add 6 oz. ***chopped California walnuts,*** a few at a time, until they are reduced to a fine paste. Scrape contents of broiler pan into machine, add remaining wine and blend until well incorporated with walnut mixture. Add ¼ lb. (1 stick) room-temperature ***sweet butter,*** ¼ tsp. ***mace,*** 1 small pinch ***cayenne pepper*** and ½ tsp. ***powdered thyme*** and blend well. Empty contents of machine into a serving bowl, chill thoroughly and serve on a large ***lettuce leaf,*** with thin pepper-dusted rounds of ***cucumber,*** to 6.

• FLOWER-CUT CHICKEN GIZZARDS •
(Cantonese cookery)

Quarter 4–5 skinned husbanded ***chicken gizzards*** and, using a very sharp knife or cleaver, score each to ⅔ of its depth, making 3 or 4 parallel cuts. Give each piece a quarter-turn and repeat process, cutting at right angles to first cuts. Drop gizzard pieces into rapidly boiling water and cook about 60 seconds, or until they assume a set flowerlike shape. Strain off water and plunge gizzards into ice water. While gizzards chill, heat enough **peanut oil** in a wok or skillet to cover the bottom thinly. Add ½ **clove garlic,** finely minced, and salt to taste. Stir-fry briefly until garlic perfumes the immediate surroundings but not the outlying suburbs, add drained gizzards and continue to stir-fry for a few seconds. Add ¼ cup **chicken stock*** and ¼ cup finely diced **carrot,** cover pan and bring to boil. Add ¼ cup fresh shelled **peas** and ¼ cup **roasted unsalted cashews,** stir briefly and stir in a blend of 1 tsp. each **cornstarch** and water. Continue to cook, stirring steadily, until all ingredients are thinly coated with sauce. When sauce has thickened slightly add 1 tbs. finely **diced scallion** and 1 tsp. **oyster sauce** (available at Chinese groceries). Stir briefly and serve immediately as a first course to 4.

• FRICASSÉE OF CHICKEN GIBLETS •
(German-American cookery)

Wash, drain and quarter 4–6 husbanded **chicken gizzards** and as many **hearts**. Cut into small dice 2 **carrots,** the white of 1 **small leek** (reserving the green for other uses), 2 medium **onions** and 1 stalk **celery.** Add all the foregoing to a large saucepan, along with boiling water to cover and salt and pepper to taste. Return water to boil, reduce heat to maintain a gentle simmer and cook about 40 minutes, skimming as necessary, or until innards are tender. Strain mixture, reserving fluid and putting aside vegetables for other uses. Make a *roux* of 2 tbs. each **butter** and **flour.** Over low heat gradually add 2 cups reserved cooking liquid, stirring slowly. Likewise 1 cup leftover **dry white wine**. Bring to boil, stirring, and cook, still stirring, until mixture attains the thickness of heavy cream. Stir in 1 tbs. **lemon juice.** Off heat, stir in ½ cup **heavy cream** mixed with 2 beaten **egg yolks.** Return chicken innards to mixture, heat through and pour into a casserole over a bed of 2 cups leftover **cooked rice**. Serves 4.

• SAMBAL HATI-HATI •
(Indonesian cookery)

If previously frozen, thaw 1 lb. mixed husbanded ***chicken livers, hearts and gizzards***. Trim and halve livers and cut hearts and trimmed gizzards into ⅛″ slices. In a skillet heat 3 tbs. ***peanut oil,*** add 1 large ***onion,*** chopped, 3 ***cloves garlic,*** minced, and 3 small ***hot chili peppers,*** seeded, cored and minced (or 2 dried chilis, seeded and crumbled). Sauté, stirring, 2–3 minutes and stir in 2 anchovy fillets, finely minced. Add 2 small slices ***ginger root,*** finely minced, 1 tsp. ***turmeric,*** ½ tsp. powdered ***coriander*** and 1 ***bay leaf.*** Stir-fry 2 minutes. Add chicken innards and continue to stir-fry 3 minutes. Add 1⅓ cups ***Coconut Cream*** (recipe below) and simmer 20–25 minutes, covered. Add 6 ***hard-boiled eggs,*** cubed, 2 tbs. ***lime juice*** and salt to taste. Discard bay leaf and serve to 4 on beds of leftover ***boiled rice***.

• COCONUT CREAM •

In a bowl steep 1⅓ cups fresh shredded (or unsweetened packaged) ***coconut meat*** in 2 cups ***scalded milk.*** After 20 minutes strain mixture through cheesecloth, pressing coconut as dry as possible and reserving all liquid. Cook liquid 1 hour in the top of a double boiler, over simmering water. Chill well until a thick cream forms on surface. Lift off cream and use as directed above.

A salient exception to the shopper's rule against buying poultry in parts: turkey legs. These often can be found in supermarkets at astonishingly low prices for the amount of good eating they provide. They may be prepared all sorts of ways but the view here is that few other approaches deliver as much mileage as . . .

• STUFFED TURKEY DRUMSTICKS •
(Original recipe)

Legs usually come two to a turkey—a characteristic, among others, that the bird shares with humans, among others. Hence turkey legs usually are sold two to a package. Ergo, this recipe calls for two legs, but any number can play if the proportions are adjusted accordingly.

* * *

Remove the skins from 2 ***turkey legs*** by cutting around the circumference of the "ankle" and then rolling the integument down as you would a pair of stockings. (If your inclinations are so oriented, it might be pleasant to think of dancer Ann Miller while performing the latter operation.) Reserve the skins for later use (they freeze well if the use is to be *much* later) and of the naked limbs make a stock,* which you may want to serve in the form of consommé* as a prelude to the main event, or at some other time in some other form. From the finished stock salvage the turkey legs and strip the meat from the bones, reserving about half for other uses and coarsely hand-chopping the remainder. Set the chopped flesh aside and in a skillet sauté, in an ounce or two of ***butter,*** 1 medium ***carrot,*** 1 stalk ***celery*** and 1 medium ***onion,*** all minced, until onion wilts. Combine contents of pan with chopped turkey and 1 ***small egg,*** lightly beaten, a handful of ***chopped parsley,*** an ounce or two of chopped leftover ***cooked ham, sausage*** or ***tongue,*** a pinch each of ***nutmeg*** and ***crumbled dried*** (or minced fresh) ***sage,*** and salt and fresh pepper to taste. Lace the whole business with a little ***Cognac, bourbon*** or ***Marsala,*** blending ingredients well.

You are now ready to stuff the reserved skins but the skins aren't quite ready to comply, so tie off or sew up the narrower ends. *Now* we're all set. Fill the skins with the stuffing, not quite to the brim on the shorter side, packing them well. At this juncture you will notice a flap of unfilled skin on what was the outer side of the leg when the turkey was in full possession of its anatomical faculties. (Unlike chair or table legs, the legs of most bipeds are not joined at right angles to a plane surface, hence the lopsidedness of their cutaneous coverings when they are detached from the whole.) Pull this convenient awning across the exposed stuffing and effect tight closure by means of a little hemstitching, using a needle and thread or very light twine. Using the same needle, prick the stuffed legs here and there lest they erupt while cooking.

In a skillet, preferably of black iron, melt 2 tbs. ***butter*** or fat (husbanded ***duck or goose fat*** would be ideal) and sauté stuffed legs over moderate heat, turning occasionally, until well browned on all sides. When legs are done, allow them to stand at room temperature for some minutes, then remove sutures and serve one per portion. Rice would be a fine accompaniment, wild rice would be even finer and, if you like, you can tell your guests they're having *jambonettes de dindon,* which translates as "little hams of turkey," little hams being the French descriptive term for anything smaller than a ham that happens to be more-or-less ham-shaped.

NOTE—Stuffed Turkey Drumsticks can be served cold in slices as an hors d'oeuvre. Hot, they can be eaten as is (or, more precisely, as are) or variously sauced. One of the most felicitous—and most economical—of the sauce options is simply leftover turkey gravy to which a few chopped green olives have been added.

Your lamb shall be without blemish.
—Exodus 12:15

Good lamb is not come by cheaply and less than good lamb is no good at all. Like any other foodstuffs, lamb can be prepared and enjoyed economically, but the false economy often encouraged in the marketplace is altogether self-defeating. New Zealand lamb, for example, is priced appreciably below the domestic product and may look like a real buy as it lies seductively—albeit stiffer than a woolly mammoth in thirty feet of permafrost—in the supermarket display case. Don't be deceived. Like Kipling's Gentlemen Rankers, these are poor little lambs who have lost their way and they ultimately invite William Blake's question: "Little Lamb, who made thee?" New Zealand lamb may have been excellent meat on the hoof, but it smells mummified and tallowy when thawed and cooked God alone knows how many months after slaughter.

Insofar as the better cuts are concerned, lamb is best economized on only *after* it has been purchased. Go for the best and then see how much you can make of it. A fine leg of lamb, for example, usually is sold only by the whole piece or half and there is no getting around that at the source of supply. Unless you cook for a large group, though, you'll usually find that, whole or half, your leg is a good deal more than you need for a single meal. Let's take a case in point.

Easter Sunday was only forty-eight hours away and our old

pal J, heeding the dictum of Greek folklore that states "Easter without lamb is a thing that cannot be," had resolved to feast that day with his lady on leg of lamb. For reasons that needn't be gone into here a whole leg was out of the question at that particular moment and even the smallest half he could find was much more than the two of them could consume at a sitting. J brought his meat home and attacked it with a boning knife. Three minutes later it lay butterflied on the cutting board as he surveyed its possibilities. Rolled and tied, the thing would take a somewhat conical shape that would not cook evenly and that in any case would yield more meat than was needed for the paschal tête-à-tête. He sliced off the narrower end and set it aside. Then he stabbed the mantling of fat of the main segment all over with the point of a knife, slivered some garlic and inserted the slivers into the wounds. He turned the meat over, flesh-side-up, gave it a healthy whack with the side of a cleaver, rubbed it with good Luccan olive oil, seasoned it and spangled it successively with chopped fresh rosemary and parsley. After considering and rejecting the notion of laying a couple of slices of prosciutto over the herbs (a nice touch, much used in Italy, but not consonant with his mood of the moment), he rolled the meat, tied it with butcher's string at one-inch intervals, wrapped it in plastic and put it in the refrigerator for safekeeping.

This done, he turned with heightened enthusiasm to the reserved tail-end of the leg and thoughts of that night's dinner. He had dined a week or so earlier at an Italian restaurant where the *ragú di abbacchio con papardelle,* a specialty of Abruzzi, was superb. He decided to duplicate—or at least approximate—the dish for the evening meal. Of the half-pound-or-so of excess meat at his disposal he cut away 50 percent, which he proceeded to hack into small bits. He sawed the previously excised bone into segments and set it to simmering in a blend of leftover red wine and meat stock. Then he brought a jar of home-canned marinara sauce up from the cellar, added the reduced stock-wine mixture to it after the bones had yielded up their goodness, and added the chopped lamb to *that,* along with a few dried mushrooms, some crumbled rosemary, a bay leaf and a jolt of Cognac.

While the sauce cooked down to a mellow coppery sheen J rifled the pantry for the components of the *papardelle* he planned to make. Damn!—No flour and no egg, and the food stores had closed for the night. There was, however, a package of commercially produced frilly-edged lasagna ("Do as I say, not as I do"), of which he set half to cooking, figuring he'd trim away the curly borders and hack the remaining flat expanses of pasta into some semblance of the irregularly cut-up rectangles distinctive of *pappardelle.* Lo! Two altogether different pastas were born of one. When the lasagna was cooked, refreshed in cold water and trimmed of its edges, a heap of long rippled strips had materialized—a new, inadvertently invented form. J tossed them in a little oil to prevent their drying out and refrigerated them for some later, as-yet-undetermined use. The remainder he cut roughly into strips of varying dimensions.

The *ragú,* as it turned out, was magnificent. The pasta base, although not half as good as the real homemade McCoy, was adequate. All in all, the dish was delectable.

The following day, Sunday, J and his lady had their roast (which was basted from time to time with lemon juice), along with the traditional flageolets, a few of the garden's first asparagus of the season and the last of the previous season's shallots, which latter were roasted whole in their skins with the meat. There were also some very small russet potatoes, baked, scooped out of their jackets, mashed and stuffed back into the skins with butter, grated Romano cheese and a little crumbled sage. Returned to the oven for a few minutes before the meal was served forth, these puffed like miniature soufflés, their brown caps jauntily tilted this way and that.

On Monday evening J put the remaining quarter-pound piece of uncooked lamb in the freezer for a while to facilitate slicing it very thin. For dinner that night he and his friend had . . .

• SLICED LAMB HUNAN-STYLE •
(Chinese cookery)

Having previously trimmed ¼ lb. of ***lamb leg*** of fat and membranes, slice the semi-frozen meat very thinly into strips about 1″ × 2″, cutting against the grain. Place meat in a bowl and allow it to thaw completely, draining off whatever liquid accumulates. In a separate bowl beat together until frothy ½ ***egg white***, 1 pinch salt and ¾ tbs. ***dry sherry.*** Pour mixture over lamb and toss well, covering meat with sauce. Sprinkle meat with ¾ tbs. cornstarch and blend latter in thoroughly, using the hands. Cover bowl and refrigerate at least 20 minutes and up to 24 hours (the longer the better).

While meat marinates, mince enough ***garlic*** to fill half a teaspoon and prepare the same amount of fresh ***ginger root,*** cutting the latter into paper-thin ¼" squares. Cut 1 ***whole scallion*** into ⅓" lengths, combine the three ingredients in a small receptacle and set aside. Trim ⅓ bunch ***watercress,*** discarding lower inch of stems (or, preferably, reserving them for other uses) and set remainder aside. Then prepare a sauce by dissolving ¾ tsp. ***cornstarch*** in a blend of 1½ tbs. ***soy sauce,*** ¾ tbs. ***dry sherry,*** ½ tsp. ***vinegar*** and ½ tsp. ***sugar.*** Set sauce aside.

In a wok or skillet heat 2 cups ***peanut*** or ***vegetable oil*** to 280°F. Turn up heat to maximum and quickly add marinated lamb, stirring well to separate slices. Stir-fry 30 seconds until meat changes color, then drain in a colander set on a receptacle to catch the oil. Return 1 tbs. oil to pan and add 6 small dried ***hot chili peppers,*** stirring over high heat until chilis turn a deep mahogany color. Quickly add reserved scallion mixture and sizzle for a moment. Add lamb and stirred sauce and stir-fry until sauce has thickened slightly and meat is heated through. Successively stir in ½ tsp. each ***vinegar*** and ***sesame oil*** and transfer contents of pan to a heated serving dish. Wash wok and place it over high heat. When pan is quite hot add 1 tbs. ***oil,*** swirling it to coat pan thoroughly. Add the prepared ***watercress*** and salt to taste and stir-fry until cress is just wilted and bright emerald green. Drain cress and arrange around meat. Serve immediately to 2 with ***boiled rice*** and/or ***sautéed bean sprouts*** on the side.

NOTE—Chili peppers should be left in the dish but not eaten.

Of course, it isn't always possible to manufacture "leftovers" in advance. The cook who calculates the size of a roast too parsimoniously runs the risk of shortchanging guests with unexpectedly hearty appetites and so, to play it safe, most of us cook more meat than turns out to be needed. No harm done;

a cupful or so of unconsumed roast lamb will feed eight regally when incorporated into . . .

• MOUSSAKA (Turkish cookery) •

Halve 3 ***eggplants*** lengthwise and, using a sharp stainless steel knife, separate the skins, intact, from the pulp, leaving the latter inside the former. Using the point of the knife, cut almost through the pulp of each half, scoring it deeply in a crosshatch pattern but taking care not to damage the skin. Using 2 or 3 large skillets, heat 2 tbs. ***light oil*** (safflower or some such) in each, add eggplant halves, pulp-side-down, and cook 60 seconds. To each skillet add a blend of 1 tsp. ***lemon juice*** and 2 tbs. hot water and cook 10 minutes over moderate heat, meanwhile peeling a fourth eggplant and slicing it into ½″-thick rounds. When the 10 minutes are up, remove eggplant halves from pans and slip pulp from skins, reserving both. Dredge uncooked eggplant rounds in ***flour*** and brown on both sides in as much oil as needed, adding a little oil at a time to compensate for absorption. Lay browned eggplant on paper towels to drain.

In a skillet heat 1 tbs. ***butter,*** add ¼ lb. ***chopped mushrooms,*** 1 small ***onion*** minced, and 1 ***clove garlic,*** minced, and sauté until onion is transparent. Roughly chop pulp of reserved eggplant halves and combine with cooled contents of pan. Stir in 1 cup ground or chopped leftover ***roast lamb,*** 2 ripe medium ***tomatoes,*** diced, and 2 tbs. ***chopped parsley.*** Add 2 lightly beaten ***eggs,*** 3 tsp. salt and ½ tsp. freshly ground pepper, blending all ingredients well. Line bottom and sides of an oiled 2-qt. charlotte mold (or any similarly shaped ovenproof vessel) with the reserved eggplant skins, overlapping them slightly, leaving their exteriors in contact with the mold and allowing sufficient skin to hang, dog-ear fashion, outside the mold, so that the filling will be entirely covered when the skins are folded back over it.

Starting and ending with the lamb mixture, alternate it in inch-thick layers with thin layers of browned eggplant rounds until mold is filled. Fold dangling eggplant skins back over the filling, overlapping them slightly and completely covering the filling. (If you come up short, some aluminum-foil jiggery-pokery will do the job, however unaesthetically.) Place mold in a pan of sufficient capacity to accomodate hot water to ⅓ the depth of the mold and bake 90 minutes in a preheated 375°F oven. When *Moussaka* is done, remove from oven and allow to stand 10 minutes at room temperature. Unmold onto a serving platter and serve to 8 with hot tomato sauce on the side.

Legs of lamb are (or should be) sold with the shanks attached. These are easily detached and should be husbanded for use as . . .

• BRAISED LAMB SHANKS •
(Everyone's cookery)

Allowing 1 shank per serving, dredge them in ***flour*** seasoned with 1 pinch each ***crumbled dried oregano*** and finely ***minced fresh rosemary,*** and salt and pepper to taste. In a skillet brown shanks on all sides in ***stockpot fat,*** husbanded ***duck fat*** or something similar, using about 1 tbs. lubricant per shank. Transfer shanks to a casserole or Dutch oven, leaving remaining fat in the skillet. To the fat add 2 tbs. each chopped ***onion, celery*** and ***carrot*** and a pinch of ***minced garlic*** per shank and cook 5 minutes, stirring, over moderate heat. Distribute contents of pan over shanks and to the casserole add a half-and-half blend of leftover ***red wine*** and ***beef stock**** sufficient to cover the bottom to a depth of ¼″. Cover and bake 90 minutes in a preheated 350°F oven, or a little longer if necessary, until the meat is tender. Serve immediately, to a chorus of "Shanks for the memory."

Needless to say, there *are* cheaper cuts of lamb than the leg, shoulder, rack, saddle and the like, and most are better suited to their particular uses than the fancier, pricier portions would be. Lean meat from the neck, for example, is excellent for use in stews, curries and most sautés, for shish kebab and its various derivatives, and for almost any dish that calls for ground lamb. Unfortunately lamb innards usually are hard to come by in this country. If you're on friendly terms with a real honest-to-God butcher, however, such inexpensive items as lamb's liver, kidneys, sweetbreads, tongue, brain, testicles and heart lend themselves to a great many splendid dishes that the virginal squeamishness of most American eaters has left largely untried. The indispensable French culinary compendium *Larousse Gastronomique* will tell you how to prepare most of these oddments in any number of delicious, often surprisingly elegant ways.

One thing *Larousse* won't tell you, however, is how to rid mutton or lamb kidneys of the distinctive characteristic that appealed to James Joyce's Leopold Bloom more than it may to you: "Most of all he liked grilled mutton kidneys which gave to his palate a fine tang of faintly scented urine." A vestigial pissiness may be unavoidable when kidneys are grilled but can easily be eliminated if you slice them thin, as Italian cooks do for *rognoncini trifolati,* and briefly marinate them in milk before cooking them.

• LAMB KIDNEYS WITH MUSHROOMS •

Remove membranes from ***4 fresh lamb kidneys,*** split each kidney lengthwise and remove fatty cores with the point of a knife. Slice kidneys laterally and very thin and pack them loosely into a cup or tumbler large enough to hold them with ¼" of space at the top. Fill container with ***milk*** (a very little will do the job with the kidneys taking up most of the space) and allow to stand 15 minutes or so. Meanwhile slice ½ lb. very fresh ***whole white mushrooms*** vertically, to about the same thickness as the kidneys. Drain kidneys, rinse in cold water and pat dry with paper towels. In a sauté pan or skillet brown 1 clove lightly crushed ***garlic*** in 1 tbs. ***olive oil.*** Discard garlic when browned and add 2 oz. ***butter*** to pan, cooking over moderate heat until butter is melted. Add kidneys and stir-fry just until color begins to change. Add mushrooms and stir-fry 1 minute with salt and pepper to taste. Stir in a squirt of ***lemon juice,*** remove from heat, sprinkle with ***chopped parsley,*** and serve with rice to 2.

As with lamb, the more so with veal, which can be dauntingly pricey these days. (Indeed, that huge succulent grilled veal chop that set you back a cool sixteen bucks at your favorite Italian restaurant probably represents a net loss to the *padrone,* who hopes he can stave off bankruptcy by selling lots of pasta, chicken and booze to the rest of his clientele.) Moreover, veal innards—given away as cat food to earlier generations of shoppers—now are in such demand among the cognoscenti that only a few still irrationally despised organs remain economical. Again, the tactic to fall back on here is the one developed by such innately frugal cooks as the Chinese and Italians: Make a little go a long way. As is the case with beef, there is no valid reason why outsized portions of veal should be served. Insofar as the overwhelming majority of veal dishes are concerned, a quarter-pound of meat, appropriately garnished and accompanied, is enough for anyone but a professional linebacker girding up for a Superbowl appearance.

All things considered, the most economical cut of veal is the breast, which, with its natural wallet-like configuration, almost cries out to be stuffed. Whether or not you plan to stuff and cook your breast of veal whole, with the bones attached, *buy* it whole, for the bones and trimmings (which you'll pay for in any case) are of inestimable value and separating them from the meat to be stuffed is the simplest of chores.

If you go to a village butcher in France and ask for the makings of a *blanquette de veau*, you will be asked in turn, "*Avec os ou sans os?*"—With or without bones? *Le boucher* will regard you quizzically while awaiting your reply, for he is testing your culinary and gastronomic perspicacity. With bones your meal will be not only cheaper but better, although you'll never find them in a *blanquette de veau* at a posh restaurant. The "bones" in question are the highly cartilaginous ends of the ribs, where they join the breast, and are much prized by true connoisseurs of the white ragoût, for they lend body and character to the sauce and are esculent in their entirety, their slight bounciness to the tooth notwithstanding. Separate these, then, either before or after stuffing and cooking the breast, either for subsequent use in a *blanquette* or for the rich viscosity they impart to stock. The true bones (easily distinguishable and separable from the rib ends by means of a sharp knife) also go into the stockpot, of course, either before or after the breast is cooked.

There are myriad ways of stuffing breast of veal, whether it is to be roasted or braised. Extrapolating from the three that follow, you should be able to devise innumerable recipes that put various leftovers to good use.

• TÖLTÖTT BORJUSZEGY VÁROSIASAN •
(Hungarian cookery)

Remove crusts from 3 ***stale rolls*** or 6–8 slices ***stale white bread*** and soak bread in 1 ***cup milk*** until soggy. Squeeze soaked bread, expressing as much milk as possible and reserving milk for another use. To the bread (by now pretty well broken up) add 2 tbs. ***lard*** or husbanded ***duck or goose fat,*** 3 lightly beaten ***eggs,*** 1 small ***onion,*** grated, 1 tbs. ***chopped parsley,*** 1 tbs. salt and ¼ tsp. freshly ground pepper. Blend well and allow the mixture to rest 3–4 hours in the refrigerator. Cut a pocket in a 3½-lb. ***breast of veal,*** working along the natural division between the two layers of meat and opening the cavity fully but without tunneling through to daylight. Salt meat well on all surfaces, fill the pocket with the bread stuffing, sew up the open end of the breast, and brush the surface with 2 tbs. melted lard or husbanded ***duck or goose fat.*** Place veal breast in a baking dish or roasting pan, add ½ cup leftover ***white wine*** and bake, covered, in a preheated 350°F oven 90 minutes, or until tender, basting often with pan juices, turning meat 2 or 3 times and adding small amounts of ***wine*** as needed. Ten minutes before meat is done turn heat up to 425°F. Allow meat to stand 10 minutes at room temperature before slicing and serving to 8.

Variation

Its authenticity can't be vouched for here, but a "Hungarian style" stuffed breast of veal was served for years at that great New York hotel, the Plaza. It, too, made use of a ***stale-bread stuffing*** bound with ***eggs*** (***yolks*** only in this case), but omitted the onion and added 8 ***asparagus spears,*** lightly cooked and chopped, as many cooked ***shrimp,*** also chopped, and a pound of fresh ***peas,*** which were briefly sautéed with the shrimp before both were added to the stuffing. The boned breast was then rolled and tied, baked with ***tomato juice*** and served with a warmed blend of ***sour cream*** and the pan juices.

• PETTO DI VITELLO RIPIENO •
(Italian cookery)

Form a pocket in a 3½-lb. ***breast of veal*** and stuff with a blend of the following: ½ lb. lean ground or chopped ***raw beef trimmings;*** ½ cup ***breadcrumbs;*** 2 slices ***prosciutto,*** chopped, or 4 oz. chopped leftover ***cooked ham;*** 3 tbs. freshly grated ***Parmesan or Romano cheese;*** 2 tbs. chopped ***Italian flat-leaf parsley;*** 1 ***clove garlic,*** minced; 3 lightly beaten ***eggs;*** and salt and pepper to taste. Sew up opening tightly and rub surface of veal with 1 tbs. ***olive oil.*** Sprinkle with 1 tbs. ***rosemary*** (preferably fresh) and salt and pepper to taste. Place in a roasting pan, drizzle 2 more tbs. ***olive oil*** over the meat and bake uncovered in a preheated 400°F oven until meat begins to brown. Add 1 cup leftover ***dry white wine*** to pan, cover and bake about 50 minutes, basting often. Add 3 large ***potatoes,*** peeled and sliced lengthwise, to pan and bake about 20 minutes longer, turning potatoes occasionally, until they are tender and lightly browned. Let meat stand at room temperature about 10 minutes and serve, with potatoes, to 8.

Variations

Make a little less stuffing to compensate for the displacement of volume, trim the ends off 3 shelled ***hard-boiled eggs,*** so that they will abut snugly when aligned, and center them in the stuffing to reveal white-and-yellow "eyes" when the meat is sliced and served.

Add to or replace ham with chopped leftover ***cooked sausage.***

• BREAST OF VEAL FLORENTINE •
(Origin deponent knoweth not)

If memory serves this is not an original recipe, but its source has long since been forgotten and its name, arbitrarily assigned here, doesn't necessarily reflect the cuisine whence it derives. Apologies are extended to anyone whose franchise may here have been trespassed upon. The dish is particularly appropriate as a summer buffet offering. With its concentric circles of pale pink, bright yellow and deep green, its appeal is visual as well as gustatory.

* * *

Lay a boned breast of veal on a sturdy work surface and have at it enthusiastically with a few whacks of the flat side of a cleaver or the bottom of a heavy skillet. (The interposition of a sheet of wax paper between weapon and meat won't injure the enterprise.) Very lightly scramble 4–6 ***eggs,*** depending on the surface area of the meat, and spread them evenly over the latter, leaving a border of about ¾″ on all sides. Briefly steam 2 lbs. ***spinach,*** chop it coarsely, express as much liquid as possible by hand-squeezing the greens and spread this over the egg, again leaving a border like the first. Dust spinach with ***nutmeg*** and salt and pepper to taste and dot with ***butter.*** Roll up the veal breast laterally and tie it with butcher's string at 1½″ intervals. Lightly oil a baking pan, center the veal roll in it and roast 90 minutes in a preheated 375°F oven, basting occasionally with pan juices. Remove veal roll from oven, allow to stand at room temperature until cool, and refrigerate several hours. Before serving, remove string and return meat almost to room temperature. Trim off ends, surreptitiously devour them in the kitchen and cut veal roll in ¼″ slices. Number of servings will vary according to the nature of the occasion and size of the roast.

As noted earlier, such veal innards as kidneys, sweetbreads, brain and liver have commanded increasingly stiff prices as their popularity in this country has increased. Two organs that still may be obtained cheaply, however, are the heart and lungs, which are much appreciated abroad, and for good reason. Properly prepared, they can be delectable.

• COEUR DE VEAU RÔTI (French cookery) •

Cut 2 ***calves' hearts*** open without completely separating the halves, remove any clotted blood to be found therein, trim off any other material that offends your aesthetic sensibilities, wash hearts in cold water and pat dry. Season hearts to taste with salt and pepper, drizzle them successively with a little ***lemon juice*** and ***olive oil,*** and allow them to absorb these substances for 30 minutes or so. Re-form hearts, wrap them in ***caul*** fat softened as for ***Crêpinettes**** and spit-roast them 35 minutes over very hot coals or alongside brisk flame. Serve, moistened with leftover ***beef pan drippings***, to 4.

NOTE—Alternatively, if not so effectively, the hearts may be baked 90 minutes to 2 hours in a 350°F oven. A nice accompaniment in season would be ***Deep-Fried Zucchini Blossoms****—hearts and flowers.

• BAKED STUFFED CALF'S HEART •

A number of cuisines have their distinctive versions of this dish. The recipe that follows borrows from several.

* * *

Figuring on 2 portions from each, open, trim and clean ***calves' hearts*** as above. Re-form hearts, tie them loosely with butcher's string to preserve their shapes and arrange them on a rack in a baking pan. Drape 2 slices ***bacon*** over each heart and add 2 cups ***stock**** to pan. Bake 2 hours, tightly covered, in a preheated 325°F oven. Allow hearts to cool to the point where they can be handled and fill their cavities with leftover ***bread dressing***, leftover ***herbed rice***, whatever leftover ***cooked sausage*** you may have on hand or just about anything else of a congruous nature that takes your fancy. Sprinkle hearts with paprika and briefly heat them through in a 400°F oven. Serve immediately, sans string, with flour-thickened pan liquids.

• SUFRITTO DI CUORE E POLMONE •
(Italian cookery)

In a large bowl or pan soak ¾ lb. each ***veal heart*** and ***lung*** 1 hour in salted cold water to cover. Drain meats and cook 5 minutes in rapidly boiling water to cover. Again drain meats and pat dry with paper towels. With a sharp knife trim off any fat, nerves, arteries, etc., and cut meats into ½" dice. In a skillet heat ½ cup ***olive oil***, add meats and cook over high heat, stirring, about 5 minutes. Add salt and ***hot pepper flakes*** to taste (don't stint on the latter) and moderate heat once meats have begun to brown at the edges. Add ½ cup leftover ***dry white wine***. Lower heat to maintain a very gentle simmer, cook 3–4 minutes and add 3 small ***onions***, sliced, and 2 ***cloves garlic***, minced. Cook another 3–4 minutes, meanwhile bringing 2 cups chopped seeded ***tomatoes*** to boil in ¼ cup water. Add tomatoes (with water) to meats, stir in 1 tsp. dried ***oregano*** and simmer, covered, 30 minutes. Serve piping hot to 6.

• COEUR DE VEAU À L'ANGLAISE •
(French cookery)

Figuring on 2 servings from each heart, clean, trim and wash ***veal hearts*** and cut them into ¾" slices. Season with salt and pepper to taste, brush with melted ***butter*** and dredge in crumbs made from leftover ***day-old bread***. (A processor will turn out a very nice product.) Grill under a slow broiler, turning once, until browned evenly on both sides. Arrange meat on a heated serving platter, alternating slices with crisp rashers of ***grilled bacon***. Top slices of heart with dollops of ***Maître d'Hotel Butter*** and serve with small boiled ***parsleyed potatoes***.

• MAÎTRE D'HOTEL BUTTER •

In a blender or processor combine 4 oz. (1 stick) ***butter***, cut in pieces, with 1 tsp. ***chopped parsley***, 1 pinch freshly ground pepper, 1 dash ***lemon juice*** and salt to taste. Run machine until mixture forms a smooth paste.

As we've already seen, pre-cut pork "leftovers" and trimmings may be put to superb use in countless varieties of sausage. The same items also may be incorporated (along with similarly husbanded veal, game, domestic rabbit, duck, poultry livers, etc.) into many a fine pâté. Pork trimmings also may be put to good use in an almost limitless number of Chinese stir-fry dishes and, along with tender, moist leftover cooked pork, in the making of . . .

• RILLETTES (French cookery) •

Aside from their delectability, the great virtue of *rillettes* is their availability for instant use once they have been packed and stored. Because a goodly batch will afford fine offhand eating for weeks, there would be little point in preparing *rillettes* in small quantities.

* * *

Using a ratio of 5 parts lean ***pork trimmings and leftovers*** to 2 parts ***fatback,*** cut meat into 2" cubes and dice fatback. (If roasted or otherwise cooked pork is to be incorporated into the recipe, any hard browned surface flesh should be trimmed away.) In a heavy ovenproof pan combine the foregoing with 1 chopped ***onion*** and ½ cup water for each 2½ lbs. pork and fatback. Add salt to taste and a ***bouquet garni*** of ***bay leaves,*** dried ***sage,*** thyme and a few ***peppercorns.*** Cook about 4 hours in a preheated 350°F oven, turning meats every half-hour or so and adding water a little at a time as needed. (The meat should be very tender and quite moist.) Remove lean meats from pan with a slotted spoon and allow to cool, meanwhile allowing any remaining water to "cook out" of the rendered fat. When the last vestiges of water have evaporated, strain off and reserve fat, discarding unrendered bits (or, better, saving them to add crackle to sausage), and allow it to cool.

At this juncture the meat is reduced to fragments, either by pounding it in a mortar or separating it, with two forks, into fine strands. (A quick whirl in a food processor will do a creditable job, but care should be taken not to reduce the meat to anything resembling a paste.) Thoroughly blend ***fragmented meat*** and ***reserved fat*** and pack the mixture into sterilized earthenware crocks or glass jars, filling them solidly but leaving a ⅜" space at the top of each container. Refrigerate until *rillettes* are firmly set, cover with a layer of ***rendered fat*** or ***lard*** and chill until covering sets solidly. Cover each jar with a round of non-porous paper (not foil) and refrigerate for use as needed. Serve as a spread with good crusty ***French bread.***

Variations

Rillettes may be cooked over an open, very gentle flame instead of in the oven. ***Leftover duck, goose, turkey or rabbit*** may be combined with or substituted for pork, and husbanded ***duck or goose fat*** may be substituted for pork fat. Toss a couple of pieces of ***orange rind*** into the pan to add a pleasant bouquet to *rillettes* of duck.

• ROAST PORK WITH VEGETABLES •
(Cantonese cookery)

Preliminary procedures

Slice ½ lb. lean leftover ***roast pork*** (preferably loin) into half-inch-thick 1″ × 1″ squares. In a bowl blend ¾ cup ***chicken stock***,* 3 tbs. ***soy sauce*** 1 tbs. ***dry sherry***, and 1 tsp. ***sugar***. Drain, discard tough stems from, and slice 6 pre-soaked dried ***black Chinese mushrooms***. Remove stems and strings from ½ cup ***snow pea pods***. Halve lengthwise ½ cup ***drained whole baby ears of corn***. Slice ⅓ cup ***drained water chestnuts***. Thinly slice on the diagonal 2 medium carrots. Separate enough ***broccoli florets*** to measure 1 cup. Mince enough peeled fresh ***ginger root*** to measure 1 tsp. Dissolve 2 tsp. ***cornstarch*** in 1½ tbs. water.

Preparation

In a wok or skillet bring 3 tbs. ***peanut oil*** to moderately high heat, add ginger root, and stir briefly. Add carrots and broccoli and stir-fry 1 minute. Add chicken stock mixture, bring to boil, and cook 2 minutes. Add remaining vegetables and pork and stir briefly, blending all ingredients well. Add cornstarch mixture and cook about 1 minute, stirring, or until sauce thickens. Serve immediately to 2 or more, depending on the composition of the menu.

> NOTE—To follow the recipe as given, you almost certainly will have to resort to commercially packed water chestnuts and baby corn. If this regrettable fact of life cannot be faced, both can be omitted without fatal consequences to the finished product.

Although pork kidney still is considered infra dig by most Americans, millions of perceptive feeders in Europe, Asia and Latin America dote on it. It is not only highly nutritious and damned fine eating but, thanks to its general unpopularity in this country, still a great buy in the market.

• COLD PORK KIDNEY IN HOT SAUCE •
(Szechuanese cookery)

This recipe was provided by Manhattan's Dumpling House restaurant, where the dish is served in a particularly luminous version.

* * *

Slice 2 very fresh ***pork kidneys*** in half, cutting as though halving kidney beans along their seams, and remove fatty white cores. With the point of a sharp knife score outer surfaces of kidney halves lengthwise, making four or five ¼″-deep incisions in each piece. Semi-freeze kidneys to facilitate slicing, then lay them cut-side-down and slice crosswise, as thinly as possible and slightly on the bias. Allow the meat to return to room temperature and marinate 30 minutes in 2 tsp. ***sesame oil,*** tossing to coat meat evenly with oil. (This procedure is designed to rid the kidneys of their pissy smell.) In a pot bring 2 qts. water to a rolling boil, plunge kidney slices into it and cook 30 seconds, stirring. Drain immediately in a colander and plunge meat into ice water. Test meat for doneness by cutting into one slice. (If any pink shows, boil again for a few seconds.) Refrigerate until well chilled.

While kidneys chill prepare a sauce by blending the following: ¼ tsp. minced ***ginger root;*** 2 cloves ***garlic,*** minced; 2½ tsp. each ***soy sauce*** and ***sesame oil;*** 1 tsp. each ***sugar*** and ***vinegar;*** ½ tsp. ***peppercorn powder*** (available by that name at Chinese food shops and not to be confused with freshly ground peppercorns); and 1 tsp. ***hot pepper oil*** (also available at Chinese markets). When kidneys are well chilled pat them completely dry with paper towels and arrange on a serving platter. Garnish with whites of 2 or 3 ***scallions,*** cut into inch-long pieces and shredded, and with 2 tbs. ***cloud-ear fungus*** (*a.k.a.* tree ears), softened in warm water and patted dry. Pour sauce over kidneys and serve to 2–6, depending on the size of the entire meal and your guests' tolerance for incendiary spicing.

• STIR-FRIED KIDNEY WITH VEGETABLES •
(Pekingese cookery)

Set aside a sauce prepared by blending 1 tsp. each ***rice wine,*** salt, water and ***cornstarch,*** 2 tsp. ***soy sauce,*** ½ tsp. each ***sugar*** and ***vinegar*** and ¼ tsp. each ***sesame oil*** and freshly ground black pepper. Halve and trim 2 ***pork kidneys*** as for preceding recipe, but score inner, rather than outer, surfaces. Slice kidneys as above and soak 30 minutes in cold water to cover. Trim 12–18 ***snow pea pods*** of stems and "strings," blanch 45 seconds in rapidly boiling water, remove from pan with a slotted spoon and plunge into very cold water. Repeat process with 12–18 slices bamboo shoot, each about ⅙" × ½" × 1". (If canned bamboo shoots are used, simply drain and set them aside.) Cut the same number of carrot slices to the same dimensions, blanch them in boiling water 90 seconds and plunge them into cold water. Using the same cooking water, lower heat, add drained and rinsed kidney slices and simmer 20 seconds before returning them to cold water. In a wok or skillet heat ¼ cup ***peanut oil*** and add 6 inch-long pieces ***green scallion,*** 6 paper-thin slices ***ginger root*** and 3 ***cloves garlic,*** minced. Stir-fry mixture until its aromas are released and add reserved veggies, drained and patted dry. Stir-fry a few seconds, then add kidney slices and reserved sauce mixture. Toss all ingredients until well blended and cooked through and serve immediately on a heated platter. As is usually the case with Chinese dishes, the number of servings will depend on the context.

• ROGNONS DE PORC EN CASSEROLE •
(French cookery)

In an ovenproof casserole heat 1 oz. ***butter*** and add ⅓ lb. ***slab bacon,*** cut in small dice, and 16 pearl ***onions.*** Sauté (to use the word loosely) until bacon is translucent and onions are lightly colored, then remove both ingredients with a slotted spoon and set them aside. To the same pan add 4 whole ***pork kidneys,*** stripped of outer membranes and well soaked in several changes of cold water, and cook lightly, just until they change color. Return onions and bacon to pan, add 1 lb. ***new potatoes,*** three-quarters cooked, 1 oz. ***butter,*** 2 cloves ***garlic,*** minced, and salt and pepper to taste. Place uncovered casserole in a preheated 400°F oven and cook 20 minutes. Add ⅓ cup strong ***meat stock,**** cook 5 minutes longer and serve in the casserole, sprinkled with chopped ***parsley,*** to 4.

NOTE—Pork kidneys may be substituted for veal kidneys in almost any standard French recipe calling for the latter.

Even the French, who will eat almost anything that doesn't eat them, haven't much heart for the hearts of pigs. Indeed, *Larousse Gastronomique,* which soberly considers the gastronomic appeal and culinary treatment of everything from rats to silkworms, is utterly mum on the subject. *Tant pis!*—The Italian peasant knows better and makes a fine hearty soup of the organ, in combination with various leftovers. Find a real butcher, buy a couple of pounds of ***pork heart*** at near-giveaway prices and, on a cold winter's night, have a go at . . .

• ZUPPA DI CUORE DI MAIALE •

Open and clean 2 lbs. very fresh ***pork heart*** as for *Coeur de Veau Rôti** and cut the meat into small dice. Also dice 2 oz. leftover ***salt pork rind.*** Place both ingredients in a heavy soup kettle, along with 1 tbs. ***rendered pork fat,*** and brown well over a brisk flame. Add salt and freshly ground black pepper to taste and continue to cook, tossing occasionally, until meats are quite brown all over. Add ½ cup leftover ***red wine*** and continue cooking until wine has evaporated completely. Lower heat to moderate, add ½ tsp. dried ***rosemary,*** ½ ***bay leaf,*** crumbled, and 2 tbs. ***tomato paste*** diluted in the same amount of water. Cook 5 minutes, stirring, add 1 qt. water and cook, covered, 1½ hours over a very slow fire. Place 3 thin slices ***semi-stale Italian bread,*** lightly toasted, in each of 6 soup dishes, pour soup over toast and serve immediately.

A Sentimental Passion 8

Then a sentimental passion of a vegetable fashion
must excite your lanquid spleen,
An attachment à la Plato for a bashful young potato,
or a not too French French bean!
—W.S. Gilbert, *Patience*

IF THE AMERICAN cooking craze of recent years has accomplished nothing else it has made a great many of us far more aware of the inherent goodness, variety and heretofore barely exploited culinary and gustatory potential of vegetables. It little matters that much of this awareness is rooted in faddism and ego-tripping, for there is a fundamental decency about any fresh vegetable that only willful abuse can diminish, and even if some exotic tuber, legume or salad green is served merely for the sake of novelty it will somehow manage to maintain its self-possession in circumstances where flesh, fish or fowl might not escape unscathed. Significantly, even the most outré of the *nouvelle cuisine* adherents—"inventors" of mustard ice cream, honeyed beefsteaks and flatfish in marmalade—seem instinctively to recognize and respect the innate dignity of vegetables. (Growers, on the other hand, do not; what passes for a tomato on the supermarket shelf bears about as much resemblance to anything organic as King Tut's mummy does to Pete Rose.)

If American cooks are learning not to subject vegetables to sins of commission, they are still subjecting them to sins of omission. If we are no longer much abusing what we cook, we are still not cooking all there is to *be* cooked. Consider peas, for example. We purchase a pound of peas for, say, sixty cents and promptly throw away thirty cents' worth of what we've paid for: namely, the shells, not to mention the cost of labor from which we derive only half the compensation we should. As it happens, that jettisoned "trash" is not only at least as nutritious as the edible seeds but delectable in its own right. It can be prepared and served as a handsome purée, or shredded, steamed and used as a component in innumerable dishes, or incorporated into . . .

• PEA POD AND SPINACH SOUP •

The recipe is reproduced from *Gourmet* magazine.

* * *

Remove the strings from and shell 1 pound ***peas,*** reserving the peas for another use. [Good old *Gourmet* has *its* priorities straight.] There should be about 1 quart ***pea pods.*** In a large heavy saucepan cook 1 small ***onion,*** minced, in 3 tbs. ***unsalted butter*** over moderate heat, stirring, until it is softened; add 4 cups ***chicken stock*** . . . and bring the liquid to a boil. Add the pea pods and simmer them, covered partially, for 30 minutes, or until they are soft. In a food processor fitted with the steel blade or in a blender blend the mixture in batches. Strain the mixture through a fine sieve set over another pan, pressing hard on the solids, bring it to a simmer, and keep it hot.

In the food processor fitted with the steel blade or in the blender mince together 2 cups firmly packed, well-washed, trimmed, spun dry, and chopped fresh ***spinach leaves*** and 2 tbs. chopped fresh ***parsley leaves.*** With the motor running add 2 cups of the hot soup mixture and purée it. Add the purée to the remaining soup in the pan, season the soup with salt and pepper, and simmer it, stirring occasionally, for 2 minutes. Let the soup cool until it is room temperature, transfer it to a tureen, and garnish it with a dollop of salted ***whipped cream.*** Serves 4.

Consider potatoes. Of late, restaurants across the country have been doing all they can to popularize the consumption of potato skins minus potato pulp. Well they might, for the detritus they had traditionally thrown away or sold for pittances as pig fodder suddenly was recognized for what it was: a highly profitable source of revenue. Why (went the reasoning) sell a baked Idaho potato for, say, $1.50, when the self-same spud could be peddled in two stages for nine dollars or more? Suddenly, baked potato skins popped up on à la carte menus everywhere, and *gnocchi* became a very chic item. Insofar as ingredients and labor are concerned, both dishes together are not appreciably more costly to produce than the simple baked potato, but their cost to the restaurant customer is another story altogether.

• BAKED POTATO SKINS (American cookery) •

In a preheated 450°F oven bake 4 ***Idaho potatoes,*** well washed and dried, 30–40 minutes, or until tender when pierced with the point of a knife. When potatoes are cool enough to handle comfortably, quarter them lengthwise and pare skins away in whole boat-shaped segments, following the natural contours of the potato, leaving a ⅛″ layer of pulp attached and taking care not to fold, spindle or mutilate skins or attached pulp. Reserve inner pulp for *Gnocchi* (below) or other uses. ***Butter*** pulp sides of potato skins very lightly, covering surfaces thoroughly, and run under a hot broiler for a few minutes, just until edges begin to brown. Serve to 6–8, with salt and pepper handy, as a cocktail hors d'oeuvre or accompaniment to simple red-meat dishes.

• POTATO GNOCCHI (Italian cookery) •

Rice or finely mash reserved ***inner pulp of potatoes*** baked for preceding recipe (or an equivalent amount of any leftover ***cooked potatoes***) or, if a processor is to be used, simply break cooked potatoes into pieces and load into work bowl of machine. To the potatoes add 1 ***egg,*** lightly beaten, 1 cup sifted ***flour,*** and salt and pepper to taste. Mix and knead, or process, ingredients together until they form a smooth stiff dough. On a lightly floured board shape dough into long "ropes" about the diameter of a finger and then cut them into ¾″ lengths. Corrugate each piece by rolling it outward on the tines of a fork and, as it leaves the end of the fork, indent it slightly with the thumb, forming a shallow well. (Both operations will facilitate adhesion of sauce.) Poach *gnocchi* a few at a time in a large pot of boiling salted water and remove from pot with a slotted spoon as they rise to the surface. Sauce or gratinée according to preference and serve to 4 as a first course or 2 as a main dish.

Variation

For green *gnocchi* add ⅔ lb. ***spinach,*** steamed, puréed and squeezed dry, to dough ingredients before kneading. (If a processor is used to blend and knead dough, just add dried cooked spinach as is. If dough is to be kneaded by hand, rub dried spinach through a fine sieve before adding it to other ingredients.)

> **NOTE**—*Gnocchi* marry well with many of the sauces used with various pastas. ***Bolognese, mushroom, marinara, cream, pesto*** and ***Amatriciana*** sauces all go well with the little dumplings, which also may be arranged in a baking dish, drizzled with melted butter, dusted with grated ***Parmesan*** and baked in a preheated 350°F oven for a few minutes, until the cheese melts.

All sorts of good things can be done with whole baked potato skins once the pulps have been scooped out for other uses. At least one professional New York chef, for example, fills them with a mixture of very lightly scrambled ***eggs, oysters*** and ***clams*** and bakes the whole business just until the egg filling sets. Alternatively, the skins may be filled with any timbale mixture, such as that used for *Timbales d'Epinards.** The good uses to which leftover cooked potatoes may be put are also legion and an exhaustive examination of soups alone would require more space than is available here. A few examples:

• VICHYSSOISE (French-derived American cookery) •

This soup was created (if that's the word) by a French-born chef, Louis Diat, who simply gussied up an old bourgeois classic, chilled the result and served it to early patrons of New York's Plaza Hotel. It has remained inordinately popular on these shores ever since and has been a constant source of bemusement to restaurateurs in France, who are bombarded by American tourists with requests for a "French" dish they know only by hearsay.

* * *

Sauté 1 medium ***onion*** and the whites of 4 ***leeks,*** all thinly sliced, in 1½ oz. ***butter*** just until vegetables begin to color. Add 4 leftover medium ***potatoes***, peeled and cut in large pieces, along with 3 cups ***chicken stock**** and salt and pepper to taste. Bring to boil, reduce heat to simmer and cook about 30 minutes. Transfer to a blender or processor in batches and reduce to the finest possible purée. Return mixture to pot and add 1 cup each ***milk*** and ***light cream*** (or 2 cups half-and-half). Season to taste with salt and white pepper, bring briefly to boil, stir well and allow to cool. Chill and serve, garnished with snipped ***chives***, to 8.

Variations

Leftover ***mashed*** or ***puréed potatoes*** may be substituted for potato solids, in which case they should not be added to mixture until just before transference to the blender or processor.

When puréeing ingredients, ½ cup ***watercress*** may be added to the basic mixture, which then should be garnished with chopped ***cress.***

In season (late spring), a ***chive blossom*** floated in the center of each portion of soup makes an attractive, surprisingly pungent garnish.

The soup may be served hot as well as cold.

• POTAGE PARMENTIER (French cookery) •

Antoine-Auguste Parmentier (1737–1817), a French economist and agronomist, was largely responsible for the popularization of the potato, which thitherto was regarded as a mere ornamental curiosity and stubbornly resisted as a potentially delicious form of nutriment. Hence the name of this fine, simple soup.

* * *

In a heavy soup kettle cook roughly chopped whites of 2 ***leeks*** in 1½ oz. ***butter*** until soft. Add 1 qt. ***white stock,**** bring to boil and cook 5 minutes. Reduce heat to a gentle simmer and add 3 cups leftover ***cooked potatoes,*** sans skins and cut in pieces. Simmer until potatoes are very tender and strain soup through a colander, reserving liquid. In a blender or processor purée solids, together with a few tablespoons of the reserved liquid, and return the mixture, with remainder of the liquid, to the soup pot. Bring briefly to boil, stir well, stir in 4 tbs. (½ stick) ***butter*** and 1 tbs. fresh ***chervil*** and simmer 3–4 minutes longer. Serve piping hot with croutons of leftover sliced ***French bread,*** fried golden-brown in ***butter,*** on the side. Serves 6–8.

Variations

As you've probably noticed, both the foregoing soups are minor variations on a basic theme. The possible combinations and permutations are virtually limitless and a judicious use of any number of leftovers can produce a first-rate "different" soup day after day. Leftover cooked ***carrots,*** for example, may be incorporated into the basic mixture in any proportion, as may leftover cooked ***turnips, peas, string beans, spinach, Swiss chard, squash, onions*** or just about any other vegetable that comes to hand, as well as such leftover soups as minestrone, mixed vegetable, *pistou*, etc. Leftover cooked ***dried beans*** may be substituted for potatoes, and all manner of fresh herbs may be used in combination with the basic stock-starch mixture to add variety and elegance to very inexpensive menus. The addition of ***watercress,*** for example, will yield a fine soup prepared as for *Potage Crème de Capucine Nancy*,* with a bunch of watercress leaves and stems substituted for nasturtium leaves and blossoms.

On solider ground, leftover cooked potatoes are eminently usable for puréed and piped garnishes (e.g., *duchesse* potatoes), all sorts of croquettes (e.g., *chevreuse,* with chervil; *à la parmesane,* with Italian cheese; *à la lyonnaise,* with onions) and for . . .

• VEGETABLE HASH (Original recipe) •

There would be no point here in pinpointing quantities or proportions. Essentially this is an improvisation designed to exploit whatever veggies come to hand. The finished product may be served as an entrée accompaniment or, topped with a fried or poached egg, as a light main dish.

* * *

Finely chop leftover ***cooked potatoes***, cooked (or raw grated) ***carrots***, cooked ***turnips, parsnips, kohlrabi, mushrooms***, etc., husbanded ***broccoli stems, asparagus stalks*** or any other non-leafy vegetables that come to hand. Add some chopped raw ***onion,*** a little minced ***garlic*** and, if desired, grated raw ***zucchini, summer squash, pumpkin,*** etc., and sauté the whole mess in a little ***butter*** in a black-iron skillet, pressing down hard with a spatula from time to time until a light crust forms on the bottom. Repeatedly tossing the mixture and duplicating the process to form new crusts, continue to sauté, breaking up components with the edge of the spatula and adding butter as needed, until the mixture is crusty, fairly dry and well browned throughout. Season to taste with ***nutmeg,*** salt and pepper, dust with ***Parmesan,*** if desired, and serve piping hot.

NOTE—Husbanded ***bacon fat***, used in lieu of butter, makes an even tastier hash.

An obvious use for unconsumed boiled potatoes—especially in conjunction with leftover cooked sausage, other cooked meats or fish and shellfish—is potato salad. If the potatoes are particularly firm, though, use them for . . .

• RÖSTI (Swiss cookery) •

Cut 4 large peeled non-mealy leftover ***boiled potatoes*** into julienne strips. In an all-metal skillet of a size that will accommodate a wall-to-wall layer of potatoes about ½" thick heat 4 tbs. (½ stick) ***butter.*** Add potatoes and salt to taste and cook over low heat, tossing potatoes until all butter is absorbed. Spread potatoes to fill pan with a level layer and sprinkle with 1 tbs. ***milk*** or water. Cover potatoes with a heavy lid or dish fitted inside the pan and cook over low flame, occasionally shaking pan to prevent sticking, 18–20 minutes, or until potatoes are crusty and golden on the bottom. Invert pan and lid together and slide potatoes from lid onto a heated serving plate. Cut in wedges and serve to 6–8 as an entrée accompaniment.

• TORTA DI PATATE ALLA TARANTO •
(Italian cookery)

Many and varied are the uses for leftover mashed potatoes. This, from Apulia, is one of the most toothsome.

* * *

To leftover ***mashed pulp*** of 3 medium ***boiled potatoes*** add 1¼ cups ***flour*** and ¼ tsp. salt and knead until ingredients are thoroughly blended. (A processor will do the job quickly and well.) Grease a large shallow ovenproof casserole, preferably earthenware, and fill bottom with a level layer of potato mixture about ½″ thick. Drizzle surface evenly with 1½ tbs. ***olive oil*** and cover mixture with ¼ lb. ***mozzarella cheese,*** diced, and 6 very ripe (or canned) ***plum tomatoes,*** peeled and hand-squeezed of their juice. Dust evenly with 2 tbs. grated ***Parmesan,*** ¼ tsp. freshly ground black pepper and 1 tbs. ***dried oregano.*** Drizzle surface with another 2 tbs. olive oil and bake in a preheated 400°F oven 30 minutes, or until cheese is golden-brown. Serve to 4–6, with a tossed green salad, as a light lunch or supper.

Many of the good, hearty, somewhat heavy breads of central and eastern Europe are made with mashed potatoes. For example . . .

• KÖMÉNYMAGOS KRUMPLIS KENYÉR •
(Hungarian cookery)

Using a large bowl pour 1 envelope ***dry yeast*** into ½ cup warm water and stir in 3 tbs. ***flour*** (preferably the hard-wheat bread flour used by small ethnic bakeries; otherwise unbleached all-purpose flour). Allow to rise 30 minutes in a warm corner. In succession, add 2 cups lukewarm water, 1½ tbs. salt, 1½ tsp. ***caraway seed,*** a scant 6 cups ***flour*** and mashed pulp of 3 leftover ***medium boiled potatoes***. Knead mixture 10–12 minutes, or until it comes away cleanly from sides of bowl. Allow dough to rise until doubled in bulk, transfer it to a floured baking sheet, knead for a minute or two and shape into a loaf. Allow dough to rise another 30 minutes, then brush top lightly with water and slash center with a sharp knife. Bake 45–50 minutes in a preheated 400°F oven. Yields 1 large loaf.

Tossed green salads have an unfortunate propensity toward rejection, and nothing is quite as depressing to the home cook as the sight of a large bowlful of dressed greens left unconsumed at the end of an evening. Knowing all too well from previous experience that it will be a limp sodden mass by morning, most cooks simply will jettison an uneaten salad after resolving never again to add dressing until assured that the dish is wanted. A much more satisfying alternative would be to add the neglected greenery, vinaigrette and all, to *Gazpacho,* which is a sort of liquid salad anyway and which very hospitably will absorb both the neglected rabbit food and an uncomplicated oil-and-vinegar dressing.

Gazpacho has virtues galore. Besides being a wasteless disposal medium for green salads and other leftover veggies, it is a magnificent dish in its own right and a real antidote to the hot-weather blahs. Moreover, it has remarkable longevity under refrigeration and will keep the superb flavor of high summer on tap long after the garden is bereft of its tomatoes.

As is the case with most originally improvisatory dishes derived from peasant cookery, there is no such thing as a "definitive" recipe for *Gazpacho.* In *The Spanish Cookbook* (a fine, uncompromisingly honest volume), Barbara Norman refers to "some thirty classic versions and many variations of this ancient dish." The non-recipe that follows conforms precisely to none of them, but evolved over the course of several summers, each of which produced a glut of home-grown tomatoes, and derives in part from a constitutional inability to dispose of potentially useful leftovers. Like Gumbo,* this particular *Gazpacho* never will be quite the same when prepared in separate batches and, indeed, a single batch won't remain the same from day to day, as various useful additions turn up in the kitchen.

• A NON-RECIPE FOR GAZPACHO •

Cut the stem bases from as many good, firm vine-ripened ***tomatoes*** as you care to use and chop the fruit coarsely. For each 3 large tomatoes or the rough equivalent thereof core, seed and thinly slice 1 or 2 ***green bell peppers,*** chop a small ***onion*** and whack flat a clove of ***garlic*** with the side of a knife. Put everything into a blender or processor and add any or all of the following: leftover tossed ***green salad vinaigrette*** (a mayonnaise-based dressing won't appreciably injure the enterprise, but *don't* add dressings made with cheese, sour cream or the like); sugarless leftover ***cucumber salad***; crustless leftover ***stale white bread***; leftover ***tomato salad***. Let your proportions be guided by your culinary common sense; a *loaf* of bread for each tomato might result in an interesting new dish but would constitute a somewhat detrimental imbalance in anything masquerading as an acceptable *Gazpacho.* Purée the mixture, together with 5–6 tbs. ***olive oil*** and 2 tbs. ***wine vinegar*** for each 3 tomatoes included, and pour it into a large receptacle, preferably an earthenware pot such as beans are baked in, with sufficient capacity to hold a good deal more. For each 3 tomatoes in the mixture add 2 cups (or less) of ice water and salt to taste and stir vigorously until all elements are thoroughly blended. Cover and refrigerate for use as needed, adding congruent leftovers as they turn up.

> **NOTE**—Many *Gazpachos* are served with garnishes of the diced or cubed solid ingredients on the side (e.g., ***peppers, tomatoes, cucumbers, onions, stale bread***, etc., the last often toasted or fried). To these may be added chopped hard-boiled ***egg*** and/or ***parsley.*** Chopped ***blanched almonds*** would not be amiss and some *Gazpachos* incorporate raw beaten ***eggs.*** None of these garnishes should be added directly to the storage pot. Incidentally, that punchbowl set that has been gathering dust since your wedding will come in very handy when you serve the soup.

• BRAISED LEFTOVER TOSSED SALAD •

Lightly braised in its own vinaigrette dressing, leftover ***tossed salad*** (greens only) makes an interesting accompaniment to duck, goose or the fattier cuts of pork or lamb, especially if a little extra garlic, a few white ***seedless raisins*** and a scattering of ***pine nuts*** are added to the wilted greens. A topping of crumbed leftover ***bread*** won't hurt, either, if browned briefly under the broiler.

Jota (or *Iota*) is a big, hearty belly-filling soup that plays much the same role in the lives of Triestine and neighboring Yugoslav revelers that onion soup traditionally has played in the lives of Parisian stay-out-lates. It's a legendary hangover preventive but, even for those who haven't overindulged, it's fine cold-weather fare and an excellent way of using up nothing but husbanded leftovers. Amounts and proportions are unimportant here; the main point is to make use of the components in whatever amounts are available, so long as the flavors of all *three vegetables come through and the soup is thick.*

* * *

Combine leftover cooked ***white beans***, leftover cooked ***sauerkraut*** (or ***cabbage***) and leftover diced ***boiled potatoes*** with water or ***meat stock**** and, if you like, husbanded ***pork cracklings*** and/or bits of leftover ***smoked pork or pork sausage***. Cook over moderate heat, stirring occasionally, until soup is well thickened with starchy throw-off from beans and potatoes. (If the latter disintegrate, no harm done.) Season to taste and serve very hot, preferably in earthenware crocks.

Vegetable Purées

Just about any known leftover cooked vegetable can be converted to a purée that will lend visual and textural variety to a subsequent meal. The simplest procedure for boiled or steamed vegetables is to feed them into a blender or processor and run the machine until a smooth consistency is attained. The vegetable in question then is heated and, if the consistency is too thick, a little reserved cooking liquid or stock* may be stirred in. At the last moment stir in 1½ tbs. butter for each half-pound of vegetable matter and season to taste.

Singly or in combination with one another, leftover boiled or steamed carrots, peas, fresh beans, cooked dried beans, potatoes, parsnips, turnips, kohlrabi, salsify, asparagus and the like all can be prepared in the same manner. In the case of more watery leafy vegetables, such as leftover lettuce and spinach, the greens should be heated over a lively fire until their moisture has evaporated and may be combined with leftover boiled potato to add body to the purée. For chestnut purée (a traditional accompaniment to red game), add a little heavy cream along with the butter.

An extremely attractive purée can be made with red bell peppers or such frying varieties as Cubanella. For this, roast peppers should be used, olive oil should be substituted for both pot liquor and butter and it should be borne in mind that a very little of the vivid red finished product goes a long way.

• ROAST PEPPERS •

Arrange very firm ***red bell*** or ***frying peppers*** in any amount you like in a shallow foil-lined baking pan and broil 3–4″ beneath high flame, turning peppers occasionally until skin is blistered all over, keeping oven door closed between turns. When skins are thoroughly blistered, transfer peppers to a brown paper bag, crimp the opening shut and allow peppers to cool until they can be handled comfortably. Strip skins from peppers with the fingers, cut around and discard stem bases, halve peppers lengthwise and scrape out seeds and ribs.

> **NOTE**—Roast peppers will keep a week or more under refrigeration if smeared over with ***olive oil*** and covered with plastic wrap. Similarly treated, they freeze fairly well, too. (Capsicum peppers, incidentally, may be frozen raw in dice or julienne strips and, for use in most dishes, transferred directly from the freezer to the cooking vessel.) A dish of roast peppers, garnished with anchovy fillets, makes so irresistible a first course or assorted antipasto component that it's unlikely you'll have much left over with which to concoct a purée.

Whereas most vegetable purées are used as main-dish garnishes, *hummus*, a chickpea purée common to many Eastern Mediterranean cuisines, usually is served as a separate course.

• HUMMUS BI TAHEENI (Lebanese cookery) •

In a blender or processor purée leftover cooked ***chickpeas*** in any desired amount, along with salt to taste and 1 clove ***garlic***, ¼ cup ***taheeni*** (sesame seed paste, available at Middle Eastern food shops) and ⅙ cup ***lemon juice*** (or less, to taste) for each cup of chickpeas. Transfer mixture to a serving dish, drizzle surface with ***olive*** or ***sesame oil,*** sprinkle with chopped ***parsley*** and serve as a dip with ***crudités*** or ***pita**** bread.

> **NOTE**—The sesame paste and oil used in Chinese and other Far Eastern cookery is not interchangeable with the Near Eastern products.

In this volume, as in life, one thing seems to lead willy-nilly to another. A momentary digression, then, for . . .

• PITA (Common to most Near Eastern cookery) •

Dissolve 1 envelope dry ***yeast*** in ¼ cup warm water and allow to stand 10 minutes. To the work bowl of a food processor fitted with the steel blade add 3 cups ***flour,*** ¾ tsp. salt, the yeast solution and, if desired, 1 tsp. ***sugar.*** With machine running pour ¾ cup warm water through feed tube and process dough 40–60 seconds. (If machine automatically cuts off, process dough in two or more stages.) Turn dough out onto a lightly floured surface and knead another minute or so by hand. Divide and form dough into 5 balls and roll each into a flat pancakelike disc about 5½″ in diameter. Arrange cakes on a greased baking sheet or pizza pan and bake 10–12 minutes in a preheated 475°F oven.

> **NOTE**—Resist the temptation to peek; the oven door must remain shut during the baking process.

• VEGETABLE PURÉE SOUPS •

Just as any cooked vegetable can be converted to a purée, so can any vegetable purée be converted to a soup. As is the case with the various consommés, vegetable purée soups for the most part ring minor changes on a single basic theme, and to sedulously describe the small variations that distinguish each of myriad examples of the genre would be to bore all concerned stiffer than a Birdseye fish fillet. In essence, any vegetable purée soup (*potage*) is a blend of vegetables and stock* or consommé* in a ratio of roughly 3 cups vegetables (before they are puréed) to 1 qt. liquid; often incorporating a *mirepoix* of cut-up vegetables cooked slowly in butter and themselves puréed; in some cases thickened by the addition of puréed potatoes, rice or other starchy material; in many cases garnished, according to traditional usage, with anything from croutons (as for *potage Crécy*) to rashers of bacon (as for French split-pea soup); and quite often finished with cream and/or small amounts of butter.

The beauty of vegetable purée soups is that it is practically impossible to concoct a poor one, however improvisatory it may be, and altogether impossible to make one that isn't cheap and nourishing, unless the dictates of culinary common sense are willfully flouted. Moreover, the foresighted connective cook can turn out a perfectly good *potage* on the spur of the moment by puréeing whatever leftover cooked vegetables come to hand and combining them with previously frozen stock* or consommé melted right in the soup kettle.

For detailed descriptions of innumerable standard vegetable purée soups, consult *Larousse Gastronomique,* which will tell you all you want to know of the subject and a good deal more.

Garnishes and soups by no means exhaust the good uses to which vegetable purées may be put. Baked in unsweetened custard mixtures, for example, they can be served as side dishes or even brunch, light luncheon or late-supper entrées. With seasonings appropriate to their individual natures and the addition of complementary ingredients (e.g., a little leftover cooked ham with puréed peas or Parmesan cheese with asparagus), any puréed leftover vegetable may be prepared as for . . .

• TIMBALES D'ÉPINARDS (French cookery) •

Combine ⅔ cup ***spinach purée,**** 1½ cups ***milk or cream,*** ⅛ tsp. ***nutmeg*** (preferably freshly grated) and salt to taste and blend well with a rotary beater. Thoroughly beat in 2 large ***eggs*** and pour mixture into 6 well-buttered custard cups. Arrange cups in a pan filled to ⅔ their depth with hot water and bake in a preheated 350°F oven 25–30 minutes, or until the tip of a knife inserted at the center of a mold comes away clean. Allow molds to stand a few minutes at room temperature, run a knife around the inside of each and turn *timbales* out onto serving dishes. Serves 6.

NOTE—*Timbales* may be mounted on butter-fried rounds of semi-stale leftover ***white bread*** and variously sauced as you deem fit. As a general rule, the color of the sauce should contrast vividly with that of the *Timbale* and the flavors, of course, should be complementary.

Soufflés, too, may be made with just about any puréed veggie (although beets might produce something of an eyesore), whether used singly or in combination with symbiotic ingredients (e.g., anchovies with cauliflower, chicken livers with avocado, Roquefort with spinach). Proportions given in the following recipe apply to any savory soufflé, including those made with meats, poultry, fish and cheese, as well as vegetable purées.

• BASIC SOUFFLÉ •

In a heavy non-aluminum saucepan prepare a *roux* of 4 tbs. each ***butter*** and ***flour*** and cook, stirring constantly, about 3 minutes, or until mixture is frothy but unbrowned. Gradually add 1 cup ***hot milk,*** beating constantly with a wire whisk until the resultant sauce (Béchamel) thickens appreciably. Off heat beat in salt and pepper to taste and, if appropriate to the salient ingredient, a generous pinch of freshly ***grated nutmeg.*** (Don't underseason, for we'll be dealing with some fairly bland elements anon.) Allow mixture to cool slightly and add 4 ***egg yolks,*** one by one, beating each in well. (Reserve whites.) (To this juncture, the soufflé may be prepared for later completion, in which case cover it tightly with plastic wrap.)

Combine the foregoing with 1½ cups of the ***vegetable purée*** (or whatever) of choice. In a separate bowl or with a suitable electrical contrivance beat 4 reserved ***egg whites*** and 2 husbanded ***egg whites***, salted to taste, until they hold firm gleaming peaks, then beat about ⅓ of this froth into the soufflé mixture. Pour the latter into the remaining egg whites and gently fold in with a rubber spatula. Correct seasonings. Butter a 2-qt. soufflé dish well and coat thoroughly with flour or grated cheese, whichever is appropriate to the nature of the soufflé, and shake out excess. Pour soufflé mixture into dish and bake 35 minutes in a preheated 475°F oven. Serve immediately to 6.

NOTE—The soufflé may be prepared in individual serving dishes, in which case half the baking time will be adequate. A simple potato soufflé, it might be noted, will convert dreary cold leftover spuds into a dish of great elegance and character. A flour-lined mold is advisable for meat, poultry and fish soufflés; a cheese-lined mold for vegetable and cheese soufflés.

Onward and upward with the vegetable purées! In various combinations, they all lend themselves to cold terrines of great style, savor and visual appeal, which can be served as a first course at dinner, a light summer luncheon entrée or a buffet offering. Flavorful as it may be, a terrine made from a single vegetable purée is less interesting to look at than a multicolored affair, so the tactic here is to construct your terrines in layers of contrasting colors, to reveal flag-like or heraldic patterns when they are sliced and served. With a little practice, further visual interest can be added by packing the terrine mold with diagonal or undulating layers of different vegetable purées, or purées in juxtaposition with various cheeses and such substances as smoked salmon or ham mousse, forcemeat of white- or pink-fleshed fish (studded or not, as you will, with diced shrimp, whole mussels or whatever). The visual possibilities here are limited only by your own patience and imagination. Marbleized patterns, abstract-expressionism—you name it—are well within the realm of the possible, and there's more than a fair chance that the finished product will taste at least as good as it looks.

A superb tricolor meatless terrine is served at the great New York French restaurant Lutèce. The following recipe was adapted from one graciously supplied by that establishment's *chef-propriètaire,* André Soltner, and its basic construction in turn can be adapted to whatever leftovers you have on hand.

• TERRINE DE LÉGUMES LUTÈCE •

In a bowl combine 1⅓ cups thick ***tomato purée,*** 1⅓ cup ***heavy cream,*** 4 very fresh ***whole eggs*** and salt, pepper and freshly grated ***nutmeg*** to taste. Whip together until thoroughly blended and set aside. In a second bowl similarly treat 3 oz. ***shredded Swiss*** or ***Gruyere*** cheese, 3 whole ***eggs*** and scant ½ cup ***heavy cream,*** with salt, pepper and ***nutmeg*** to taste. Same story with 6 oz. puréed leftover ***spinach***, 3 whole ***eggs*** and ⅓ cup ***heavy cream,*** with salt, pepper and ***nutmeg*** to taste. Line a terrine mold 3″ × 4″ × 12″ with wax paper and fill bottom with the tomato mixture, smoothing surface with a rubber spatula. Place mold in a pan partially filled with hot water and bake 10–15 minutes, covered, in a preheated 350°F oven, or until mixture has set to the point where it will support a layer of the cheese mixture. Pour cheese mixture into mold and bake as before, then repeat process with spinach mixture, baking until a knifepoint inserted into its center comes away clean. Allow terrine to cool, unmold onto a presentation platter, remove wax paper and slice, as needed, in ⅜″ thicknesses. Garnish as desired and serve with a light vinaigrette sauce.

A FINAL WORD ABOUT PURÉED LEFTOVER VEGETABLES

To feed an infant store-bought baby food, with its questionable additives and outrageously inflated prices, would be criminally negligent in view of the ease and economy with which a better product can be prepared in the home kitchen.

Found Money

Such usually discarded vegetable matter as beet and radish tops (leaves) is eminently esculent and may be incorporated into salads or cooked in any manner applicable to spinach, while carrot, turnip, parsnip and celery tops make excellent additions to the stockpot.

You're unlikely to find them in the market but, if you grow your own, the broad upper leaves of the Brussels sprout plant (which sheds water like a duck's back) are as delicious as they are versatile and nutritious. They are particularly good when wrapped envelope-fashion around any stuffing suitable for cabbage, make a fine addition to many peasant-style soups and may be used for a very interesting variant on conventional sauerkraut. (For the dilettante farmer, the unavoidable task of trimming away those leaves in order to provide the sprouts themselves with their full share of nutrients is as onerous as any that noncommercial gardening demands. To put out *that* much time and sweat and to spurn immediate and delectable recompense, as is usually the case, would be sheer idiocy.)

Stems of broccoli, cauliflower, artichokes and similar succulents, normally cut off and discarded, also have manifold culinary uses. Broccoli stems in particular are much used in Chinese cookery. Peel the stems as you would asparagus before cooking them.

Potatoes wastefully are peeled far more often than can be justified by the dubious aesthetic enhancement provided by a process that consumes working time while doing away with both flavor and valuable nutriment. Roasted, fried and boiled potatoes need not be stripped naked, nor need the spuds used in potato salad. Indeed, you may find that, like a PG movie, they're more interesting with a bit of skin in evidence.

Those goddam dandelions spreading all over the lawn can, of course, be converted to salads, but what is less well known is that they can be cooked and eaten almost any way that spinach can be.

Such garden flowers as lilies, carnations, gladiolas, chrysanthemums, honeysuckle, pansies, peonies, lilacs, tulips, marigolds and roses all are edible. They not only make strikingly beautiful salads, soups and garnishes, but delicate fritters as well, and the more fragrant varieties can be used to perfume butter, vinegar, tea and honey, among other things. Marigolds make a marvelous, somewhat saffron-like addition to rice dishes.

A WORD OF CAUTION

One *can* get carried away—in more senses than one—by a desire to exploit all that *looks* edible. While it is highly unlikely that any stems, leaves, blossoms, etc. found attached to store-bought vegetables are not benign, at the very least, foraging indiscriminately in the garden may abruptly punctuate one's curriculum vitae. Potato, tomato and eggplant leaves, for example, all members of the nightshade family, should not be nibbled in any form, nor should anything else about which you're not absolutely certain.

Can a sentimental passion of a vegetable fashion *really* excite your languid spleen? Well, the otherwise omnivorous *Larousse Gastronomique* isn't terribly encouraging in this respect:

> Pig's spleen. RATE DE PORC—This part of the viscera is rather mediocre in taste. It is mainly used in pork butchery for making ordinary sausages.

"In cookery," *Larousse* adds without much enthusiasm, "the spleen, together with the lungs and the heart, can be made into a stew." Not a word about bashful young potatoes or not too French French beans.

Use Your Noodle 9

> Macaroni is in England a common name given to many preparations of Italian paste, as well as to that particular kind which Theodore Hook described as "tobacco pipes made easy". . . . In Chaucer's time the English name was macrow, and it was applied especially to little balls or puddings of paste.
>
> Macaroni is a form of wheat flour—a bread, in fact—so palatable, so cheap, and so easily managed in cookery, that it is a wonder to see it so little used in this country.
>
> —E.S. Dallas, *Kettner's Book of the Table* (1877)

THE CATCHALL term in use today is "pasta," and, increasingly, the pasta we use is no longer *pasta secca,* the dried, packaged factory-made product of the Italian south (or etiolated domestically produced versions thereof), but instead the recently chic so-called "fresh" pasta more typical of north-Italian cookery.

To make your own fresh pasta from scratch (even using a food processor and pasta machine, both of which do quite creditable jobs) requires a bit more time and effort in most cases than would a trip to the nearest belly boutique, whose product, though costly, may not be half bad. In general, however—and particularly for such filled pastas as ravioli, capelletti and tortellini—both the satisfactions and economy to be derived from producing the stuff yourself far outweigh the convenience of buying it ready-made to a mass-production formula.

The myth of Marco Polo's having introduced pasta to Italy from the Far East has long since been discredited. In one form or another, the noodle evolved independently in both regions and was familiar to inhabitants of the Italian boot centuries before Polo flouted advice that Horace Greeley would not get around to formulating for some centuries longer. It is safe to say that in each case the responsible party was a connective cook.

Whatever form it may take, pasta is the connective cook's staple food par excellence. It is one of the simplest of all culinary compounds and yet perhaps the most sophisticated and versatile culinary prop ever devised, a medium beside which any other grain food—even rice, with its protean adaptability—seems to have little more multiplicity of function than the telephone, the alarm clock or the dashboard cigarette lighter.

A second, more persistent myth would have it that pasta is inordinately fattening. This misconception is traceable in large part to misguided ideas of pasta's function, ideas implanted in the minds of American diners by restaurateurs who were only too happy to stuff their clients to the ears with cheap spaghetti, instead of relatively unprofitable meat, fish or fowl, and who deliberately cultivated the erroneous notion that pasta properly was eaten as a main course.

Eaten in immoderate quantities, *any* food is fattening and pasta is no exception. What many Americans fail to realize, though, is that pasta almost always is eaten in Italy as a prelude to a light entrée, and that its primary function is not to induce satiety but to serve as a vehicle whereby its sauce can be most pleasurably savored. As the late Waverley Root remarked in his definitive book *The Food of Italy,*

> In France, a sauce is an adornment, even a disguise. . . . In Italy, it *is* the dish, its soul, its *raison d'être,* the element which gives it character and flavor. . . . Pasta unadorned would quickly become monotonous. The whole point of *tagliatelle alla bolognese* or *spaghetti con le vongole* is the sauce.

The pattern for pasta-eating in Italy had been more or less shaped at least as early as the onset of the Renaissance and was epitomized by the dining regimen of a prominent fourteenth-century Tuscan merchant, Francisco Datini. On the urging of his doctor, Datini took the larger of his two daily meals around dusk, beginning it with either a light soup or a small portion of ravioli or lasagna dusted with Parmesan cheese. This usually was followed by a thin collop of veal, sautéed with local mushrooms and served with fresh young beans. A portrait of Datini by Fra Lippo Lippi shows him as a man well past his prime but in splendid shape, with a knife-edge jawline and—as far as can be judged from the meager evidence revealed by a voluminous cloak—not a superfluous ounce on his frame.

The fact is that pasta is one of the most healthful of all foods. The flour used in any Italian pasta worth the name is semolina, which is ground from hard durum wheat and contains more protein and vitamins than ordinary baking flour. An unsauced standard portion (which is to say, two ounces dry weight—a figure that may astonish Americans accustomed to snaffling up a half-pound at one go) provides 35 percent of the recommended daily thiamine allowance, 15 percent of the recommended riboflavin intake, and 10 percent of the iron requirement, while committing to the battle of the bulge only one gram of fat and a very modest 210 calories.

In its simplest form, pasta is nothing more than flour and water and it isn't appreciably more complex than that even in its most elaborate manifestations. Eggs are incorporated into most fresh (i.e., undried) pastas and into some dried pastas (e.g., packaged egg noodles), too, but, aside from the addition of a finely puréed vegetable and/or a little oil to the dough, there isn't much more that can be done with the stuff. Stock could be substituted for water, which may or may not be a hitherto unpublished idea, but the amount of liquid in either case would be so negligible that the difference in flavor probably would not be perceptible.

Machines exist for the home-fabrication of such hollow tubular pastas as *penne* and *ziti* and for such solid extrusions as spaghetti and vermicelli, as well as a variety of fancy shapes, but whether their products are any improvement on store-bought counterparts of decent quality is debatable. (Your own made-from-scratch dried spaghetti may taste every bit as good as the version produced by some factory in Naples but it certainly won't *look* as good, in its disheveled uncooked state, as those ruler-straight strands from the package.) Our concern here, then, is not with dried pastas (although any unfilled pasta can be dried successfully), but with the family of fresh pastas, which are cooked while still moist and pliable. More particularly, our concern is with such filled pasta dumplings as *tortellini, tortelloni, cappelletti* and *ravioli,* for, aside from the saucing of pasta, it is here that pasta and Connective Cookery are most closely intertwined.

• BASIC PASTA DOUGH •

Kneading dough by hand will produce much lighter and airier bread than you're likely to turn out by letting a processor do the job for you. Pasta dough, on the other hand, is not activated by yeast and consequently doesn't require the sort of kneading that creates a glutenous network of air bubbles. The purpose of kneading pasta dough is simply to blend its elements as thoroughly as possible and to achieve a velvety consistency, and a processor will do this in a fraction of the fifteen or twenty minutes that hand-kneading entails.

* * *

In the work bowl of a processor fitted with the steel blade, combine desired quantity of ***semolina*** (or, if semolina is unavailable, unbleached flour) with 3 ***eggs*** per 2 cups of flour and salt to taste. Allow machine to run until dough forms a ball above blade-spindle, adding lukewarm water a few drops at a time if dough is too mealy and fails to cohere. Turn dough out onto a lightly floured surface and knead briefly by hand until its texture is smooth and velvety, adding a little flour if the mixture is too moist and sticky. Roll dough into a ball. (If more than 1 cup of flour was used, divide dough into units equivalent to 1 cup of flour apiece and roll each into a ball.) Flatten dough so that it resembles an Edam cheese, rub all over with a few drops of ***olive oil*** and wrap each piece separately in plastic or foil. Allow dough to rest 1 hour or more at room temperature before rolling it out.

Hand-made Pasta Dough

Using above ingredients in the same proportions, place ***flour*** and salt together on a work surface and form a well in the center. Break requisite number of ***eggs*** into the well and beat them with a fork, working in surrounding flour bit by bit until about half is absorbed. Using the hands, gradually work remaining dry flour into the moist center, moving the elements in a circular pattern and scraping work surface occasionally, until all particles are absorbed into the whole. Little by little, add about 2 tsp. lukewarm water per cup of flour, kneading constantly and adding more water, if necessary, a few drops at a time, or sprinkling with flour if mixture is too moist and sticky. When the texture is smooth and velvety, proceed as above.

• ROLLING OUT THE PASTA •

Opinions differ, but the view here is that the best implement for rolling out pasta dough is a tapered wooden pin about an inch and a quarter in diameter and some eighteen inches long. After a preliminary flattening, pasta dough can be rolled out in a crank-operated machine designed for that purpose, and the resultant product will be quite creditable. Take the time and effort to master the technique of rolling pasta by hand, though, and you'll probably consign your expensive machine to your next tag sale. The hand-rolled product—harder, lighter and thinner—is not only appreciably better but the satisfaction of making it is roughly analogous to creating a master drawing instead of photocopying someone else's creation.

* * *

Place a round of pasta dough in the center of a lightly floured work surface, allowing yourself plenty of elbow room, and flatten it to a thickness of about ¼″ with a rolling pin, giving the dough a quarter-turn after each pass of the pin. Gradually roll dough flatter, wrapping it completely around the pin from time to time, stretching it outward from the center with the heels of the hands and dusting with flour as needed to keep overlapping layers from sticking to one another. When dough is quite thin (⅙″ or so), lay it out flat and, giving it a quarter-turn from time to time, roll it from the center outward toward the edges until it is thin enough so that you can see your own silhouette through it if you drape it vertically between yourself and a mirror. You can? Marvelous. Your pasta is now ready for conversion to any of the filled dumplings mentioned earlier. (For *linguine, fettucine, papardelle* or similar flat noodles, the dough needn't be quite so thin as for filled dumplings.)

Machine-rolled Pasta
After hand-rolling dough to a thickness slightly in excess of the machine's largest opening, cut it into rectangles about ⅔ the width of the machine's rollers. Further flatten one end of each strip, so that it will feed easily into the machine, and crank dough through rollers. Repeat process, decreasing feed-slot width 1 setting, and continue in the same manner until dough has passed through the narrowest setting the machine allows.

• RIBBON NOODLES •

For any long flat noodle, such as *linguine* or *fettucine,* roll up a sheet of pasta dough lengthwise into a cylinder, having first dusted it lightly with flour to prevent sticking. With a sharp knife slice the cylinder into sections of the desired noodle width. Unroll noodles on a lightly floured surface and allow to dry for at least 1 hour, turning occasionally, before use. Alternatively, use a machine and feed prepared dough through the noodle-cutting attachment of your choice.

> **NOTE**—Racks for semi-drying cut pasta will hasten the process and may be purchased or improvised. An old-fashioned laundry rack will do. The cooking time for fresh ribbon noodles is 3–5 minutes in rapidly boiling salted water.

Filled Pasta Dumplings

> The variety of tortellini stuffings is endless. . . . There are so many that it is almost rare to come upon the original.
>
> —Waverley Root, *The Food of Italy*

What applies to *tortellini* applies equally to filled pasta dumplings of any other type. A few specific suggestions will be outlined anon, but the enterprising connective cook will produce a more-or-less original recipe every time out.

• TORTELLINI (Bolognese cookery) •

The technique of fashioning *tortellini* and their larger siblings, *tortelli* (a.k.a. *tortelletti*) and *tortelloni,* is not easily described. If you're unfamiliar with the form, you'd be well advised to inspect a commercially produced example before tackling the job yourself, just to get a clear idea of what it is that you're setting out to achieve. Failing that, you might have a good look at a female navel—the model, according to Italian folklore, on which these ring-dumplings were based.

* * *

Using a small cookie cutter, jar lid or the like, stamp circles about 1½″ in diameter from a sheet of thinly rolled-out pasta dough. Slightly off-center in each circle place a small gob (about the size of a chickpea) of the filling of your choice. Moisten half the circumference of each circle with water, treating a few at a time, to facilitate closure. One at a time, fold circles in half over filling and press edges to seal, forming convex crescents. Stretch and flatten the points of one of these crescents slightly and lay it, flat-side-down and folded edge facing the wrist, over back of index finger of the left hand (assuming right-handedness). Wrap points of crescent around finger and press them together on underside, forming a ring. With a finger of the right hand give pressed edge of the dumpling a wristward flip, so that it forms a shallow backward fold. Continue until filled dough is used up.

NOTE—You will find this slow, messy going at first, but take heart. According to Waverley Root, practiced Italian women are able to turn out as many as 6,500 of the dumplings an hour. The figure is somewhat harder to swallow than the products of their labors.

• CAPPELLETTI •

Stamp circles from a thin sheet of pasta dough, as for *tortellini.** Before filling, moisten edges of each circle with water to facilitate later adhesion. Place a lump of the desired filling (about ⅓ tsp.) in the center of each circle and fold pasta over filling, covering the latter completely and pressing dough surfaces together to form little peaked caps. Allow about 8 pieces per serving for use in soup, about 12 for service with sauce. Cook *cappelletti* 5 minutes in boiling consommé* for soup (*cappelletti in brodo*) and serve in the cooking liquid. Boil 5 minutes in salted water and drain for any sauced dish.

• RAVIOLI •

Arrange a very thin sheet of pasta dough on a lightly floured surface. Measuring desired filling in half-teaspoons, dispose it in uniform rows on one side (a little less than half) of the sheet of dough, leaving each dollop isolated from its neighbors by about 1½″ on all sides. Lightly brush surface of remaining dough with water (for adhesion) and fold it back over filled side, completely covering the latter. Using the edge of the hand, tamp pasta down firmly between rows of filling, working vertically and horizontally so that dough adheres thoroughly to dough all around each "bubble" of filling. Run a wheeled ravioli cutter between rows of bubbles in both directions to simulate a pane of lumpy postage stamps. Bring plenty of salted water to a rapid boil and cook *ravioli,* a few at a time, 2–3 minutes, or until they surface. Remove cooked dumplings from water with a slotted spoon or similar device, drain briefly and arrange in 1 layer in a heated serving dish. Cover with a small amount of sauce of choice, dust with grated Parmesan or Romano cheese; stack layers of *ravioli,* sauce and cheese until dumpling supply is exhausted, finishing with layers of sauce and cheese. Allow about 8 pieces per serving.

• CANNELLONI •

Cut thin sheets of pasta dough into 4″ squares and cook them a few at a time about 2 minutes in boiling salted water. Drain and dry on flat cloth towels. Center 4"-long cylinders of desired filling on pasta squares and roll up latter. Arrange *cannelloni* overlap-side-down in a lightly greased baking dish, cover with sauce of choice, and cheese if desired, and bake 15 minutes in a preheated 400°F oven. Allow 2 pieces per serving.

• PASTA VERDE •

What we're concerned with here is green pasta—and a very good use for leftover cooked spinach. *Pasta verde* may be substituted for ordinary egg pasta in the preparation of any of the foregoing forms and may be used in conjunction with egg pasta to produce dishes such as the popular *paglia e fieno* ("straw and hay").

* * *

Using ½ cup (or more to taste) of leftover ***cooked spinach*** per 3 cups of ***flour,*** press as much moisture as possible from the spinach and purée it as finely as possible, using a processor or blender or rubbing it through a fine sieve. Combine purée with ***Basic Pasta Dough**** ingredients, add a pinch of ***nutmeg*** and proceed as for that recipe.

NOTE—Variously colored and flavored pastas can be produced by substituting ***carrots, beets, tomato paste*** and the like for spinach.

SOME PASTA FILLINGS

As remarked earlier, pasta is the ideal vehicle whereby the connective cook can exercise his ingenuity and talent for improvisation. *Tortellini, cappelletti, ravioli* or *cannelloni* all may be filled with the products of the following recipes, which are more-or-less conventional, but the combinations and permutations that can be achieved with various trimmings and leftovers are virtually infinite. Pure cheese fillings, on the other hand, properly lie outside the scope of Connective Cookery (one doesn't have *leftover* cheese; one has only what might be termed primary cheese until the last of it is consumed), but one cheese filling is included here because some fanciers believe that *ravioli,* in particular, wouldn't *be ravioli* without it.

• RICOTTA FILLING •

Mash together until well blended 1¼ cups ***ricotta cheese,*** 1 lightly beaten ***egg,*** ⅛ tsp. freshly ground pepper and 2 tbs. freshly grated ***Parmesan cheese.*** Yield: about 1½ cups.

• BASIC MEAT FILLING •

In 1 tbs. melted ***butter*** sauté ¾ cup ground leftover ***cooked beef or veal*** 5 minutes. Allow meat to cool and blend thoroughly with 2 tbs. each ***dry breadcrumbs*** and grated ***Parmesan cheese*** and a pinch of ***nutmeg.*** Yield: about 1 cup.

• SPINACH-MEAT FILLING •

Thoroughly blend 6 tbs. each completely drained and chopped left-over ***cooked spinach*** and ground leftover ***cooked beef, veal or pork*** (some fat included), or any combination of those meats. Add 2 tbs. grated ***Parmesan cheese,*** 1 heaping tbs. dry ***breadcrumbs*** and 1 pinch ***nutmeg*** and blend well. Yield: about 1 cup.

• CHICKEN FILLING •

In a processor or blender combine and reduce to a fine paste ½ cup salvaged ***stockpot chicken,*** ¼ cup thoroughly drained leftover ***cooked spinach,*** 2 tbs. grated ***Parmesan cheese,*** ½ clove ***garlic,*** 1 small ***egg,*** 3 tbs. ***heavy cream,*** 1 pinch ***nutmeg*** and salt and pepper to taste (easy on the salt). If mixture is too runny blend in enough dry ***breadcrumbs*** to firm it up. Yield: about 1 cup.

• PORK FILLING •

In a skillet melt 1 oz. butter or husbanded ***fat***, add ¼ cup ground leftover ***cooked sausage*** and ½ cup ground leftover ***cooked pork*** and sauté briefly. Allow meats to cool and blend in 1 small ***egg yolk***, lightly beaten, ⅓ cup grated ***Parmesan cheese***, 1½ tbs. dry ***breadcrumbs***, a pinch of ***nutmeg*** and salt and pepper to taste. Yield: about 1 cup.

• SPINACH-CHEESE FILLING •

Blend together and season to taste ½ cup thoroughly drained, finely chopped leftover cooked ***spinach***, ¼ cup drained ***ricotta cheese***, 2 tbs. grated ***Parmesan cheese*** and 1½ tbs. dry ***breadcrumbs***. Yield: about 1 cup.

Needless to say, what we have here is only the proverbial tip of the iceberg. A little leftover ***cooked ham*** will add a bit of spark to any of the foregoing fillings and others may be made with leftover ***cooked duck*** (add a little ***grated orange peel***), ***rabbit***, ***turkey***, ***game*** or what you will. (One Manhattan restaurateur fills ravioli with chocolate and serves it as dessert, a practice for which there is ample precedent in the *ravioli dolci* of various regional Italian cuisines.) Fresh ***chopped basil*** makes a fine addition to any dumpling to be served in conjunction with ***tomato sauce***, and if you're lucky enough to have some ***venison trimmings*** on hand, try blending them with ground ***black walnuts***, crushed ***juniper berries*** and a little ***grated orange rind***.

Stuff ravioli with a blend of ***lean veal***, ***calf's brain***, ***sweetbreads***, ***egg***, ***breadcrumbs***, ***Parmesan*** and ***chopped chard***, and you'll have something much like a specialty of Genoa—although it won't be altogether authentic without the inclusion of heifer's udder and borage. Fill your dumplings with veggies and no meat, and you'll have the *ravioli magri* of Ligurian fast days. Use minced ***fish*** and ***cheese*** in your *cappelletti*, and you'll have approximated a dish of Ravenna, where the same dumplings also are filled with a sauce-bound purée of ***mushrooms*** and ***crawfish tails***. In short, there is almost no way to fill pasta that hasn't been tried before, at least in broad outline, and found good.

As is the case with pasta fillings, so is it with pasta sauces: Recipes abound for producing classic sauces from a standing start, but the imaginative connective cook will concoct all manner of "original" sauces by combining whatever trimmings and leftovers that may come to hand. Moreover, he will usually learn that his creation has been enjoyed for generations in one section or another of Italy. Pasta can be sauced and enjoyed with nothing more complicated than **butter** (*al burro*), **cream** (*alla panna*) or **olive oil** (*all'olio*), but it also can be dressed, and approach sublimity, with everything but the kitchen sink thrown into the sauce, and the most frugally made whatever-comes-to-hand sauce often turns out to be as delectable as any concocted of the rarest and costliest of ingredients.

Classical French cookery is largely dependent on a few "mother" sauces from which derive a multiplicity of other sauces. For the connective cook who works extensively with pasta (and many other Italian dishes), the mother sauce is marinara, and if a goodly batch be cooked and put by in small jars, all sorts of other sauces quickly can be knocked together from all sorts of salvaged and husbanded oddments.

Marinara sauce freezes fairly well, but it takes up valuable freezer space and thawing time. The view here is that the home-canned product is preferable by far. It is easily and safely put up, its quality is better and it is always ready for instant use. Make a big enough batch in late summer or early fall, when good vine-ripened tomatoes are plentiful, and you're free of the task for a full year.

• A NON-RECIPE FOR MARINARA SAUCE •

"What is the basic difference between French and Italian cooking?" Enrico Galozzi, the noted Italian gastronomic expert, echoed my question. "French cooking is formalized, technical and scientific. Order Béarnaise sauce in 200 different French restaurants and you will get exactly

> the same sauce 200 times. Ask for Bolognese sauce in 200 different Italian restaurants and you will get 200 different versions of *ragù.*"
>
> —Waverley Root, *The Food of Italy*

Have marinara sauce in two hundred Italian restaurants or homes and you'll encounter a similar diversity of interpretation. Some cooks insist on simmering the stuff for aeons; others hold that the longer the sauce cooks the more bitter it becomes. Some include tomato paste, others consider its inclusion heretical. A considerable body of opinion holds that sugar must be added for sweetness, which is demonstrable nonsense. What follows is one home gardener's formula, and if information is sketchy on quantities and proportions it's because the cook never has bothered to keep precise track of what he's about or to make the sauce exactly the same way twice. He has, however, turned out a consistently agreeable and highly adaptable sauce year after year.

If you don't grow your own tomatoes, purchase good firm vine-ripened locally grown produce and sedulously avoid the etiolated Frankensteinian supermarket stuff that produces a lymphatic mush of no discernible flavor or acidity when crushed—if it *can* be crushed.

* * *

Gather enough ***tomatoes*** (including a fair proportion of the Italian plum, or Roma, variety) nearly to fill a large (16-to-20-qt.) stockpot when they are reduced to pulp. (The weight of fresh tomatoes of a given size may vary, depending on their density and moisture content. As a rule of thumb, two pounds will produce about a quart of sauce.) Plunge them briefly, a few at a time, into rapidly boiling water, retrieve them, cut away stem bases, and slip the loosened skins from the fruit. Roughly hack the peeled tomatoes into pieces and feed them in batches into a processor, running the machine until they are coarsely puréed. When all the tomatoes have been processed, run them in batches through a food mill equipped with perforations small enough to prevent the seeds from passing through. Transfer the strained purée to the stockpot. In the processor reduce to a mealy consistency 4–5 roughly chopped ***carrots,*** as many ***onions*** and 10–12 ***cloves garlic.***

Sauté carrots, onions and garlic in ***butter*** until soft but not browned and add mixture to stockpot. Toss in a scant palmful each of chopped ***fresh basil*** and ***oregano*** (⅓ that much if dried), along with a cupful or so of ***olive oil*** and salt and pepper to taste. Bring the pot nearly to a boil, stirring occasionally, and reduce heat to maintain a lively simmer. Cook about 2 hours, occasionally ladling off any watery liquids that rise to the surface, until sauce has thickened appreciably and can be held without noticeable loss in an ordinary strainer.

Sterilize sufficient collar-and-dome-lid canning jars in boiling water. Likewise their tops. Ladle hot sauce through a funnel directly into drained jars, filling to within ¼″ of their tops, seal and allow to cool. (The dome lids will give off a series of *pings* as they cool and each convexity becomes a shallow concavity.) Affix dated labels to jars and store in a cool dry dark place for future use.

> **NOTE**—If a thicker sauce is wanted for any specific later use, a small quantity of your basic marinara can be reduced in minutes to the desired consistency, with no risk of the bitterness that prolonged cooking may induce.

MARINARA-BASED MEAT SAUCES

In principle, most red Italian meat sauces are the result of a process that combines in one operation the procedures for preparing stock* and marinara sauce. By commingling these two husbanded compounds and adding a small quantity of meat trimmings during the preparation of a given meal, the resourceful connective cook can turn out a perfectly creditable meat sauce in minutes, whereas making it from a standing start would consume several hours.

Just about any meat, used singly or in combination with others, will produce a sauce for which a precedent can be found somewhere in regional Italian cookery. To take one example, our friend J thought he had invented something with the recipe that follows (which, as it happened, produced a superb sauce). He described his creation excitedly to an Italian maître d'hôtel of his acquaintance. "Oh yes," he was told, "that's a specialty of Rome. I've eaten it many times there."

• SALSA DI CODA DI BUE •
(Not-so-original recipe)

This sauce was "originated" in the aftermath of a dinner at which a couple of meaty segments of oxtail unaccountably went unconsumed. The original ragout was magnificent but the next day's pasta was even better.

* * *

Strip the meat and any other detachable matter from 2 or 3 pieces of leftover ***cooked oxtail*** and chop it roughly with a sharp knife. In a saucepan combine 2 oz. each ***consummé**** (preferably oxtail) and left-over ***red wine***. Bring to boil and reduce by ¾. Lower heat and add 1 cup ***marinara sauce***,* chopped oxtail and 1 ***bay leaf*** and simmer 10 minutes, stirring often to prevent sticking, or until sauce reaches desired consistency. Discard bay leaf and serve over pasta of choice (8 oz. dry weight) to 4.

MARINARA-BASED FISH AND SEAFOOD SAUCES FOR PASTA

With few exceptions, most fish and seafoods do not benefit from a heavy involvement with tomato-based sauces, which tend to overwhelm the delicacy of their flavors and textures. The robustly sauced classic Lobster Fra Diavolo is one such exception and, somewhat contrary to culinary logic, a Neapolitan cook can get away with blanketing mussels or *scungilli* in a sludgy, alarmingly red, hellishly spicy tomato sauce; but most seafoods won't stand up to this sort of assault. A favorite phrase of restaurateurs and professional chefs, when describing seafood sauces (whether or not they are served in conjunction with pasta) is ". . . and just a *touch* of marinara."

Justly revered as it may be for most purposes, *The Joy of Cooking* (or at least the 1953 edition that comes to hand) contains what may be the two most horrendous recipes ever devised for pasta with red seafood sauce. One of these combines cooked or canned seafood with a sort of bastard marinara concocted of canned condensed tomato soup(!), chopped onion and green peppers (which are simply stewed as is), either stock of an unspecified type or milk(!), flour(!) and diced cheese(!) of an unspecified type (*Feta*? Monterey Jack? Caerphilly?). The other—which is entitled "Italian Spaghetti with Seafood" and which, significantly, suggests that cooked ham or tongue may be substituted for seafoods—posits a sauce made up in equal parts of meat stock(!) and tomato purée, along with (among other things) paprika(!), Worcestershire sauce(!), butter(?) and "1 cup cooked seafood" (type and form unspecified; a whole baby octopus, perhaps?). Into this misalliance is stirred half a pound of pre-cooked spaghetti, whereupon the whole mishmash is steamed(!) for half an hour(!) and served with grated cheese, which, as most Italians will tell you, is an arrant barbarism with seafoods.

As non-Italians, Mesdames Rombauer and Becker, the perpetrators, may perhaps be forgiven their transgressions, but even in Italy it is possible to come upon egregiously maladroit seafood sauces. One that comes to mind was served some years ago at a picturesque *ristorante* perched high on a sunny hillside overlooking the Mediterranean. The sauce was a profusion of minuscule sea creatures of ineffable vulnerability and irreproachable freshness: clams the size of thumbnails, shrimp hardly bigger than mosquitoes, ringlets of squid of the diameter of cigar bands. Lamentably, the sauce was a heavily spiced, tar-thick, barely diluted tomato paste that utterly obliterated all that subtlety.

The plea implicit here is that you refrain from overuse of your marinara when preparing fish or seafood sauces. In judicious quantities, the stuff can be a marvelous perker-up of clam, fish and similar pasta dressings—but only if the inherent goodness of the salient ingredients is allowed to shine forth undiminished. In short, undiluted marinara is fine by itself or in combination with various robust seasonings and substances but, used in full force, it will murder more delicate ingredients.

• FRESH LINGUINE WITH FISH-HEAD SAUCE •
(Original recipe)

Poach 2–3 very fresh ***fish heads***† 20 minutes in simmering *court-bouillon** to cover generously, having removed their gills if there is any question about their freshness. Set fish heads aside to cool; strain and reserve poaching liquid. Pick over cooled heads, first removing and discarding skin and then separating all bits of flesh from bones. In a large pot bring reserved poaching liquid to boil and add ½ lb. freshly made ***linguine,*** stirring briefly to prevent unseemly entanglements. While pasta cooks, sauté 1 tbs. ***minced garlic*** in 4–5 tbs. ***olive oil*** in a large skillet, just until garlic begins to color. Drain pasta when *al dente* (after 3–4 minutes), reserving a little of the cooking liquid, and add to skillet, along with ¼ cup ***marinara sauce,**** 2–3 tbs. reserved ***pasta liquid, red pepper flakes*** to taste and ⅓ cup chopped ***Italian (flat-leaf) parsley.*** Toss briefly and serve immediately to 4.

If marinara sauce has received most of the attention here, it's only because it's the most adaptable compound for use with pasta and the progenitor of more different quickly made pasta sauces than any other in the connective cook's arsenal. With the addition of minced hot chili peppers, for example, it becomes *salsa arrabbiata* ("angry sauce"), a superb dressing for tubular dry pastas such as *penne;* with the addition of meats, stock and wine it becomes *salsa ragù,* and so on. There is, however, an infinitude of fine pasta sauces in which tomatoes play no part whatever. Many of these can be made with rich stock bases; many more incorporate the natural liquors of shellfish, fish roe, cuttlefish ink, and the like. Others, such as *pesto* and *primavera,* are made exclusively with vegetable matter or herbs in conjunction with cheese, and still others are made with nothing but dairy products. As Waverley Root has noted, most of these sauces are not rigidly codified, as sauces are in France, and leave much more leeway for improvisation. Speaking of Root, his book *The Food of Italy,* though not a compilation of recipes or cookery instruction per se, comprises what is probably the most comprehensive guide in English to the authentic saucing of pastas and to the whole repertory of Italian cuisine.

†Needless to say, we are dealing here with the heads of neither sardines nor marlin, but something between those extremes.

Just Desserts 10

FOR THE MOST PART, desserts lie outside the realm of Connective Cookery. One reason is obvious: However exalted many of its products may be, Connective Cookery is rooted in the culinary traditions of the poor—a societal element that historically has been far too preoccupied with filling its collective belly with sustaining nutrients to indulge its sweet tooth at relatively high cost. Moreover, the very nature of most known desserts requires that they be prepared from a standing start, using raw staples that in no legitimate sense may be termed trimmings, oddments or leftovers. Flour is flour and sugar, sugar. Like them, such dessert elements as chocolate, fruit, butter and cream do not lend themselves to recycling, as various other culinary elements and compounds do. Still, there *are* desserts that with some legitimacy may be termed products of Connective Cookery. To take one rather magnificent example, if you've been wondering what's to be done with all those egg whites that have been accumulating in the freezer, consider . . .

• SOUFFLÉ DE FRAMBOISES GLACÉ •
(French cookery)

The recipe was kindly supplied by André Soltner, the redoubtable *chef-proprietaire* of New York's Lutèce restaurant. The almond topping is an unauthorized addition to his basic formula and may constitute lily-gilding, but no dinner guests have yet complained about it.

* * *

Allow 15 frozen ***egg whites***, divided into batches of 10 and 5, to thaw to room temperature. In a chilled bowl thoroughly beat 5 of the egg whites until they form stiff peaks and thoroughly blend in 1½ cups ***almond flour.*** Using a pastry bag, squeeze mixture onto wax paper in concentric cricles, forming 2 discs, each slightly smaller in diameter than the inside of a 9″ soufflé dish. Bake in a slow 200°F oven about 2 hours, or until meringue discs are crisp and firm throughout. Set aside to cool.

In a blender or processor purée 1½ pts. ***raspberries*** and refrigerate until needed. Prepare two 9″ ceramic soufflé dishes by fitting wax paper to their exteriors. (Collars should be double-thickness and fastened with cellophane tape, and should extend at least 3″ above tops of dishes.) Beat remaining egg whites until they form stiff peaks. Cook 1 lb. ***sugar*** in 1 cup water until temperature reaches 260°F on a candy thermometer and slowly pour resultant syrup over beaten egg whites, beating until cooled. Gradually add reserved raspberry purée and juice of 2 ***lemons,*** blending gently. Fold in without overmixing 1 pt. unsweetened ***cream stiffly whipped.*** Half-fill each soufflé dish with the mixture and smooth surfaces with a rubber spatula. Lay 1 meringue disc on each portion of soufflé mixture and cover discs with remainder of the mixture, which should project well above the tops of the soufflé dishes. Place soufflés in freezer after covering their surfaces completely with lightly toasted crushed blanched almonds. Freeze at least 3 hours until soufflés are set solid. Invert briefly to remove excess almond topping, remove paper collars and serve 6 portions per soufflé.

> **NOTE**—These soufflés keep very well in the freezer and for that reason there is little point in making them one at a time, but quantities may, of course, be halved for a single soufflé.

Variations

If so desired, meringues may be omitted, or ***strawberries*** substituted for raspberries.

Frozen soufflés can be produced in virtually limitless variations and combinations of flavors. One further example:

• SOUFFLÉ GLACÉ GRAND MARNIER (French cookery) •

Whip together 1 pt. ***heavy cream*** and ⅓ cup ***Grand Marnier*** until stiff peaks form. Chill mixture briefly. In the top of a double boiler beat 3 whole ***eggs*** and 6 tbs. ***sugar*** over boiling water until ribbons form. Off heat, gradually fold in chilled whipped cream mixture and refrigerate. Meanwhile, beat ⅓ cup ***egg whites***, thawed to room temperature, until soft peaks form. In a saucepan heat another 6 tbs. sugar over very low flame until it melts and coats a spoon thinly. Slowly pour resultant syrup into egg whites, stirring, then whip until mixture is fairly stiff. Fold into whipped cream mixture, spoon into individual soufflé dishes and refrigerate at least 2 hours before serving. Garnish each portion with a ***berry, crystallized violet, mint sprig, rose petal*** or the like and serve to 6–8.

• MOUSSE D'HIVER (Swiss cookery) •

Another elegant use for husbanded egg whites, this chilled dessert is a specialty of Manhattan's Dézaley restaurant.

* * *

Thaw 4 frozen ***egg whites*** to room temperature and reserve. Break four 3-oz. bars ***Toblerone white chocolate*** into small pieces, place in top of a double boiler and add ⅔ ***cup milk.*** Melt chocolate slowly over simmering water, stirring occasionally with a wooden spoon, until smooth and well blended with milk. Allow mixture to cool to room temperature. In a chilled bowl beat reserved egg whites together with ⅛ tsp. ***lemon juice*** until mixture stiffens. With a rubber spatula gently fold cooled chocolate mixture into egg white mixture. Whip 1 cup ***heavy cream*** until it forms peaks and fold into chocolate mixture. Spoon into tulip glasses and refrigerate at least 2 hours. Garnish as desired, with ***candied cherries, crystallized violets, fan-shaped wafers*** or the like. Serves 8.

• OEUFS À LA NEIGE (French cookery) •

Pour 3 cups ***milk*** into a large enameled skillet and bring to a very gentle simmer (the stage when, according to French cooks, "the pan smiles"). Meanwhile, beat 6 husbanded ***egg whites***, thawed to room temperature, until fluffy. Gradually beat 1 cup ***sugar*** into egg whites until mixture forms stiff peaks. With a large spoon scoop up egg-shaped globs of the mixture and set gently into simmering milk, poaching a few at a time for 30 seconds, or until just lightly colored. Remove "eggs" with a skimmer and drain on napkins until cool. Pour cooked *Crème Anglaise* (recipe below) into a crystal serving bowl, mound "eggs" over sauce to form a pyramid and serve to 4–6.

• CRÈME ANGLAISE •

For 1 cup of sauce, gradually add ¼ cup ***sugar*** to 2 ***egg yolks***, beating constantly until mixture forms a ribbon when lifted. In a very thin stream add ⅞ cup boiling milk, beating vigorously. In a heavy-bottomed saucepan cook mixture over moderate heat, stirring slowly but thoroughly, until thick enough to coat spoon lightly. Off heat, beat 2 minutes longer, adding ½ tsp. ***vanilla extract.***

As is the case with frozen and chilled soufflés and mousses, hot dessert soufflés may be flavored innumerable ways. Here are two.

• SOUFFLÉ AU CHOCOLAT (French cookery) •

Lightly ***butter*** the inside of a 1½-qt. soufflé dish. Dust lining thoroughly with granulated ***sugar***, swirling it about and then pouring out excess. Refrigerate at least 30 minutes. In top of a double boiler melt 3 oz. ***semisweet chocolate*** over gently simmering water. Beat melted chocolate (and, if desired, 2 tbs. ***powdered instant coffee***) into hot *Crème Patissière* (recipe below) and set mixture aside, covered. Beat 8 husbanded ***egg whites***, thawed to room temperature, together with a pinch of salt, until they form fairly stiff peaks and beat in 1 tbs. ***sugar.*** With a wire whisk vigorously beat about ⅓ of the egg white mixture into chocolate mixture, then gently fold in remainder of the egg whites. Pour soufflé mixture into prepared dish and bake 35 minutes in a preheated 375°F oven. Sprinkle confectioners sugar onto soufflé surface through a fine sieve and bake another 7–8 minutes. Serve immediately to 6.

• CRÈME PATISSIÈRE •

Bring 2 cups ***milk*** just to boil and set aside. In a bowl combine 4 ***egg yolks,*** ¾ cup ***sugar*** and ¾ tsp. ***vanilla extract*** and beat until ribbons form. Add ¼ cup ***flour*** and beat until mixture is smooth. Gradually add reserved hot milk, beating constantly. Transfer mixture to a saucepan and slowly bring to boil, stirring constantly. Continue boiling, still stirring constantly, about 5 minutes. Strain through a tamis or several layers of cheesecloth.

• SOUFFLÉ À L'ORANGE (French cookery) •

Prepare a 1-qt. soufflé dish as for *Soufflé au Chocolat** and refrigerate 30 minutes or more. Prepare *Crème Patissière* as for the preceding recipe and into it stir 1 oz. ***Curaçao*** and the grated rind of 1 ***orange.*** In a bowl beat until stiff 7 husbanded ***egg whites***, thawed to room temperature, and vigorously whisk ⅓ of this mixture into *Crème Patissière.* Gently fold in remaining egg whites, pour mixture into prepared soufflé dish and bake about 35 minutes in a preheated 375°F oven, or until well puffed and golden. Serve immediately to 4.

• BISCUIT TORTONI •
(Franco-Italian cookery)

In its original form, this dessert was served at the Café Tortoni, which was opened in Paris in 1798 by a Neapolitan ice-cream maker. This version departs considerably from its progenitor, as do most modern readings.

* * *

Allow 4 frozen ***egg whites*** to thaw to room temperature and set aside for an hour or more, unrefrigerated. Beat reserved egg whites, together with a pinch of salt, until stiff peaks form. In a saucepan cook ¾ cup ***sugar*** in ¼ cup water over low heat, stirring, until sugar is completely dissolved. Turn up heat, bring mixture to boil and continue to boil until syrup spins a short thread when dropped from a spoon (at about 253°F on a candy thermometer). Pour hot sugar syrup over egg whites in a thin stream, beating constantly, until stiff peaks form, and refrigerate, covered, 30 minutes or more.

While egg white mixture chills, toast ¼ cup ***blanched almonds*** (whole or slivered) in a baking pan placed below a moderate broiler, shaking pan occasionally, just until they take on color. In a blender or processor grind toasted almonds to a fairly fine consistency. Add 1¼ tsp. ***almond extract,*** blend well and set aside. In a bowl whip 1½ cups ***heavy cream,*** together with a dash of almond extract, until mixture stiffens. Fold whipped cream into chilled egg white mixture, blending thoroughly. Spoon mixture into individual pleated-paper serving cups, smooth tops and sprinkle with reserved ground toasted almonds. Freeze 3 hours or longer and serve straight from the freezer, 1 cup per person.

• MERINGUE SHELLS •

These crisp "pie" shells lend themselves to all manner of fillings: ice cream, frozen soufflés, fruits in custard sauces or sweetened whipped cream, etc.

* * *

Thaw to room temperature 3 frozen ***egg whites*** and allow to rest 1 hour. Lightly but thoroughly ***butter*** inside of a 9″ pie plate. Beat reserved egg whites, together with ¼ tsp. ***cream of tartar*** and a pinch of salt, until soft peaks form. Beat in ¾ cup ***sugar,*** bit by bit, and continue to beat until mixture is shiny and very stiff. Line pie plate with an even coating of the resultant meringue and bake 1 hour in a preheated 275°F oven. Allow to cool, fill as desired and serve to 6–8.

• CREMA DE NARANJA (Spanish cookery) •

In a bowl combine 2 cups ***milk,*** ⅔ cup ***sugar,*** 2 whole ***eggs,*** 6 ***egg whites*** (thawed to room temperature) and ***grated peel of 1 orange***. Beat mixture until frothy and stiff, strain into top of a double boiler and add a large piece of ***orange peel*** (inner white removed). Cook about 20 minutes over gently simmering water, stirring occasionally to keep mixture smooth. When custard has reached the consistency of a fairly thick Béchamel sauce, remove orange peel, pour into individual serving cups and chill. Serves 4.

• ANGEL CAKE (American cookery) •

Triple-sift and set aside 1 cup ***cake flour*** mixed with ¾ cup ***sugar.*** In a large bowl beat 1½ cups (12–13) husbanded ***egg whites***, thawed to room temperature, together with ¼ tsp. salt, until foamy. Sprinkle 1 tsp. ***cream of tartar*** over egg whites and resume beating to bring them to soft peaks. Sprinkle egg whites with ¾ cup ***sugar,*** 3 or 4 tbs. at a time, gently folding in sugar after each application. Little by little, sift reserved flour-sugar mixture over egg white mixture, folding the former into the latter after each of 8–10 siftings. Fold into this mixture ½ tsp. each ***almond*** and ***vanilla extract*** and ¾ tsp. ***lemon juice.*** Pour batter into an ungreased 10″ tube pan and bake in a preheated 325°F oven 60 minutes, or until cake is lightly browned, resilient to the touch and has separated from lining of pan. Allow to cool in inverted pan and serve to 10–12, dividing cake with two forks or a tined cutter.

Rice-Based Desserts

Rice puddings and the derivatives thereof come in various guises in various parts of the world but in most cases aren't readily adaptable to the procedures of Connective Cookery. The two that follow are, as are the old New Orleans rice cakes that follow *them.*

• OLD-FASHIONED RICE PUDDING • (American cookery)

In a bowl beat together 1⅓ cups ***milk,*** 2 ***eggs,*** 3½ tbs. ***sugar,*** 1 tbs. softened ***butter,*** ¾ tsp. ***vanilla extract,*** ½ tsp. grated ***lemon rind,*** 1 tsp. ***lemon juice*** and a pinch of salt. To the foregoing mixture add 2 cups leftover ***cooked rice*** and ⅓ cup white ***seedless raisins.*** Thoroughly butter the inside of an ovenproof dish and cover with a thin coating of

breadcrumbs, inverting dish to dispose of excess crumbs. Spoon pudding mixture into baking dish and bake in a preheated 325°F oven 40 minutes, or until pudding has lightly set. Dust surface with nutmeg, chill and serve, with whipped cream if desired, to 6.

• WILD RICE AND RAISIN PUDDING •
(American cookery)

It isn't often that home cooks find themselves with significant quantities of wild rice (magnificent grain!) on their hands, but it has been known to happen after particularly festive dinner parties. This dessert (slightly adapted from the original) was served for many years by Pearl Byrd Foster at her now lamentably defunct restaurant, Mr. & Mrs. Foster's Place. It's a real winner.

* * *

In a large heavy skillet cook ½ cup ***seedless black raisins*** in water barely to cover until they are tender and all liquid has been absorbed. Combine with 2 cups leftover ***cooked wild rice*** and stir in 3 tbs. ***clover honey,*** ½ tsp. freshly ***grated nutmeg*** and a pinch of salt. In the top of a double boiler heat 2 cups ***milk,*** add ***wild rice mixture*** and stir in 2 lightly beaten ***eggs.*** Cook without boiling until mixture thickens. Stir in 2 tbs. ***Cognac*** (or other brandy of your choice) and serve, warm or cold and topped with ***whipped cream,*** to 6.

• CALAS (Creole cookery) •

These fried rice cakes once were hawked by street vendors in New Orleans' French Quarter. Although not altogether appropriate as the windup to an elaborate meal, they make fine casual eating.

* * *

Dissolve 1 pkg. (or its equivalent) active ***dry yeast*** in 2 tbs. warm water, mix thoroughly with 2½ cups leftover ***cooked rice,*** cover loosely with cloth and allow to stand overnight in a warm spot. Next day, beat in by hand 3 well-beaten ***eggs,*** ¼ cup ***flour,*** ½ cup ***sugar,*** ½ tsp. salt and a pinch of ***nutmeg,*** adding ***flour,*** if necessary, to make a thick batter.

Heat fat in a deep fryer to 370°F, or until a cube of bread browns in about 60 seconds. Drop batter into fat from a tablespoon, a few gobs at a time, and fry until golden-brown. Drain, sprinkle with confectioners sugar and serve hot.

Desserts from Other Oddments

• BREAD PUDDING •

A mainstay of Connective Cookery, bread pudding turns up in various guises in various cuisines. This, an American version, is one of the best.

* * *

Butter and diagonally quarter 4 slices stale ***white bread*** (crusts removed or not, as you will). Arrange half the bread in the bottom of a buttered 1½-qt. casserole and strew surface with ¼ cup ***seedless raisins.*** Dust with ¼ tsp. ***blended cinnamon*** and ***nutmeg,*** and repeat entire process, starting with remaining bread. Beat together 3 ***eggs*** and ⅓ cup ***sugar*** until mixture is smooth and cream-yellow. Stir in 2 cups ***milk*** and pour mixture over bread-raisin layers. Allow to rest 60 minutes at room temperature, then place casserole in a large pan and add boiling water to latter to a depth of 1″. Bake, uncovered, in a preheated 350°F oven about 1 hour, or until a straw inserted into the pudding comes away clean. Serve warm to 6.

• APPLE BROWN BETTY (American cookery) •

Work together 1½ cups dry ***bread crumbs*** and ¼ cup very ***soft butter*** until both are thoroughly integrated. Separate ⅓ of the mixture and spread it over the bottom of a buttered baking dish, tamping it down to cover the surface completely. Core, peel and slice 4 medium ***apples*** and arrange half over the bread-crumb layer, reserving remainder. Blend together ¾ cup ***brown sugar,*** 1 tsp. ***cinnamon,*** ¼ tsp. each ***ground nutmeg*** and ***cloves,*** 1 tsp. grated ***lemon rind*** and a pinch of salt. Sprinkle half this mixture over apple layer and sprinkle *that* with the ***juice*** of ½ ***lemon*** mixed with 1 tbs. water. Add about ½ the remainder of the breadcrumb mixture, distributing it evenly over the surface. Repeat all previous operations, starting with remaining apple slices and finishing with breadcrumbs. Cover and bake 40 minutes in a preheated 350°F oven. Lower heat to 300°, remove cover and bake 10 minutes longer. Serve warm to 6, with heavy cream, vanilla ice cream or the like.

• SWEET POTATO PIE (American cookery) •

In a bowl combine 1½ cups mashed leftover ***cooked sweet potatoes***, ½ cup ***brown sugar*** (well packed), ¼ tsp. ***cinnamon*** and ⅓ tsp. salt. In a second bowl mix together 2 well-beaten ***eggs***, 1 tbs. ***melted butter*** and ¾ cup ***milk***. Combine two mixtures, blending thoroughly, and pour into a chilled, pastry-lined 8″ pie pan. Bake 45 minutes in a preheated 400°F oven, or until a straw inserted into the center of the pie comes away clean. Cool, pipe ***whipped cream*** over top of pie if desired, and serve to 6–8.

The personal view from this quarter is that, except for certain rancid fried pastries favored by Kalmuck nomads, mince pie and plum pudding are the two most fearsome substances the culinary arts have to offer. Admittedly, this may be a minority view, at least in the English-speaking world. Both are included here, with some reluctance, chiefly because both fall—with resounding thuds—well within the framework of Connective Cookery.

• MINCEMEAT PIE (American cookery) •

If there is any point at all in making mincemeat, there is no point whatsoever in making it in parsimonious one-pie batches, for the stuff must be aged several weeks before use and is used almost exclusively during the winter holiday season, when it, like Steuben glass, is better to give than to receive. Unlike vitreous dolphins, however, it costs considerably less to inflict on putative loved ones.

* * *

Sterilize six 1-qt. canning jars and closures and keep hot in a 250°F oven. In a kettle simmer 2 lbs. ground lean ***beef trimmings*** 10 minutes in water to cover, separating particles with a wooden spoon. Drain off water and add to the kettle all the following: ¾ lb. chopped ***beef suet***; 5 lbs. ***tart apples,*** peeled, cored and finely chopped; 1 lb. each dried ***currants*** and ***seedless muscat*** and ***sultana raisins;*** 3 cups ***cider;*** 1 cup ***brandy*** or ***rum;*** 1 tbs. each ***nutmeg, allspice*** and ***cinnamon;*** ½ tsp. minced fresh ***ginger root;*** chopped pulp of 2 ***oranges*** and 1 ***lemon;*** and ***grated rinds*** of both those last. Simmer 1 hour, stirring from time to time, until mixture approaches the specific gravity of uranium. Ladle into sterilized jars, filling to within ⅛″ of tops, seal securely and store at least 1 month before use in a cool, dark, dry place.

For mincemeat pies, line desired number of 9″ pie plates with pastry, spoon mincemeat into shells, filling them generously, cover with a thinner layer of pastry and crimp all around the perimeters to seal. Slash pie tops in several places and bake 30 minutes in a preheated 450°F oven. Portions will vary, depending on victims' capacity for punishment.

• PLUM PUDDING (English cookery) •

Some gave them white bread,
And some gave them brown;
Some gave them plum cake,
And sent them out of town.
—Old nursery rhyme

In a large bowl mix together 1⅓ cups ***seedless raisins;*** 1 ***tart apple,*** peeled, cored and grated; ½ cup each ***chopped mixed candied fruits*** and ***dried currants; grated rinds*** of 1 ***orange*** and 1 ***lemon***; ¾ cup ***ale*** or ***stout.*** Allow mixture to stand ½ hour at room temperature. In another large bowl sift together 1 cup ***flour,*** 1 tsp. ***baking powder,*** 1 tsp. ***cinnamon,*** ½ tsp. ***allspice,*** ¼ tsp. ***nutmeg*** and ½ tsp. salt. Into this agglomeration stir 1 cup fine ***dry breadcrumbs;*** 1 well-packed cup ***dark brown sugar;*** ⅓ cup ***molasses;*** ½ cup minced ***toasted almonds;*** 1 cup ground ***beef suet***; and 3 lightly ***beaten eggs.***

Into the foregoing incorporate reserved fruit mixture, mixing all ingredients well, and spoon the resultant glop into 2 well-buttered 1-qt. rectangular baking pans. Cover pans tightly with double thicknesses of aluminum foil and set on racks in a large roasting pan or something of the sort. Add boiling water to half the height of the baking pans, cover outer receptacle and steam 4 hours at a gentle simmer, replenishing water as needed. Allow puddings to cool in their foil-covered pans and store 2 weeks or more before use in a cool dry place. Puddings yield 6–8 servings each and traditionally are served warm after a brief re-steaming. Hard sauce, rum sauce or runny custard are among the more popular accompaniments.

A Selected Reading List

AS WAS REMARKED in Chapter 2, not every good cookbook is suited to every cook's needs and preferences. The selections that follow—in some cases highly idiosyncratic—are personal favorites which most nearly accord with the selector's notions of what good, honest cooking from scratch is all about and what the literature pertaining thereto should be.

The Art of Charcuterie by Jane Grigson. Knopf, 1968.

Recipes for everything the pig yields but its grunt, along with appropriate sauces, game pâtés, goose *rillettes,* veal galantines, and just about anything else to be found in a typical French take-out shop, all to be made rigorously from scratch and all described in literate English-accented prose. Not for dilettantes and possibly not for apartment dwellers, but a fine book for serious work in a big country kitchen.

Better Than Store-bought by Helen Witty and Elizabeth Schneider Colchie. Harper and Row, 1979.

In clearly organized recipes distinguished by uncompromising integrity, the authors take dead aim on the extravagances of the belly boutiques. It's all here, from cured meats to condiments, from corn chips to home-made caviar, and the title tells the story.

Chinese Cuisine: Wei-chuan Cooking Book by Huang Su Huei, translated by Nina Simonds. Wei-chuan Publishing Co., Taipei, 1974.

There are more comprehensive Chinese cookbooks than this but none more mouth-watering or authentic. Handsome color photographs show what the finished products should look like in every case and uncommonly easy-to-follow, numerically coded recipes make a snap of even the most complex of dishes. Paper-wrapped fried chicken and egg flower soup virtually can be eaten off the page.

The Complete Book of Mexican Cooking by Elisabeth Lambert Ortiz. M. Evans and Company (distributed by Lippincott), 1967.

The title may be suspect but the contents are unimpeachable. Canned goods are recommended in cases where fresh ingredients are virtually impossible to procure north of the border, but no substitutions are made for authentic ingredients.

The Cuisine of Hungary by George Lang. Bonanza Books, 1971.

The most complete history in English and a splendid cookbook in a single fascinating volume chockful of lusty song, drink, and good living, impoverished though some sections of Hungary may be. The author's knowledge of his subject is encyclopedic and he imparts it with the flair and enthusiasm of a born raconteur.

The Cuisines of Mexico by Diana Kennedy. Harper & Row, 1972.

Mexico *has* a number of distinguished cuisines, however unlikely that may seem to gringos familiar only with Mexican cookery north of the Rio Grande. Many of the author's ingredients are hard to come by in the United States but the recipes themselves are much easier to follow than the trail of an elusive *chile quajillo.*

The Escoffier Cookbook by Auguste Escoffier. Crown (original edition), 1941.

The gussied-up *haute cuisine* of la Belle Epoque may have outworn its welcome, but this is the magnum opus and legacy of the acknowledged master of the genre. The recipes are perfunctory and presuppose extensive knowledge on the part of the home cook, and the format is cumbersome, with its constant references to secondary and tertiary recipes. Still, if you're determined to prepare *ris de veau à la régence,* you might as well get it right—with a garnish of truffled chicken *quenelles,* small fluted mushrooms, curled cocks' combs, and truffles turned to resemble olives. (Nowadays olives are cut to resemble truffles.)

The Food of Italy by Waverley Root. Atheneum, 1971.

No recipes per se here, but a reasonably resourceful cook can work from detailed descriptions of hundreds of regional specialties. This is the definitive book in English on Italian gastronomy considered from every conceivable point of view, and it is densely packed with history, lore, literature, and anecdote, all conveyed with style, grace, and enthusiasm. The index, alas, is thoroughly bollixed.

The Food-lover's Garden by Angelo M. Pellegrini. Knopf, 1970.

In which a scholar-gastronomer hymns the praises of none but the freshest herbs and vegetables. The author occasionally darts into the kitchen to demonstrate the good uses to which his produce can be put, but spends most of his time cultivating his veggies. His enthusiasm is contagious, his style felicitous, and he reaps a surprisingly abundant harvest from a plot of ground that is "bigger than a windowbox [but] smaller than a farm." A cookbook only in the broadest sense of the term, but a valuable adjunct to the library of any cook who revels in the goodness of what he grows and consumes.

Italian Family Cooking by Edward Giobbi. Random House, 1971.

Various regional and family dishes with the emphasis on economy, purity, and simplicity. The author, a child of the Great Depression whose chosen career (art) didn't augur well for his future solvency, spent his youth learning to make the most of foods that cost little or nothing. His authoritative recipes are interspersed with delightful anecdotes and reminiscences. The illustrations, by his then-small children, are equally delightful.

Kettner's Book of the Table by E.S. Dallas. Centaur Press, London, 1968.

This reissue of an 1877 work, ghost-written for a Soho restaurateur (the restaurant still exists) by a leading Victorian literary critic and philologist, is hard to find but worth the search. The recipes, sporadically interspersed among brief, alphabetically arranged essays, often are archaic and capricious and the opinions (". . . sheep's kidneys or lamb's . . . alone are of much account") often are debatable, but the scholarship is fascinating, particularly as regards the nomenclature and origin of various dishes and ingredients.

Larousse Gastronomique by Prosper Montagné. Crown, 1977.

Quite simply, the Bible of French cookery, but difficult for the neophyte to put to practical use.

The Spanish Cookbook by Barbara Norman. Bantam (paperback), 1971.

Spanish cookery is much misunderstood in this country (where the most characteristic ingredients are hard to come by, if not nonexistent) and often is confused with the cuisine of Mexico, which it in no way resembles. The author makes no compromises, omitting dishes for which no authentic ingredients can be found on this side of the Atlantic. The result is an incomplete but consistently authentic piece of work.

The Supper of the Lamb by Robert Farrar Capon. Doubleday, 1969.

As a recipe book this is a slight, somewhat quirky volume. As a philosophical and spiritual meditation on the conscientious preparation of food for the table, it is indispensable. Moreover, the style is graceful, erudite, and witty.

Waste Not, Want Not by Helen McCully. Random House, 1975.

The banality of some of her dishes notwithstanding, the late author's intentions are honorable and no usable scrap escapes her notice.

• Index •